DATE			
APR 24 '81			
SEP 28 '81			
MAY 27 '83			
AUG 18 '83			
APR 3 '84			
OCT 1 2 1986			
OCT 2 5 1988			
JUN 2 8 1993			
JAN 3 1 2000			
OCT 2 8 2008			

FOUNDATIONS OF MODERN PSYCHOLOGY SERIES

Richard S. Lazarus, Editor

JOHN B. P. SHAFFER

Associate Professor of Psychology
Queens College
of the City University of New York

Humanistic Psychology

PRENTICE-HALL, INC. ENGLEWOOD CLIFFS, NEW JERSEY 07632

Library of Congress Cataloging in Publication Data

Shaffer, John B P (date)
  Humanistic psychology.

  (Foundations of modern psychology series)
  1. Humanistic psychology. I. Title.
BF204.S49   150'.19'2   77-15044
ISBN 0-13-447698-0
ISBN 0-13-447680-8 pbk.

To Judy and Derek

© *1978 by*

Prentice-Hall, Inc., Englewood Cliffs, N.J. 07632

10 9 8 7 6 5 4 3 2

Prentice-Hall International, Inc., London
Prentice-Hall of Australia Pty. Limited, Sydney
Prentice-Hall of Canada, Ltd., Toronto
Prentice-Hall of India Private Limited, New Delhi
Prentice-Hall of Japan, Inc., Tokyo
Prentice-Hall of Southeast Asia Pte. Ltd., Singapore
Whitehall Books Limited, Wellington, New Zealand

Contents

Foundations of
Modern Psychology Series

The tremendous growth and vitality of psychology and its increasing fusion with the social and biological sciences demand a search for new approaches to teaching at the introductory level. We can no longer feel content with the traditional basic course, geared as it usually is to a single text that tries to skim everything, that sacrifices depth for breadth. Psychology has become too diverse for any one person, or group, to write about with complete authority. The alternative, a book that ignores many essential areas in order to present more comprehensively and effectively a particular aspect or view of psychology, is also insufficient, for in this solution many key areas are simply not communicated to the student at all.

The Foundations of Modern Psychology Series was the first in what has become a growing trend in psychology toward groups of short texts dealing with various basic subjects, each written by an active authority. It was conceived with the idea of providing greater flexibility for instructors teaching general courses than was ordinarily available in the large, encyclopedic textbooks, and greater depth of presentation for individual topics not typically given much space in introductory textbooks.

The earliest volumes appeared in 1963, the latest not until 1973. Well over one and a quarter million copies, collectively, have been sold, attesting to the widespread use of these books in the teaching of psychology. Individual volumes have been used as supplementary texts, or as *the* text, in various undergraduate courses in psychology, education, public health, and sociology, and clusters of volumes have served as the text in beginning undergraduate courses in general psychology. Groups of volumes have been translated into eight languages, including Dutch, Hebrew, Italian, Japanese, Polish, Portuguese, Spanish, and Swedish.

With wide variation in publication date and type of content, some of the volumes need revision, while others do not. We have left this decision to the individual author who best knows his book in relation to the state of the field. Some will remain unchanged, some will be modestly changed, and still others completely rewritten. In the new series edition, we have also opted for some variation in the length and style of individual books, to reflect the different ways in which they have been used as texts.

There has never been stronger interest in good teaching in our colleges and universities than there is now; and for this the availability of high quality, well-written, and stimulating text materials highlighting the exciting and continuing search for knowledge is a prime prerequisite. This is especially the case in undergraduate courses where large numbers of students must have access to suitable readings. The Foundations of Modern Psychology Series represents our ongoing attempt to provide college teachers with the best textbook materials we can create.

Richard S. Lazarus, Editor

Preface and Acknowledgments

The fact that Prentice-Hall has added a text in humanistic psychology to its Foundations of Modern Psychology Series is, for me, an indication that this somewhat diffuse and once radical subfield of psychology has come of age. And while currents have continued to shift within the field since I commenced work on the book three-and-a-half years ago, the humanistic viewpoint seems well entrenched within modern psychology. For example, Robert Ornstein's efforts to integrate into a humanistic framework research involving the differential functions of the left and right brain hemispheres suggests that the humanistic perspective has begun, at least for some, to attain a certain measure of academic and scientific respectability.

It has not been easy to give a coherent structure to a field that ranges from the rational intellectualism of a Heidegger to the literary mysticism of a Castaneda (within the area of theory), or from the thoroughly American and interpersonal client-centered therapy of Rogers to the Eastern-oriented, more solitary practice of meditation (within the area of technique). Yet I hope that this book succeeds in setting forth a somewhat coherent schema underlying the many diverse, sometimes bewildering manifestations of what is, again and again, labeled as humanistic. Rendering such a presentation even more complex is the fact that particular sociopolitical events of the past fifteen years have been prominently related to the emergence of humanism as a distinct field within contemporary psychology: the dissent from the war in Vietnam, the emergence of the counterculture, and the various liberation movements (women's, men's, gay, and black).

Humanistic psychology is most often described as psychology's "third force," which reaches beyond the initial two forces of psychoanalysis and behaviorism. It did not seem appropriate in this text to go into all the subtleties of psychology theory. However, as is probably clear in the book, I see a wider divergence between humanism and behaviorism than between humanism and psychoanalysis. Areas of overlapping emphasis between humanistic psychology and psychoanalysis include an interest in the concepts of growth and change, a conception of people as more than passive reactors to their environment, careful attention to the person's moment-to-moment subjective experience, and an appreciation of the vital role played by body experience and body pleasure in psychological development. More recent areas of convergence between psychoanalysis and humanism involve psychoanalytic ego psychology, which emphasizes forces within the person that help to promote autonomy and wholeness, and the latest work of Roy Schafer (1976), in which the language of psychoanalysis is revised to give greater prominence to certain key concepts within existential thought, such as intentionality and action. Actually, it was one of the first psychoanalysts, Carl Jung, who stood very early on for a humanistic union between our instinctual and our spiritual strivings (and humanistic psychology, as it has developed within the United States during the past decade, has gone in a strongly spiritual direction). In Jung's thinking, the nature of the unconscious was incompletely grasped so long as we failed to grant it cosmic and religious, as well as sexual, dimensions.

Acknowledgments

Sincere thanks go to Dr. Howard Pollio, whose perceptive and detailed criticism was of great help in my reorganization and revision of the initial draft of this book, and to my wife, Judy, who gave strong support to this project at every phase of its development.

What Is Humanistic Psychology?

chapter one

Humanistic psychology is both old and new. Old, in that its fundamental concerns with the value of life and with what it means to be human hark back to man's earliest efforts to answer the basic riddles of existence through art, religion, and philosophy. New, in that it is strongly identified with the human potential movement of the 1960s and 1970s, a movement that attempts to liberate people from a dehumanizing culture through a series of specific techniques. These human potential techniques range from small-group experiences designed to help participants contact and express their feelings more directly, to other, less verbal activities that involve massage, meditation, and dance.

Unlike other fields of psychology—e.g., physiological, personality, or abnormal psychology—humanistic psychology does not involve a specific content area so much as an attitude or orientation toward psychology as a whole. Hence, it has implications for all specializations within psychology, including psychopathology, personality theory, and even experimental research. The "Articles of Association" formulated by the American Association of Humanistic Psychology at its inception in 1962 describe the field in the following way:

Humanistic psychology is primarily an orientation toward the whole of psychology rather than a distinct area or school. It stands for the respect for the worth of persons, respect for differences of approach, open-mindedness as to acceptable methods, and interest in exploration of new aspects of human behavior. As a "third force" in contemporary psychology, it is concerned with topics having little place in existing theories and systems: e.g., love, creativity, self, growth, organism, basic need-gratification, self-actualization, higher values, being, becoming, spontaneity, play, humor, affection, naturalness, warmth, ego-transcendence, objectivity, autonomy, responsibility, meaning, fair play, transcendental experience, peak experience, courage, and related concepts (p. 2).

Essentially, then, humanism as a force in psychology questions, and at times opposes, some of the major thrusts within modern psychology, in particular: (1) the assumption that psychology should emulate the philosophy and procedures of natural science, and (2) the predominant view of human beings as primarily responding to, and being shaped by, the various determining influences that impinge upon them from within or without. One major school of psychology, psychoanalysis, sees these important influences as consisting largely of biological drives emanating from within, while another, behaviorism, regards the important determinants of behavior as originating outside the organism, in the form of specific stimuli or "reinforcers." (Reinforcement occurs when a stimulus is followed by, or is associated with, events that have either positive or negative consequences for the particular person—in other words, either reward or punishment). Of course, in distinguishing between humanistic psychology and psychoanalysis on the one hand, and between humanistic psychology and behaviorism on the other, theorists sympathetic to humanism occasionally depict psychoanalysis and behaviorism in too simplistic a way and fail to do full justice to either one. For instance, a contemporary approach within psychoanalysis known as "ego psychology" (see Blanck and Blanck, 1974) has revised psychoanalytic concepts to allow more room for elements within an individual's personality (or "ego") that are independent of biological drives, and some behaviorists, like Skinner, have attested the need for human beings to actively use their scientific knowledge to create a more just, orderly, and humane society.

Nevertheless, orthodox psychoanalysis continues in the main to regard attributes like creativity and love as derivative of more basic animal drives, or "instincts." And Skinner, who is probably America's foremost behaviorist, insists that society, if it is to effectively control urgent behavioral problems (e.g., the increase in this country of criminal violence), must renounce its concern with individual freedom and dignity (Skinner,

1971), which for him are illusory concepts without any basis in psychological reality; on the other hand, the concepts of dignity and freedom are basic to all humanistically oriented theories.

The Evolution of Humanistic Psychology

An orientation that could properly be described as humanistic had been introduced into American psychology as early as the nineteenth century by William James and G. Stanley Hall, both of whom advocated a psychology that would leave the wholeness, passion, and uniqueness of the individual intact. This emphasis was renewed in the 1930s by such personality theorists as Goldstein, Allport, and Maslow. Yet "humanistic psychology," as a specific term, had no appreciable existence before 1958. At that point, a series of related developments brought into increasing prominence an orientation that had lain fallow for about twenty-five years, with the result that suddenly, within the short span of a decade, humanistic psychology had become recognized as a distinct school or approach, with a philosophy, a research method, and an array of applications that were uniquely its own.

SPECIFIC MILESTONES

Some of these key developments are listed below. I have selected the most conspicuous events, and in this sense my selection is somewhat arbitrary. Other, less official happenings may well have been equally influential, if not more so. The milestones cited are obviously interrelated, and each of them can be seen as either cause or effect—effect, in that the milestone in question would not have occurred unless a humanistic perspective had already been in the process of formation; and cause, in that the event in turn helped to strengthen whatever humanistic currents were already in existence. The list is as follows:

1. In England, the publication of *Humanistic Psychology*, by John Cohen, in 1958.

2. The founding of the *Journal of Humanistic Psychology*, edited by A. J. Sutich, in 1961.

3. An address by James F. T. Bugental, entitled *Humanistic Psychology: A New Breakthrough*, given to the Orange County (California) Psychological Association in 1962; in a sense this constituted the first official "position paper" on humanistic psychology in the United States, and, it was subsequently published in the *American Psychologist* (Bugental, 1963).

4. The formation of the American Association for Humanistic Psychology in 1962. At a later point this association expanded into an international

organization, the Association for Humanistic Psychology, which held its first international conference in Holland in 1970.

5. The founding of a graduate program in humanistic psychology at Sonoma State College (California) in about 1963. This is a Master's level program and is one of the few specifically humanistic programs in the country.

6. The publication of several books in the area of humanistic psychology, two characteristic ones being *Humanistic Viewpoints in Psychology,* edited by Frank T. Severin (1965) and *Challenges of Humanistic Psychology,* edited by James F. T. Bugental (1967). In addition to these anthologies, a whole spate of books appeared that were concerned with the human potential movement. Several of these were addressed to the public at large, two prominent examples being *Please Touch* by Jane Howard (1970), and *Turning On* by Rasa Gustaitis (1969), both written by journalists. Others, like *Joy* by William Schutz (1967), were written by professionals specializing in one particular aspect of the movement.

7. The creation of a new subdivision within the American Psychological Association called the Division of Humanistic Psychology (Division 32), in 1970.

8. The opening, in 1962, of Esalen Institute, which had been founded for the purpose of a detailed exploration and expansion of the human potential movement.

This last milestone was probably the most significant. Esalen Institute was started by two Stanford University graduates, Michael Murphy and Richard Price, who had decided to use property belonging to Murphy in Big Sur, California, for the development of a center that would devote itself to the investigation of human potential. Murphy and Price, both nonprofessionals, were convinced that Esalen, if it were to remain consistent with a basically humanistic orientation, had to be non-doctrinaire. Therefore, while they wished to study further the sensitivity-training procedures initially developed by the National Training Laboratories in Bethel, Maine (where people met in small groups in order to learn more about themselves and about groups in general), they were receptive to other orientations and techniques as well, including Yoga, meditation, and Zen Buddhism. Starting with weekend retreats, Esalen's Big Sur program grew to a point where by 1968 it offered events throughout the entire calendar year, had a permanent staff, and ran at any one time two or three concurrent workshops. Some of these workshops lasted three or four days, others for a month or more. By 1969 the institute had opened a San Francisco branch that sponsored weekend workshops on a nonresidential basis.

Sensitivity-training groups, initially known as T-groups, had originated in the Northeastern United States and had existed primarily as a means of helping administrators and business executives become more sensitive to the interpersonal aspects of their jobs and organizations. Once transplanted to the less traditional and less academic atmosphere of Esalen, the T-group soon evolved into the encounter group, which, instead of focusing on making people more expert in their professional lives, aimed at a more complete kind of liberation wherein they might begin to consider changing their jobs or even giving up work altogether. The emotionally intense and intimate atmosphere of encounter groups seemed to have broad appeal, and many people who attended them claimed that they returned to their home situations revitalized, with a deepened appreciation of what close human contact and a renewed sense of community could mean to their lives. While the encounter group gradually became Esalen's single best-known feature, there was no well-known human potential technique or area of interest—whether extra-sensory perception, body movement, or theatre games—that did not eventually find its way into the Esalen catalog.

In this way Esalen came to spearhead and epitomize the human potential movement. Its increasing popularity, its lush surroundings, and its emphasis on sensuality (which included occasional nude encounter groups as well as sulphur baths and massage) helped it to receive more and more publicity, with the result that many mental health professionals, as well as laymen, participated in its groups. Slowly it became a prototype for the scores of growth centers that subsequently sprang up throughout the United States.

In summary, Esalen helped forge what had until then been a somewhat diffuse set of techniques and practitioners, some of whom had hardly been aware of one another, into a coherent movement—a movement that began to develop, in turn, an increasingly acute sense of its own identity and significance. Without Esalen, the human potential movement would not exist in the form that it does today, and without the human potential movement Esalen would have had no raison d'etre. As with other factors related to the popular emergence of humanistic psychology, we see cause and effect interacting in a reciprocal, mutually enhancing fashion, to a point where it is hard to determine just where one ends and the other begins.

FACTORS IN THE POPULARITY
OF THE HUMANISTIC MOVEMENT

The previous section highlighted some of the actual events that helped consolidate the humanistic movement and render it visible in psychology. However, these specific developments (e.g., the founding of the

Esalen Institute and the Association of Humanistic Psychologists) are probably best seen as a reaction not just to the theoretical determinism prevalent within academic psychology, but to deeper yearnings and currents within the larger culture. Indeed, many humanists·claimed that the aridity of modern psychological theory and its picture of man was in itself symptomatic of a deadening alienation and a dehumanization that had badly infected the entire social fabric.

Therefore, while some humanistic writers confined their criticism to the subtleties of psychological theory (see Ornstein, 1972), others were quite explicit in their negative view of our entire society. For example, William Schutz, one of the main architects of the encounter group, perceived that the typical elementary or high school fostered an emotional climate in which feelings of secrecy, shame, and depersonalization flourished (Schutz, 1971), and it was this kind of atmosphere that encounter groups, with their emphasis on openness and trust, were designed to combat. The evolution of a distinctly humanistic school of psychology must be seen within this larger sociocultural context if it is to be fully understood. Otherwise, the strength and suddenness of humanism's popularity, which gave it the dimensions of a social movement and brought it as quickly to the attention of the general public as it was brought to the psychological community, cannot be adequately accounted for.

Almost all analyses of what ails American society have focused to some degree on the concept of alienation (for instance, see Fromm, 1955; Henry, 1963; Keniston, 1965; and Reich, 1970). This includes not only alienation from our bodies and our feelings, but also from one another as members of a coherent society that inspires in us a sense of enthusiastic commitment and of shared purpose. Having suffered a decline in genuine religiosity and in deeply felt patriotism, our rational-technological society stresses a readiness for chronic change and for job performance within fairly narrow occupational specifications. A sense of continuity is hard to come by, whether it be one of historical continuity or emotional participation in a group experience that extends beyond one's immediate family or vocational boundaries.

As a result, people lack a sense of connectedness to the past, to one another as members of an organic community, and to a meaningful, readily envisaged future. The fragmentation of urban culture is such that one can no longer exist in an ongoing community in which most people know one another on a face-to-face basis. Instead people participate in a wide variety of disparate and isolated reference groups—familial, vocational, social, and civic. And of all these, the family offers the sense of intimacy, support, and emotional engagement that is all too often lacking in a person's outside social contacts. Keniston, who wrote one of the best-known analyses of alienated youth, described this phenomenon as follows (1965):

> The primacy of technology leads to the dissociation and subordination of all that is not technological, of all that we can call the affective and expressive side of life. Our society sharply splits the public and private spheres of life. . . . Feeling, family, and fun, leisure and fantasy, idealism and relaxation are split off and relegated to inferior status, deemed necessary only as the price of peak performance in public life. . . . This creates a variety of human problems. The psyche resists compartmentalization: men strive for integration. To maintain a divided life takes a heavy toll of energy; and even where it succeeds it exhausts us and leads to a sense of inner division (pp. 422–23).

Keniston's championing of a less-compartmentalized kind of life, in which several different aspects of a person's potential are realized and blended, helps us relate the concept of alienation to two central emphases within humanistic theory: man's essential wholeness and his unfulfilled potential.

The concept of alienation can be expanded to include both the oversocialized and the undersocialized man. The oversocialized person identifies too completely with his various social roles, to the point where he loses touch with a sense of an authentic, centered, personal self that goes beyond roles. The undersocialized person tends to view all roles as hollow, meaningless, and superficial (including those of the artist and the intellectual, whom he sees as having been corrupted and debased by their overly commercial culture). More obviously disturbed and troubled than his seemingly adjusted oversocialized counterpart, it is undersocialized man, alienated from establishment society and from all features of its ideology, who is traditionally thought of as being alienated.

Humanistic psychology perceives itself as a potential source of revitalization for both over- and undersocialized man. For instance, the encounter group (initially the most prominent feature of the human potential movement), was expressly designed to allow individuals to encounter aspects of their being that they had become deadened to; this included encounters with their body feelings, with their fellow group participants, and with nature. Hopefully the group would provide a sense of what it feels like to be in a face-to-face community without masks or facades and to be accepted by such a community.

Parallel to the humanistic movement because it championed similar values and rose to prominence at approximately the same time, was a segment of overtly alienated youth that gradually came to comprise a distinctive subculture known as the "counterculture" (see Reich, 1970; Roszak, 1969). While the counterculture was in part a reaction to the same alienating trends within the culture, two historical events during the 1960s were especially catalytic in its development. One was the war in Vietnam, to which many young people were deeply opposed; the other was the war against pollution, to which they were genuinely sympathetic. For many citizens, the threat to all forms of life posed by pollution, and the slow destruction of a small foreign country in the Vietnam War, were cause for deep concern. Young people, however, seemed particularly affected (1) because it was they who were called upon to serve in Vietnam, and (2) because they, as adolescents and young adults, were dramatically confronted with school and career decisions that involved implicit choices for or against established values—at a time when the orderly and humane direction of social progress was especially doubted. Consequently, American youth during the 1960s rebelled and "dropped out"—from family life, school, the draft, and the army itself. Persuaded by earlier American ethics that involved a regard for the importance of the individual conscience and a deep, abiding respect for nature, these young people searched for more natural life styles that frequently embraced group marriages and communal living in rural surroundings. They also sought a heightened sense of feeling and consciousness, often with the aid of psychedelic drugs. The counterculture, although primarily oriented to youth and lacking an official statement of aims, gradually came to represent a set of values that strongly overlapped those central to humanistic psychology: freedom, authenticity, and openness to experience.

RELATIONSHIPS BETWEEN HUMANISTIC
PSYCHOLOGY AND THE COUNTERCULTURE

Our analysis of contemporary society has explicitly criticized contemporary culture; this critique was drawn largely from the statements and writings of humanistic psychologists, who have frequently denounced sometimes strongly and sometimes implicitly our bureaucratic and materialistic society. The humanists not only complained about the dehumanization of the overall culture but also expressed their disenchantment with traditional psychology, which, in picturing human beings as victims of either animal urges or social control, had hardly helped to ameliorate this state of affairs. In this manner, the humanist movement in psychology began to assume something of an antiestablishment posture.

Similarly, it was just this element of rebellion against an alienating society that came to characterize the counterculture. Charles Reich (1970), who is often credited with having written the most complete and sympathetic depiction of the movement, describes it in the following way:

> There is a revolution coming. It will not be like revolutions of the past. It will originate with the individual and with culture, and it will change the political structure only as its final act. It will not require violence to succeed, and it cannot be successfully resisted by violence. It is now spreading with amazing rapidity, and already our laws, institutions and social structure are changing in consequence. It promises a higher reason, a more human community, and a new and liberated individual. Its ultimate creation will be a new and enduring wholeness and beauty—a renewed relationship of man to himself, to other men, to society, to nature, and to the land (p. 2).

Clearly, then, the goals and visions of the counterculture are strongly humanistic.

Along with the urges toward rebellion and change, the two movements had other points in common. Among them were an emphasis on: (1) freedom and the rejection of the idea of "role-appropriate" behavior; (2) the need to expand one's consciousness, whether through drugs or through meditation, body movement, and encounter group participation; (3) an avoidance of the Western tendency to view polarities in a dichotomous, either-or fashion (e.g., mind vs. body, male vs. female, man vs. nature, life vs. death) in favor of more Eastern, Zen-like conceptions of polarity (Watts, 1951) in which each pole dynamically relates to and interpenetrates the other; and (4) the concept of community, which the counterculture actualized by creating permanent communes, and the human potential movement, through the more temporary communality of encounter groups and resident workshops.

The points of official contact between these two movements were few, and members of one were not necessarily members of the other. Hence, many young people strongly identified with the drop-out culture but knew next to nothing about humanistic theory or the human potential movement. Yet in matters of esthetic preferences and life styles, there were many points of overlap. Consequently, a place like Esalen, which came to epitomize the spirit of the human potential movement, took on many features of the counterculture: attitudes toward drugs and nudity were casual; the dining menus stressed natural, organically grown foods; and resident workers—gardeners, janitors, and waiters—tended to be young people who had left the city for a more rural and simple environment. Indeed the Esalen Institute—simply because it could create a life style of its own miles from the city, and bring within its confines professionals with a humanistic orientation—was the single place in which the humanist culture and the counterculture became most closely merged.

On a deeper level it would seem that the two movements gave each other moral support. Since the human potential movement was staffed by professionals who could be perceived as more expert and more adult, it probably was seen by young people as offering an element of respectability and legitimacy to the counterculture. But the counterculture also had something to offer the humanistic psychologists: youthful zest, an atmosphere of revolt, and an integrated life style that promised a viable alternative to the increasing aridity of family life and the bureaucracy of most institutions. The humanist movement bridged both the establishment culture and the counterculture by being composed of mature professionals who had for the most part achieved success according to prevailing social standards, yet who tended to adopt the habits, manners, and dress of the counterculture.

Just how much the humanistic movement in psychology and the counterculture constitute a response to each other—as well as to underlying, causal factors that they share in common—is of course difficult to say. We have stressed the fundamental interconnections between them in order to underscore the extent to which humanistic psychology, in expressing its dissatisfaction with our culture and in its association with the life style of the counterculture, has been more closely linked with esthetic and cultural developments within the general society than have other schools of psychology.

Central Emphases Within Humanistic Psychology

So far we have sketched those intellectual and cultural developments that, starting in the late 1950s, helped bring into prominence humanistic conceptions of man. But what, in a more detailed sense, are these humanistic conceptions? The humanistic position is based on five central principles; as will become clear, they are interrelated and interdependent.

1. **Humanism is strongly phenomenological or experiential: its starting point is conscious experience.** According to the humanist position, conscious experience provides important and primary data for the psychologist to concern himself with, without regard to prior "causes" that might explain it. Humanistic psychology further holds this consciousness to be sacred and inviolable: each person has an unassailable right to his or her own unique feelings and point of view. However, this respect for each person's beliefs does not lead to a moral or intellectual relativism wherein all viewpoints are seen as equally valid. The humanist simply tries to retain an empathic realization that his particular stance is not the only possible one, and that the world—or "reality"—

is not so much objectively given as it is personalized and individual, somewhat different for each perceiver.

Consistent with this experiential orientation, humanistic psychology is known for its strong interest in subjective psychological events. Since many, if not most, people report moments when they feel more "free" (that is, have the sense of being in control of their lives and being relatively unconstrained by outside pressures) and moments when they feel less free, the humanistic psychologist is willing to find a place in his theory for the concept of freedom. Similarly, he is reluctant to discount psychological experiences that, because they seem to defy accepted standards of what is humanly logical or possible (clairvoyance and extra-sensory perception), are often viewed as mystical or unverifiable and as therefore not within the proper domain of science. This kind of empathic approach, wherein conscious experience is accepted on its own terms and no attempt is made to divorce reality from the attitudes and experiences of the person beholding it, is frequently described as a *phenomenological* orientation to psychology. Its roots lie in phenomenology, a distinct school of philosophy founded by the European philosopher, Edmund Husserl, at the end of the last century.

It should not be assumed, however, that humanistic psychology, because of its concern with the subjective, has disowned the scientific point of view, for it is precisely because of its interest in building *a science of human experience* that the humanistic position insists on its rightful place within psychology, as well as within philosophy. However, the humanistic view of science takes it beyond the orientation of *logical positivism* that is assumed by many contemporary psychologists, wherein no psychological phenomenon is taken seriously that cannot be precisely and consistently measured, under standardized conditions, in a relatively large number of people. This rather complex question of what attitudes and procedures best befit a research psychologist relates to the branch of philosophy known as "the philosophy of science," and will be considered at greater length in Chapter 7.

In taking consciousness as its center of interest, humanistic psychology makes a marked departure from the behaviorist position, which traditionally eschews any interest in subjective experience per se. The behavorist regards questions concerning the nature of consciousness as lying beyond the purview of the scientific researcher, since conscious experience is essentially unknowable to anyone other than the person experiencing it. In this sense, consciousness for the behaviorist is an "epiphenomenon": it is no more important for understanding man's behavior than the squeak of a wheel is important for understanding what makes it turn. Once such experiences are talked about in the form of speech, or "verbal reports," and reliably measured in that several observers agree that they have indeed witnessed such a report, they cease to be wholly private events and begin to meet some of the behaviorist's criteria for objectivity.

The humanists' interest in a person's experience renders their focus closer to that of psychoanalysts, who also are interested in the individual's subjective life, particularly that part involving his or her feelings. However, Freud and his followers regarded conscious experiences as secondary, or *manifest*, events that were derived from unconscious, or *latent*, drives and complexes. For instance, a person's extreme concern with giving to others might serve as a defense against awareness of strong dependent and exploitive tendencies, and another person's preoccupation with death might symbolize a deeper fear of castration. On the other hand, humanistic psychologists believe that conscious experience is a given in its own right and does not require any further explanation or analysis. In their insistence that consciousness is its own cause and is not a "result" of more fundamental causes (like repressed dependency), humanists remain true to their phenomenological heritage: they avoid the error of *reductionism* in which a genuine but complex human phenomenon (like creativity or altruism) is somehow explained in terms of, or *reduced to*, more basic defenses or drives. Because of this interest in consciousness as it is occurring and irrespective of whatever connections it may have to the past or to the future, humanistic psychology has become strongly identified with an emphasis on living in the *here-and-now*—i.e., in the immediate experience of the present moment.

2. **Humanistic psychology insists on man's essential wholeness and integrity.** This holistic emphasis recapitulates on the level of personality theory an earlier movement in the development of perceptual theory, when the more molecular emphasis of Wundt's and Tichener's structural psychology was succeeded by the Gestalt school's more "molar" approach to perception. As the structuralists conceptualized it, the perceiving human took in many discrete "bits," or elements, of sensation which were then, through the action of the brain in general and the cortex in particular, combined into recognizable wholes. The more molar Gestaltists, on the other hand, emphasized the extent to which organizing activities inhere in the perceptual act itself, with the result that several discrete visual stimuli, when presented close to one another on a card, are immediately taken in by the eye in terms of a patterned, dynamic "whole" that "is greater than the sum of its parts" (Koffka, 1935).

Kurt Goldstein (1940), who had been strongly influenced by Gestalt perceptual theory, applied similar holistic notions to personality and motivation. He concluded that one very basic human motivation is directed toward unity and wholeness. A similar idea was embodied in the work of other phenomenologically and humanistically oriented personality theorists such as Gordon Allport, Abraham Maslow, and Carl Rogers; these theorists saw the strivings for unity first emphasized by Goldstein as embodying a search for what they at times called "self-actualization"—self-actualization being a process wherein individuals attempt to realize some of their unfulfilled potential, to be something more than they presently are, and in so doing become more complete. In this respect, as in others, humanism has more in common with psychoanalysis than with behaviorism, for psychoanalytic models of mental health frequently equate psychological well-being with a state of integration, and emotional illness with fragmentation and inner conflict (for example, see Cameron, 1963).

The trait theories of the behavioral psychologists viewed the individual as a constellation of distinct habits that could be categorized in terms of such universal dimensions as cleanliness-dirtiness, honesty-dishonesty, strength-weakness, and so on. However, according to a humanistic personality theory like that of Gordon Allport's, behavioral trait theories missed the primary point, which is that human beings have an essential core or being that integrates their seemingly isolated traits into a unique, patterned whole which gives each of them their own, never-to-be repeated character. Hence the quality, the *feel*, of Ted's extroversion is different from Jim's, even though both men may receive precisely the same score on a carefully constructed and well standardized psychological test of extroversion. In this holistic conception, none of our outstanding characteristics or traits can be isolated from any other because they all dynamically interrelate. To leave out the central organizer, core, or "self," is to leave human beings fragmented and hollow, to make them into the alienated, center-less people they all too often, in today's impersonal world, feel themselves to be.

Recent emphases in humanistic psychology, especially those contributed by the human potential movement, have paid particular attention to the essential unity of mind and body. Humanistic psychologists are seriously concerned that psychology too readily overlooks the importance of bodily experience; and their point of view is described by Irvin Child (1973):

> Some philosophers of earlier centuries discussed psychological processes almost as though they occurred in a bodyless mind—a mode of approach that makes scientific study difficult, to say the least. The research tradition, fearful of encountering difficulties in applying a scientific approach, has often tried to confine its view of man to what can be classed as "body"—that is, to those psychological functions for

which some sort of anatomical or physiological account can at the time be given or reasonably imagined. In general, humanistic psychologists reject the timidity of this approach and view it as perpetuating an unnecessary distinction between body and mind. They tend to trust the naive impression that a person is a total functioning organism, and to conclude we should not disregard any part of its functioning just because we have at present no adequate guesses about the anatomical or physiological aspect of that part (p. 16).

Along with the mind-body dichotomy, there are other polar concepts that the humanistically oriented psychologist would like to rely upon less and less: e.g., conscious-vs.-unconscious, inner-vs.-outer, and thought-vs.-feeling. What humanism questions is whether it is meaningful to conceptualize psychological experience in either-or terms. For instance, is it possible to have a pure thought that is devoid of any feeling, or feeling tone? or a feeling without some kind of implicit thought attached to it (e.g., "I feel anxious")? Yet humanists have a problem; in discussing the relative neglect of the body in Western culture and the importance of being in touch with all aspects of our bodily experience, they unwittingly foster the idea that the mind and the body are somehow distinct. The writer of this book faces a similar difficulty, for how can he explain psychoanalysis without articulating the concept of the unconscious and thereby reinforcing the conscious-unconscious polarity? And how can he explain existentialism without focusing on the idea of the subjective and thereby reinforcing the inner-outer polarity (see pp. 24–26 below)? Because these dualisms continue to be part of our theoretical heritage in psychology, he must ask you, the reader, to bear in mind the fact that the humanistic psychologist, while frequently forced to employ either-or concepts, is at the same time determined to ultimately transcend them.

3. **Humanistic psychology, while acknowledging that there are clear-cut limits inherent in human existence, insists that human beings retain an essential freedom and autonomy.** People can at least *attempt* to remove or transcend these limits, and to choose their attitude toward limitations and toward the other conditions imposed on them. Therefore a woman who knows that her death is imminent is nonetheless free to choose the psychological stance with which she will face this unalterable fact. Choice is a central idea in existentialist philosophy, which underscores an individual's responsibility for his or her own decisions and which, like phenomenology, provides crucial philosophic underpinnings to humanistic emphases. Sartre, one of the original and most important existentialists, goes so far as to suggest that one essential aspect of the freedom of human beings lies in their ability to say No in *thought*, as

when political prisoners, albeit overtly conforming, elect to despise their oppressor and their oppressor's ideology. For some, this kind of psychological (as opposed to behavioral) freedom is of no consequence. For the existentially oriented humanist, it is of the utmost importance.

The question of freedom leads straight to an issue that has bedeviled psychology since its inception: Are human beings governed by "free will," or are their lives determined by a combination of innate endowment and significant environmental influences that obtained during their formative periods of development? Humanists have no argument with the fact that each of us is to a great extent affected by heredity, constitution, and the very limitations of existence itself. What they see as crucial, however, is the thin margin of freedom we have when we react to, and attempt to exploit, the given, usually unalterable, conditions of our lives—conditions constituting what Martin Heidegger (1962), another early and extremely important existentialist, referred to as our "thrownness" (our chronological age, our sex, our physiognomy, and the particular historical epoch into which we are "thrown," or born).

In arguing for this margin of freedom, humanists do not claim that it has been demonstrated in any directly empirical or "scientific" sense. Instead, they turn to phenomenology and to the subjective conviction of most people that human beings are essentially free. For instance, as I write and revise this sentence, I have little doubt that it is *I* who am *freely* selecting the words and phrases that I put down, despite my commitment to psychoanalytic theories of unconscious processes and critical childhood experiences. Actually, none of the three prevailing forces in psychology—psychoanalysis, behaviorism, or humanism—would challenge the contention that the average person subjectively experiences a sense of "free will" and active autonomy much of the time. Both the psychoanalyst and the behaviorist, while agreeing that this subjective sense of freedom does not accurately reflect the true state of affairs, would have serious clinical concern about persons who experience the opposite feeling sense about themselves and their lives—namely that their every feeling, every thought, and every behavior was controlled by people or forces outside themselves. Psychologists of almost all persuasions agree that these people are suffering from severe paranoid tendencies.

Yet behaviorists, while acknowledging that it is probably less than healthy to feel oneself as constantly controlled, are willing to offer us such a model of man on a theoretical basis. In their system, human behavior is primarily determined by stimulus inputs (or "reinforcements") of which we are largely unaware, while our *conscious thoughts* as to why we do what we do are essentially unimportant and not worthy of scientific study. Hence there is little match between the model of man that they depict in their theory and the phenomenological conception that most of us have of ourselves. Humanism, on the other hand, is the one school that insists on preserving a correspondence between most people's experiential sense of themselves and the theoretical model that it offers. The humanistic psychologist's intention is to create a psychological theory that includes both human behavior *and* experience and that does not contradict, but instead enhances, whatever sense of autonomy, vitality, and dignity that human beings already have (while not concealing the less attractive, more destructive side of their nature).

Indeed, a central criticism that humanists have made of contemporary psychology is that it has, in offering people the psychoanalytic and behavioral concepts of human nature as its primary models, further exacerbated the alienation and powerlessness experienced by increasing numbers of people today. The behaviorally oriented clinical psychologist is in the ironic position of holding to a theoretical position that pictures human beings as lifeless, passive, and essentially mechanical, while simultaneously diagnosing as schizophrenic patients who describe themselves as being dead or as being machines. The humanistic psychologist deplores this paradox and argues that in creating it behaviorism produces a dissociated and "schizophrenic" sense of what it means to be human. The humanist's aim is to create a psychological theory that does not do violence to a phenomenological experience of free choice and active selfhood.

4. Humanistic psychology is antireductionistic in its orientation. As we indicated above, the strongly phenomenological thrust within humanism takes conscious experiences for what they are and does not try to reduce them to more basic drives or defenses, as in psychoanalysis, or to mere epiphenomena, as in behaviorism. For this reason, creativity and brotherly love are genuine phenomena and need not be viewed as manifestations of erotic drives or as reflections of earlier states of need-satisfaction.

You may be tempted to conclude from this that humanists completely reject the notion of an unconscious mind, a central concept in psychoanalysis frequently used to explain behavior that might otherwise seem incomprehensible. However, it would be more accurate to say that humanists regard the concept of an unconscious as not especially helpful or relevant, since it can never, by its very nature, be directly known. Another reason for their disinterest in the concept is the emphasis that they place on the individual's autonomy. According to the humanist, the idea of the unconscious can easily be used by individuals to deny this autonomy, and to rationalize away their responsibility for their actions;

their "unconscious," rather than they themselves, is to blame for their behavior. Yet another factor in humanistic psychologists' conceptual discomfort with the unconscious is their emphasis on the irreducible wholeness of human beings, as opposed to the fragmented image of human beings and of the human mind that psychoanalysts encourage when they divide the mind into two distinct spheres, the conscious and the unconscious. Rollo May, a psychologist who did more than any other to introduce existential concepts into American psychology and psychiatry, expressed this point in the following way:

> They (the existential-humanists) stand against splitting the being into parts. What is called unconscious, they hold, is still part of this given person; *being,* in any living sense, is at its core indivisible (1958, p. 90).

However, these reservations notwithstanding, most existential and humanistic psychologists do not reject in spirit Freud's notion of the unconscious. They tend to agree that Freud, in developing the concept, helped reveal the darker, irrational side of human nature, and it is this darker aspect, particularly as it is exemplified in feelings of dread (of the unknown, of potential meaninglessness, of death) that existentialism strives to emphasize; indeed, one of the best-known expositions of existential philosophy is entitled *Irrational Man* (Barrett, 1962). May concludes: "The meaning of the discovery [of the unconscious], namely, the radical enlargement of being, is one of the great contributions of our day and must be retained" (p. 91).

5. Humanistic psychology, consistent with its strong grounding in existentialism, believes that human nature can never be fully defined. For if we decide to define human nature by what people actually *do* and actually *are* (or by what the existentialist prefers to call the "being" aspects of the person), instead of by an abstract statement of the essence of humanness, the limits of human capacity will never be fully clear. Chapter 2 will help clarify the existentialist distinction made between being and essence.

If the limits of human nature are not certain, then the human personality is infinitely expandable. This emphasis on the possibilities of expanding and transcending the self ties in directly with man's strivings for self-actualization, mentioned in the second point above, and with the central thrust of the human potential movement, which in general urges the individual to actualize his or her as yet unrealized potential. This point of view challenges the Freudian notion of man as a regression-oriented and tension-reducing organism forever in search of earlier, more primitive forms of gratification.

Recapitulation

Humanistic psychology is a distillation of forces that had existed within philosophy and psychology for several decades. In philosophy it had roots in the phenomenology of Husserl and the existentialism of Heidegger and Sartre. In psychology its major emphases were reflected in the personality theories of Goldstein, Maslow, Allport, and Rogers. Hence, until roughly 1955, humanistic psychology was not so much a distinct school of psychology as a common core of theory and theorists. Then, under the energizing impact of what eventually became known as "the human potential movement," these theoretical and philosophical forces (which in general stressed man's freedom, wholeness, and struggle for meaning) coalesced under the banner and rubric of Humanistic Psychology. For this reason, any account of humanistic psychology cannot omit a history of the human potential movement (see Chapter 6).

However, if the humanistic approach is to retain its integrity as a theoretical orientation, it cannot endorse any particular life style or psychological technique. Although the Esalen Institute in particular and the human potential movement in general, together with the gradual evolution of the counterculture, helped to "put humanistic thinking on the map," humanistic psychology must extend beyond any specific movement or esthetic, for it throws each person back onto his or her own aloneness and his or her own freedom. Some people may choose to live in the style of the counterculture; others may not. Some may choose to practice Transcendental Meditation, or to participate in encounter groups; others may not. And some may opt for more active forms of social protest and political reform. In this sense, the human potential movement may prove to have been a short-lived phenomenon, very much tied to the upheavals in style and values that existed during the time in which it developed. A humanistic orientation in psychology, on the other hand, will hopefully exist for as long as there are theorists who believe in the importance of the individual and human consciousness.

Basic Existential Concepts

chapter two

Existential thought encompasses four main themes: (1) a person's un-avoidable uncertainty when confronted on the one hand by a universe devoid of any clear-cut or easily fixed meaning, and on the other hand by the inevitability of his own eventual nothingness, or death; (2) his or her inherent freedom to choose the attitudes and actions that he or she takes in the face of this potentially meaningless situation; (3) the omnipresent constraints, or limits, that the person's situation places upon his or her freedom; and (4) the impossibility of successfully evading responsibility for whatever choices he or she makes.

Though eventually it led to existential-humanistic schools within both psychology and psychiatry, existentialism began as a formal movement within philosophy. Foreshadowed in the writing of such nineteenth-century philosophers as Kierkegaard and Nietzsche, it came to fruition in the twentieth century under the aegis of several writers, among them being Heidegger, Sartre, Merleau-Ponty, Jaspers, and Camus. It is of course no accident that a philosophy emphasizing the darker and more tragic side of human life took hold during an era burdened by two world wars, massive social fragmentation, and the threat of a third world war that could obliterate all mankind.

Existentialism reminded man that beneath the elaborate structure of his consensually validated, seemingly knowable, and apparently purposeful world there remains the palpable, yet indescribable, fact of sheer biological existence; this fact often leads to a felt awareness of "being" that can inspire both terror and awe and that defies succinct verbal articulation. It is this ephemeralness that accounts for our difficulty in finding words for the existential, or ontological, level of human experience; as others have pointed out, our language is much more able to detail the *characteristics* of the thing or organism that "is" than to elaborate or specify what we mean when we state that this thing or organism "exists." The kinds of personal statements that begin to approximate ontological awareness (although they now, as they appear on the printed page, are necessarily devoid of their associated emotional content) are: I am; one day I was not; one day I shall once again no longer be.

The philosophy of existentialism, then, cannot be divorced from the situation of human beings who realize that their relationship to the world is contingent and finite, and that the world, as experienced by them, will die with them. The more they face this ultimate aloneness, epitomized in the inevitability of their death, the more they sense that the meaningfulness of life, which might *appear* to be validated by the collective, and seemingly purposeful, activity ceaselessly taking place around them, can only be confirmed or refuted on the most personal level. Committing onself to life, and to various life projects, does not occur automatically; it is a specific task that faces each individual as he or she matures and becomes aware of his or her own mortality. There is no way out of the existential dilemma of why one lives, because ignorance, or neglect, of the problem in itself is an existential stance, or "decision," albeit an *inauthentic* one (inauthentic because the person, failing to explicitly acknowledge that he has made a decision, takes no responsibility for it).

Hence human beings, born into a universe whose meaning is not manifestly given, and given no guidelines as to what constitutes a legitimate purpose for their own existence (or even as to whether such a purpose is necessary or desirable) find themselves in an "absurd" situation (Camus, 1955). Yet the fact that no one but themselves can provide the measure of their life's purposefulness, and the possibility that they might be able to create their own meaning, add elements of dignity and courage to this absurdity.

The existentialists' own personal experience played an important role in the "ontology," or science of being, that they were gradually to develop, for their emphasis on the awe experienced at the mere fact of biological existence, at the simple realization that we *are*, came straight from the data of their own consciousness. In this sense existentialism was the offspring of phenomenology, a method of analysis in philosophy in which the study of any particular phenomenon had, as its starting point, a first-person description of what it feels like to directly experience that phenomenon. Credit for the original development of phenomenology is usually given to Edmund Husserl; Husserl was in turn a teacher of Martin Heidegger, who is considered to have been the single most influential figure in the development of existential philosophy. Indeed, existentialism is inextricably related to phenomenology, and for this reason the school is sometimes referred to as existential phenomenology. However, as Misiak and Sexton point out (1973), while all existentialists are phenomenologists in that their analysis of the human existential situation proceeds directly from their own experience, not all phenomenologists are existentialists, for phenomenology is the more basic method, and as such it applies to the analysis of all human subjective experiences, including the perception of color and movement. Existentialism, then, may be seen as a more specific application of phenomenology to those aspects of the person that are normally subsumed in psychology under the terms "motivation" and "personality": how do individuals relate themselves to the universe, to other people, and to their own attempts to discover meaningful values?

Existentialism is better viewed as a movement of revolt than as a formal school with firmly established principles or tenets. In this respect it strongly resembles the phenomenological movement that preceded it in philosophy and the humanism in social science that was eventually its outgrowth, and it cannot easily be given a succinct or specific definition. What we outline in the present chapter is a common core of fundamental and frequently encountered existential concepts, each of which has been given a unique twist by the particular theorist employing it.

Being and Nonbeing

By referring to our felt awareness that we "*are*"—that we have a definite existence specific to a particular body and a particular time—the concept of being has a strong phenomenological grounding. It is an existential, as opposed to essentialist, concept because it takes into account the fluidity that being alive implies: I may have a sense of what I was, and what I am, but I cannot know for certain what, during the next moment, I shall be and what I shall experience. Because human beings and their experiences are ever evolving and never fixed, they cannot validly be described by definitive attributes or characteristics——i.e., we cannot state their *essence*. As a being, a process, there is always within one a potential for totally new, never-before-evidenced behavior. Hence we can never discover the true essence of human nature, for human nature is always in the process of redefining itself.

Despite the state of openness and potential freedom that the concept of being implies, there are some circumstances over which individuals have no control. These circumstances—like their particular sex, race, physiognomy, and historical epoch—constitute what Heidegger termed man's "thrownness." In the act of being born, one is "thrown" into the world and into a particular situation within the world.

The basic conditions of a person's situation set some limits to his existence, but they cannot completely determine it. For example, a man born into the twentieth century cannot ever experience, first hand, what it was like to live during the fifteenth century. This is a clear-cut limitation on his experience. However, how he responds to that limitation is within his area of freedom. He can try to find out as fully as possible just what it felt like, for some people, to live during the fifteenth century, and he is free to *fantasize* that he is living during this earlier period. Similarly, he is free to try to feel at home in the twentieth century, just as he is free to proudly hate and curse this fact of his existence. (He is also free to shift from one of these attitudes to the other). Because this man has some measure of freedom, however slight, with regard to how he faces the limiting conditions of his thrownness, he is able to transcend his immediate situation. If he is thus open to his sense of "being"—to the fact that his attitudes and his life path have not yet been, and can never be, fully fixed—he feels his future open before him full of possibilities, some of which will be actualized by him and some of which will not.

As a means of clarifying the distinction between essence and being on a phenomenological level, some existential theorists differentiate between the experience of "self-as-subject" and "self-as-object" (Keen, 1970). Keen describes the sense of self-as-subject in the following way:

> The experience of *what* I am is at times dwarfed by the experience *that* I am. This is a second, entirely different sort of self-experience. . . . Rather than viewing myself as an object of my self-conscious scrutiny, I am now living the part of the viewer, the subject of the act, "I-see-me." The "I" experience does not contain attributes, characteristics and traits, as the "me" experience does. Rather than being experienced as a fixed entity, the "I" is experienced as a dynamic, open-ended activity without the stability of the me-as-object, i.e., without an essence. The "I" is pure existence, noteworthy because it *is*, not because it is *such and such* (p. 14).

The more the person experiences in subject terms, the more his view of himself and of the world seems to him as potentially valid as that of anyone else. While he is naturally reactive to the world around him, he realizes that he is capable of modifying, or attempting to modify, those of his reactions that displease him, and he is in turn able to have some measure of influence on the world. On the other hand, the more he experiences himself in an object sense, the more he begins to perceive himself as though from outside—to define himself in terms of how others see him and in terms of his meaning for *them*. The problem with this stance is that the person, as he experiences less and less contact with his subject side, tends to see himself as an object who (like inanimate objects) is acted upon and done to. It is then but a short step to his viewing himself as having an essence that is fixed and that has been primarily determined by external forces. (Of course, it is the rare and exceptionally unintrospective person who never becomes the object of his own self-conscious scrutiny, or who does not try to see himself through the eyes of others. Therefore the existentialist focuses on the *relative balance* between these two modes of experience and points out the consequences of a too-exclusive emphasis on the self-as-object experience.)

One cannot experience a full sense of being, however, without envisaging the possibility of nonbeing, and without feeling the dread that often accompanies such an envisagement. Being and nonbeing are in a fundamental and interdependent relationship to each other, much as are the "figure and ground" of Gestalt perceptual psychology. In Gestalt terms, a stimulus figure receives more conscious attention from the perceiver than does its ground (or background), but without the ground the figure could not be perceived. If we take a visual stimulus as an example, we find that a black circle is seen only by virtue of the somewhat lighter background surrounding it. Similarly, being can only be savored in a context permitting an awareness of the ever-present possibility of nonbeing, or death. Each moment of life becomes more precious and more fully "owned," the more one realizes that existence is finite.

BEING-IN-THE-WORLD

This concept was originally introduced by Heidegger. As with being and nonbeing, a dialectical relationship is intended—this time between the self and the world. The hyphens indicate that without the world there is no self (since the very notion of selfhood implies some kind of background, or world, against which one's self is contrasted); and without the self there is no world (for each of us, the world will die once there is no longer an "I"-perceiver to experience it; the person, in death, loses both himself and the world). Hence the expression "being-in-the-world" is meant to suggest much more than a purely spatial relationship.

This concept (like that of "intentionality"—see p. 26 below) represents an attempt to overcome the subject-object dichotomy in philosophy, which had supposedly plagued Western epistemology since Descartes first attempted to distinguish a mind, or "Soul," that is somehow detached from the body and from the sensory input impinging on it. As the existentialists saw it, the Cartesian conception fragmented what man had initially experienced as a holistic relationship to the universe into a division between "inner" and "outer" reality that isolates the knower from the known and that alienates modern man from the world he inhabits. In this model of reality, two people, each with his "self" buried deeply and obscurely within him, can only become indirectly known to each other. Such a view contrasts sharply with the existential notion of an I-Thou, dialogic relationship wherein each person fully and directly encounters the other (see "The I-Thou Relationship" immediately below). In the I-Thou concept there is no self, no "inner person," that is secreted away within one; access to the world is immediate, and the self comes into being, and continues to actualize itself, through direct intercourse with the world.

By reminding us that the self is inextricably related to the world that it is experiencing, existential phenomenology emphasized the creativity that is involved in man's formation of his own reality. Traditional Western philosophy, in particular logical positivism, had on the other hand devalued subjectivity as a potential source of error in man's efforts to acquaint himself with "objective" reality. Existentialism saw this differently. If the world pole of the self-world (or subject-object) polarity is experienced as more fundamental or "real" than the "I" who is the perceiver of that world, the being aspects of one's existence become devitalized. The more the sense of oneself as an active subject becomes devitalized, the more one begins to experience oneself as a mere object in a world of objects. It is important to remember, however, that existentialists were not attempting to reverse this order of priorities and to elevate the "I"-perceiver to a position *superior* to that of the world, or of what we normally mean by "reality." By stressing the dialectic relationship between subject and object, they were trying to transcend this polarity altogether.

THE I-THOU RELATIONSHIP

Martin Buber was an influential Jewish theologian whose philosophy was strongly existentialist in its orientation. Buber's conception of the

I-Thou relationship (Buber, 1970) has important implications for how
the existential humanist views the psychotherapist-patient relationship.
It also helps to amplify the distinction between self-as-subject and self-
as-object.

Buber contrasted the I-Thou (or I-You) relationship with the I-It relationship. In the I-You relationship I know that you, while you initially
appear within my phenomenology as an object, or "it" (in the sense that
you are part of the otherness of *my* perceived world), are actually, from
your point-of-view, the subject of *your* world. The process of empathy
enables me to try to imagine what the world looks like from your perspective.

My ability to remember that you are subject of *your* world (just as I
am subject of mine) has some important applications. When we have a
disagreement in which I see you as clearly wrong, it reminds me that you
are just as convinced of the correctness of your opinion as I am of mine.
When I am tempted to define you in essentialistic terms ("you are a
kind, stable, and studious person"), it reminds me that you are a *process*
and not a fixed thing (you are not always kind, stable, or studious). Even
in terms of your immediate behavior, the action that I deem kind you
may view differently. In your eyes, your behavior may be activated by
very mixed motives and feelings. It may also foster in other people a
subtle dependency and may therefore, in your perception, be less than
kind. One way in which I can become less concerned about what you
are like, in essentialistic terms, is to attend to my *feeling* response to
you. I may discover that I like you, and that I feel good about myself
when in your presence. Now I am owning the being and subject aspects
of my perception, and my perception of you as kind has as much to do
with my immediate, warm feeling for you as it does with your (alleged)
"kindness."

I "thing" you and turn you into an "it" every time I use you, or attempt to do so, for my purposes. I "thing" you when your admiration
becomes necessary for my sense of importance or status, or when I
need you (a patient) to improve in order for me (a therapist) to feel
helpful or competent. It is here that the I-Thou relationship applies to
psychotherapy, for it states that the patient is more than an object whose
every movement toward integration is a function of the therapist's effectiveness (or whose every move toward retrogression, a function of the
therapist's ineffectiveness). The more the therapist reminds himself of
the patient's freedom to remain ill or get well, the more he can respond
to the patient as the subject of his (the patient's) own world. The more
he attributes a patient's sense of well-being, or lack thereof, to his success or failure as a therapist, the more he tends to render the patient

an "it" who is the passive object of his (the therapist's) competence. Does this mean that the patient's improvement has *nothing* to do with the therapist? Not quite—we shall have more to say about this issue in Chapter 3, where we discuss existential-humanistic approaches to psychotherapy in more detail.

Intentionality

Intentionality bears some resemblance to the principle of *psychic determinism* within psychoanalysis, which postulates that no mental event occurs purely by chance (i.e., without, at some unconscious level, having been "intended" by the person). In a similar vein, but with a different emphasis, the present concept implies that some degree of meaning and intent colors the most fundamental acts of consciousness. Indeed, it was the contention of Husserl (the founder of phenomenology) and of Brentano (his teacher, and therefore generally considered to be the forerunner of phenomenology) that intentionality is built into the very fabric of consciousness. As Rollo May put it (1969, p. 226), "consciousness is defined by the fact that it *intends* something, points toward something outside itself—specifically, that it *intends the object*." In the act of consciousness one is therefore already reaching out toward the world with some degree of purposiveness, and in this way the concept of intentionality helps bridge the gap between subject and object. In other words, although psychologists tend to locate consciousness *inside* a person's head, the *contents* of his or her consciousness embrace the world immediately and concretely. We are again confronted with an apparent polarity, one that the existentialist wants to transcend, this time between "inner" and "outer" reality. In an effort to show the artificiality of this dualism, Sartre (1956) goes so far as to insist that the table seen by him is not *in* his head (or his consciousness) but is instead *"out there"* in the spaces of the real world.

Some degree of intentionality, then, is built into the act of perception. For instance, what we view must be in part guided by our intentions, since what we see is a direct consequence of where we choose to look. We could not see at all if our eyes were closed; thus the very fact of perception demands some degree of "cooperation," or readiness, on our part. As we have emphasized throughout, the world that impinges on us is not wholly independent of our being.

Let's take this a step further. Your eyes are open and are fixed on a particular object (both these facts, as we just indicated, are in part a function of your intentionality). Those aspects of the object that you now choose to attend to will also be a function of your intentionality. May (1969, p. 224) gives the illustration of a man going to see a house in the mountains. What he focuses upon will be affected by his purpose in going. Is he the owner, checking to see whether the house can easily be rented? (If so, he is likely to miss seeing many of the house's features that are already familiar to him, but he will quickly notice those things that are in need of repair). Is he a visitor hoping to spend a pleasant afternoon? (If so, he is likely to experience the house in a passive and sensual way). Or is he an artist who wishes to paint a picture of the house? (If so, he may see it in a more fresh and detailed way than either the owner or the visitor). A rather extensive research literature has developed around the finding that our perceptions are strongly contingent on the assumptions, expectancies, and "sets" that we bring with us to the perceptual situation (Allport, 1955).

Similarly, one's intentions help to create his or her interpersonal experience. If one's intention is to use other people to justify feelings of inferiority, one will find much in them to admire and to envy. If one's intention is to pick a fight, then one will find things to disagree with. In this way most of us, from time to time, illustrate the phenomenon of the "self-fulfilling prophecy" wherein we manage to bring about just what we most feared (or hoped) would happen.

Unlike psychoanalysis, existentialism does not concern itself with a careful distinction between conscious and unconscious events. Therefore, while related to the Freudian notion of psychic determinism, the concept of intentionality ends up with a quite different emphasis, for it places the responsibility for a person's perceptions and thoughts, not on his unconscious, but on *him*. One's way of relating to the world is a matter of one's intentions, even though these intentions are activated at a level of being that is far more profound than the volitional level involved in our usual everyday choices. (Should I wear red or blue? Should I read my newspaper or my book?) In this sense, intentionality is best divorced from our usual notion of intentions, in which one plans an action and then carries it out. In intentionality, there is no essential separation between intention and action. One doesn't necessarily decide and then choose; one may choose without rational aforethought, and in the act of choosing experience his or her intentionality. The meaning of our action often emerges in the act itself, not before. Sometimes the meaning only emerges afterwards, when our "intention," in the more usual sense of this word, is to discover the intentionality that informed our act (it is this kind of exploration that psychotherapy usually encourages). Thus by being alive, and by doing things, the person intends.

Despite the fact that we often are not directly aware of the intentionality informing our acts at the moment that we perform them, we are nonetheless, in an existential framework, responsible for our "choices" and our "decisions." Thus the task of existential psychotherapists is a difficult one, for they ask their patients to "own up to" their choices at the same time that they empathize with their patients' feelings that the problems of their lives are *not* of their choosing and are beyond their control. Keen put this matter well when he wrote:

> It violates an implicit moral tradition to attribute an active role to the person for what he is and at the same time to have compassion for his plight and to make the commitment to try to help him do something about it. And yet that is exactly the paradox that the clinical psychologist must live with. To assume the individual is purely a passive recipient of forces playing upon him is not to do him a favor clinically. The goal of clinical psychology is to help the person appreciate and participate in the authorship of his self-world relationship, not to reinforce passivity by making it more comfortable; the goal is to promote responsibility, not to condone escape from it (1970, pp. 83–84).

Authentic and Inauthentic Existence

The concepts enumerated thus far help pave the way for understanding the existentialist's definition of authentic and inauthentic existence. In inauthentic existence one seeks to confirm himself in ways that will help one avoid confronting the specter of nonbeing. In today's society, inauthentic goals often stem from grandiose and competitive notions of existence in which the self is perceived as an essence that must achieve certain fixed characteristics, often involving tangible signs of "success." In trying to confirm oneself inauthentically, one plays status-seeking games and tends to view others as a means of gaining applause for one's life "performance." (In doing this one treats the other person as a thing, as an "it.") Because the security that the person longs for involves protection from the threat of nonbeing, the quest is doomed to failure and each apparent success is usually tinged with some sense of disappointment.

Sartre's concept of "bad faith" (1965) describes an inauthentic situation in which one refuses to take responsibility for one's decisions. An example would be a man who explains his stealing by stating that he is a thief. This person has an essentialist conception of identity in which the self is defined in terms of what one has been, or what one appears to be in the eyes of others. As a being in the process of becoming, the "thief" will remain a thief only if he chooses to continue his stealing. For him to claim that he had until now been unaware of the possibility of choice (that it had not occurred to him that he could be anything but a thief) constitutes another act of bad faith, for unawareness is not without some degree of intentionality and choice.

In an authentic existence a person confronts directly the ever-emergent possibility of nonbeing, makes decisions in the face of uncertainty, and takes responsibility for them. When it comes to his human relationships, he is secure enough to respect the autonomy of other people; he appreciates that they have their own purposes to fulfill and do not exist simply for his own pleasure and self-enhancement.

A completely authentic existence is an ideal. It is something that most people hopefully approximate from time to time, some perhaps to a greater degree, or more frequently, than others. To perceive a person's entire life span as characterized by authenticity (or inauthenticity) would be to view him in too essencelike a way. If we instead look at a person in "being" terms, he or she exists only now, in the immediate moment, and it is within this moment that he or she lives either authentically or inauthentically.

EXISTENTIAL VS. NEUROTIC ANXIETY

As we indicated earlier, a healthy sense of being entails some awareness of the threat of nonbeing. However, an appreciation of death as a constant possibility must produce a certain amount of anxiety. Since it is an unavoidable consequence of living, this anxiety is referred to as existential anxiety. While the visualizing of nonbeing provides the most dramatic context for existential anxiety, other contingencies in human existence may also account for its appearance. One is the necessity to act and to make choices in the face of uncertainty, with the result that there is no one to blame but ourselves for actions that are bound to have unpredictable, and sometimes unfortunate, consequences. Even behavior that is genuinely designed to benefit others can inadvertently bring harm to them. Another source of existential anxiety is individuation, which guarantees that despite the possibilities of communication and empathy, we can never fully discover just what it feels like to be someone else. We are born alone and we die alone.

Existential anxiety is not pathological. Neurotic anxiety is, and it results whenever a person evades existential anxiety by failing to confront it directly and make active choices in spite of it. Although neurotic anxiety can manifest itself in a variety of ways, the existentialist sees it as typically involving some diminishment of the sense of self-as-subject and a corresponding increase in the sense of self-as-object. Now one begins to live according to the expectations of others, and he behaves as he *ought* to behave (in terms of externalized criteria). The more one experiences oneself as an object, the more one limits life's meaning to the avoidance of harm from others, whether this harm appears in the form of negative evaluations of oneself, or the threat of actual physical abuse or attack (in which case the neurotic symptoms become more serious, and we often describe them as "phobic" or "paranoid"). Once there is a real breakdown in the person's more autonomous relatedness to the world, experiences of disorganization, depersonalization, and meaninglessness can occur (here we move from situations usually described as neurotic to those that are termed psychotic).

EXISTENTIAL GUILT VS. NEUROTIC GUILT

According to the existentialist, most psychodynamically oriented personality theories—especially psychoanalysis—too often ignore the question of actual guilt and regard a person's guilt feelings as inappropriate and irrational. For the existential phenomenologist, however, there is such a thing as ontological, or genuine, guilt. Such guilt is experienced whenever we have, for whatever reasons, brought real hurt or disappointment to another. Existential guilt is also experienced when we neglect certain potentialities within us. Since we can never fulfill all our potentials, some degree of existential guilt is inevitable.

As was the case with existential anxiety, ontological guilt, when it is evaded, becomes neurotic. And as with anxiety, the neurotic form of this emotion usually involves a curtailment of a person's sense of himself as an active subject; instead he objectifies himself, accusing himself of having failed to meet arbitrary standards involving fair and loving treatment of others. Of course, many of our actions do bring hurt to others, whether or not this was our conscious wish. To the degree to which we take responsibility for these actions and feel pain because we care about these other people (self-as-subject), we experience either existential anxiety (in anticipating the possibility of hurting them in the future) or existential guilt (after an actual hurt has occurred). All too often, however, guilt involves a breakdown in the experience of self-as-subject. Instead of he whom we have hurt being of prime concern, we focus on our self as an object or essence, wondering if we are evil or good, and if we deserve damnation or salvation (either at the hands of others or of God).

The fields of the three theorists to be discussed in the next chapter—Maslow, Szasz, and Laing—lie within medicine and social science. Yet these men, while not formal philosophers, take an approach to personal development, and to the individual's relationship to his society, that is strongly existential in its central thrust and spirit. In this way we shall see in slightly greater detail some of the implications that existentialism has for theories of personality and psychological adjustment.

Humanistic Theories of
Personality and Adjustment

chapter three

Several personality psychologists have developed theoretical approaches that might properly be described as humanistic, among them being Kurt Lewin, Kurt Goldstein, Gordon Allport, Erich Fromm, Henry Murray, Carl Rogers, Charlotte Buhler, and Abraham Maslow. It is beyond the scope of this book to describe each of their theories in detail, and the reader who is interested in this kind of presentation should refer to Hall and Lindzey's *Theory of Personality* (1970). Here we shall focus on a very few representative theories.

We begin with an outline of Maslow's holistic-dynamic theory of personality. One of the reasons for choosing Maslow as an exemplar of the humanistic position in personality theory is the fact that his writings manage to incorporate each of the major conceptual emphases that the theorists cited above share in common. These emphases are: (1) a holistic thrust wherein the person is viewed as a unique totality: each trait must be seen in dynamic relationship to all other traits and cannot be meaningfully studied in isolation; (2) the assumption that those personal attributes that seem most distinctively human (like self-awareness, compassion, and creativity) are not derived from, or secondary to, more fundamental and physiologically based drives, but instead constitute primary phenomena in their own right; (3) the view that the human organism has inherent capacities for development and growth that originate independent of the environment, however much the latter may enhance, modify, or thwart these potentialities; (4) the conviction that these predispositions or potentials are either basically good or at least neutral (i.e., neither good nor bad); therefore the distorting effects of a misguided or hostile environment are always responsible for whatever overweaning selfishness, greed, or cruelty emerge in the developing child; and (5), the equating of emotional maturity or health with the ability to realize one's inherent potential and to accept one's individuality and fundamental aloneness.

Another reason for our selection is that Maslow, because of his active attempts to give greater structure and visibility to the humanistic position in contemporary psychology (as well as because of the theoretical thrust of his work), has been cited as the spiritual father of humanistic psychology (Misiak and Sexton, 1973). While he was hardly the first psychologist to articulate a humanistic conception of personality, Maslow, more than any other single person, specifically took American academic psychology to task for its emphasis on determinism and animal drives and its concomitant neglect of man's capacity for nobility and freedom. As a result of his efforts, the American Association of Humanistic Psychologists was founded in 1962, and in 1970 the Division of Humanistic Psychology was added to the several subdivisions of the American Psychological Association.

Carl Rogers is another personality theorist who has been a guiding force in the formal development of a humanistic movement in psychology. However, since Rogers has exerted the greatest influence in his client-centered school of counseling and psychotherapy and in his innovative approaches to classroom teaching, a summary of his contributions will be reserved for Chapters 4 and 5.

Following the presentation of Maslow, the theories of Thomas Szasz and Ronald Laing are summarized. Laing and Szasz are two psychiatrists who have been strongly critical of society's prevailing approach to mental illness and to problems of emotional adjustment. Because they are so concretely concerned with the mental patient's emotional and political freedom (which they cherish) and with what they see as active efforts on the part of institutional psychiatry to curtail this freedom, these writers clearly fall within the humanistic tradition.

Maslow's Holistic-Dynamic Theory of Personality

Maslow was born in 1908 and grew up in New York City. He died in 1970, during his first year as resident fellow at the W. Price Laughlin Foundation in California. He was at the foundation to investigate the implications of humanistic psychology for related academic disciplines such as economics, political science, and ethics; the previous year he had taken a leave of absence from Brandeis University, where he had taught for eighteen years and had been chairman of the Psychology Department for ten years.

Briefly attracted to behaviorism as an undergraduate student at the University of Wisconsin, Maslow during the early phases of his career concentrated on primate behavior, in particular reaction time, food preferences, and patterns of dominance and submission. Although interested in discovering continuities between primate and human behavior, especially the needs for sex and affection, Maslow was also convinced that there existed a fundamental human nature that was unique to *homo sapiens* as a distinct species within animal life and that could not, beyond a certain limit, be modified by various social, political, or historical conditions. As Lowry (1973, p. 77) has pointed out, this search for man's higher nature had constituted a remarkably consistent theme in Maslow's life, for as early as 1928 Maslow had written in an undergraduate paper the following phrase: "At the moment of the mystic experience we see wonderful possibilities and inscrutable depths in mankind. . . ."

THE MOTIVATIONAL HIERARCHY

Maslow saw human needs operating in a multilayered and dynamic fashion. For example, some needs are more salient at a particular stage of human development than others—a person's need for security is usually more pronounced during childhood than adulthood. Similarly, needs differ in their prepotency, or degree of priority; some press for satisfaction harder than others. Thus the food-deprived person, in the immediate moment of intense hunger, worries more about eating than about an unrequited love affair. If he were suddenly deprived of oxygen, his concern with breathing would quickly take precedence over his concern with food (Lowry, p. 27).

However, Maslow was unwilling to view one need as somehow based on, or derived from, another. Each level of need, whether *seemingly* sophisticated because it bears a less obvious relationship to physical survival and is not openly manifest in every member of the human species (e.g., the striving for artistic expression), or *seemingly* primitive and primary because its physiological aspects and clear-cut relationship to survival can be more readily described (e.g., hunger), was as human and basic as any other. In arguing that the various levels of need are reasonably independent of one another, Maslow was rejecting the tension-reduction principle of both the psychoanalytic and behavioral theories of motivation. According to Freudian thought, all behavior satisfies instinctual longings (even activity that seems to create tension rather than reduce it, like writing a book or engaging in scientific research). Hence the work of the professional detective might reflect the sublimation of a repressed childhood wish to spy on the sexual activities of his parents. In this view, overt behavior that the person rationalizes with socially acceptable reasons really expresses—or can be reduced to— the operation of unconscious needs.

Similarly, in a behavioral framework, seemingly adult motivations can be traced, via behavior chains, to more primitive gratifications. For example, a woman's absorption in crossword puzzles is associated with an identification with her mother. The identification is based on strong love for the mother, a love that in turn relates to more primitive need-satisfaction (i.e., the mother's satiation of her hunger through feeding). Maslow was remaining true to the strongly *antireductionistic* thrust of humanistic thought (see Chapter 1), wherein distinctively human and complex responses like love and creativity are not explained in terms of earlier experiences.

From a developmental point of view, lower-level needs manifest themselves earlier in life than do higher-level needs and must be tended to before higher-level needs emerge. Hence Maslow was able to devise a motivational hierarchy postulating five distinct levels of need. These were:

> Level 1—Physiological needs: survival-related needs such as those for oxygen, food, sex, and sleep.
> Level 2—Safety needs: needs for order, stability, routine, economic and job security.
> Level 3—Belongingness and love needs: physical contact, affection, family membership, informal social networks, clubs, and organizations.
> Level 4—Esteem needs: includes both the need for self-esteem (e.g. a sense of competence, autonomy, and mastery) and for esteem and indications of esteem, from others (e.g. praise, recognition, status, and reputation).
> Level 5—Self-actualization needs: can involve playfulness and curiosity, the search for truth and understanding, the attempt to secure equality and justice, the creation and love of beauty.

Need levels 1 through 4 were described as "deficiency" needs by Maslow, while level 5 needs were at different times termed self-actualization needs, higher-order needs, growth needs, and "metaneeds." Metaneeds differ from deficiency needs in that they are long-term and forever active (and in this sense, can never be easily satisfied), whereas deficiency needs, like hunger, or the need for order, or the search for belongingness, can be appeased, however temporarily (assuming that they have not reached seriously neurotic, or insatiable, proportions). Hence it is only deficiency needs that lend themselves to a homeostatic model wherein the individual, after a period of need-related activity, finds himself or herself "at rest," in a state of relative satiation. How can one ever satisfy the search for artistic excellence or spiritual fulfillment? In a corollary fashion, the means-end dichotomy often employed in looking at deficiency motivation (e.g., one drinks water so as to assuage a sense of thirst) no longer applies to metaneeds; here one's activity (e.g., the writing of a poem) is not so much a means of reaching a specific goal as it is a gratifying activity in its own right.

For the mature or healthy person, the satisfaction of deficiency needs has ceased to be the critical issue that it was earlier in his or her life. If more or less satisfied on a reasonably periodic basis and woven into the daily fabric of living, deficiency needs do not have to become especially prominent or problematic in one's life. It is only the neurotic or seriously immature individual who, perhaps deprived of security and affection as a child, finds himself perpetually seeking love and acceptance from others. Lowry puts it as follows:

> Thus, to be healthy is to be good and self-actualizing, and if one falls short of being good and self-actualizing, he does so only because he is sick. This, of course, is not to say that people are all good and self-actualizing; it is only to say that they are all good and self-actualizing *underneath*. If only their basic needs are adequately fulfilled, they would be good and self-actualizing on the surface as well (p. 29).

What Maslow tried to emphasize was the fact that metaneeds, simply because they are less prepotent than deficiency needs, are in no way less rooted in the fundamental nature of the human being. According to him, the search for self-actualization, whether via intellectual, esthetic, or spiritual pursuits, was endemic to man and was what made him truly human. We have a need to transcend the more animalistic and security-conscious side of our beings. "What a man *can* be, he *must* be" (Maslow, 1970, p. 46). And for Maslow the ultimate direction that the satisfaction of such needs may take in the case of any particular individual has as much to do with the person's basic constitution or inherent capacities as it does with specific learning or environmental influences.

Nonactualizers have not yet grown into their mature or full humanness and therefore have yet to fulfill their basic nature. Maslow's thinking here reverses the usual connotation of the terms "human" and "humanness," which typically refer to man's weakness and fallibility. Instead he sees people as becoming most completely human when they strive for some kind of perfection and fulfill their highest possibilities by discovering a nonegocentric, creative engagement with the world.

THE STUDY OF SELF-ACTUALIZATION

Maslow had postulated the existence of level 5 needs on a more or less a priori basis, although he had no dearth of actual historic figures who seemed to personify the kind of creativity he had in mind. He then decided to study at closer hand a group of people who, on the basis of their achievements, seemed to merit the description of "self-actualizers." This research involved his well-known study of self-actualizers and was initially reported in the first edition, published in 1954, of his book *Motivation and Personality* (1970).

The research subjects included people whom Maslow knew personally and people who were well known in the past and present. He looked for a person who fulfilled the self-actualization criteria while at the same time exhibiting no outstanding signs of serious emotional or personality disturbance. In articulating what he had in mind by self-actualization Maslow wrote:

> ... it may be loosely described as the full use and exploitation of talents, capacities, potentialities, etc. Such people seem to be fulfilling themselves and to be doing the best that they are capable of doing, reminding us of Nietzsche's exhortation, "Become what thou art!" They are people who have developed or are developing to the full stature of which they are capable (1970, p. 150).

Keeping in mind another important selection criterion, he also searched for indications that these people had fulfilled lower-level needs like those for safety and belongingness.

Maslow knew from the first that his study would not be well controlled, with precise measures of observation, and this was not his intention. Impressions were formed on the basis of relatively informal contacts, sometimes with friends and relatives of the subjects; his interviews with these people did not follow a standard outline. Subjects were often self-conscious or seemingly embarrassed by the research effort, perhaps out of modesty, and it was usually impossible to ask them very personal questions or to administer psychological tests. However, he was able to administer tests to a group of younger subjects.

Gradually Maslow purified his sample. Some cases turned out not to meet the original criteria as much as he had hoped and had to be discarded. Others furnished new insights into the nature of self-actualization, and these insights in turn led to some modifications of the original criteria. Then, on the basis of these somewhat revised criteria, new subjects were tentatively added. With these procedures Maslow eventually wound up with a sample of about sixty subjects, some of whom successfully met all his criteria, and some of whom fell slightly short of them but who nonetheless shed some light on the self-actualization process. Approximately three-quarters of the people were public figures, either past or present, such as Einstein, Eleanor Roosevelt, Eugene Debs, Adlai Stevenson, Freud, Thoreau, and Lincoln (many of the subjects who are now dead were alive at the time of the original study).

Maslow's findings suggested that there are certain basic preconditions for successful self-actualization. One, of course, is that the person's lower-level needs have been reasonably satisfied. Another is that the person feel motivated by, and loyal to, values going beyond personal gain or gratification—in other words, values such as truth, justice, or beauty, that can somehow be construed as lying *outside* the self. Still another is that of age; although Maslow studied young people who gave every indication of having embarked upon a path that would ultimately lead to self-actualization, he found that those subjects who had the most self-actualizing styles of life were usually sixty years of age or older.

What traits are associated with self-actualization? Maslow highlighted the following characteristics: (1) spontaneity and creativity; (2) an ability to transcend the immediate environment (for instance, self-actualizers often have more in common with creative people from different cultures than they do with other people in their own social context); they also perceive the world in relatively novel and unstereotyped ways—they experience other people as they *are*, and not as they used to be or are expected to be; (3) while their friendships tend to be intimate and open, they do not have an overriding need for company and instead frequently seek out privacy and solitude; (4) they have a nonjudgmental, accepting attitude toward both themselves and others; (5) they are deeply democratic and ethical—i.e., they tend to treat all people with a certain measure of respect and nonexploitiveness; however, this does not mean that they have a laissez-faire, indifferent attitude toward cruelty and evil; (6) their sense of humor tends toward the ironic and is directed toward the failings of humankind rather than mocking or "slamming" a specific individual; (7) a healthy ability to differentiate between what is real and authentic (however disappointing) and what is imagined or false; and (8) an inclination toward mystical and "peak" experiences.

THE PEAK EXPERIENCE

As we have just seen, one trait that Maslow found characteristic of his self-actualizing subjects was their ability to have mystical or spiritual experiences. He found that most people had experiences of this kind, but perhaps no more than onee or twice during their entire lives. (Yet the ability of the average person to have such an experience, however rarely, offered proof that a capacity for deeper, or higher, states of existence was very much present within him or her, thereby bearing out Maslow's contention that most of us have many untapped potentials). Maslow came to call this experience a "peak" experience, and he himself was no stranger to it. He wrote in one of his journals: "I think I used to call it 'exultation' to myself, with lump in throat, tears in eyes, chills, prickles, slight feeling of (pleasant) nausea, and all sorts of other autonomic reactions plus impulse to shout and yell, etc." (Lowry, p. 53).

The concept of the peak experience gradually came to occupy a key position within Maslow's theory, partly because of its ecstatic nature and partly because it implied a reverence for life and an ability to see the world as it really was that for him epitomized the self-actualizing attitude. Among the distinguishing characteristics of the peak experience were the following: (1) Wholeness and concreteness: the object perceived is seen as complete and as utterly unique. It is viewed in terms of itself and does not have to be related, or compared, to anything else in order to be appreciated. "It is seen as if it were all there was in the universe, as if it were all of Being, synonymous with the universe" (Maslow, 1968, p. 74). (2) It is perceived with care, if not love: "The caring minuteness with which a mother will gaze upon her infant again and again, or the lover at his beloved, or the connoisseur at his painting will surely produce a more complete perception than the usual casual rubricizing which passes illegitimately for perception" (1968, p. 76). (3) The object is seen in a noninstrumental and nonegocentric way; hence the peak-experiencer "can then more readily look upon nature as if it were in itself and for itself, and not simply as if it were a human playground put there for human purposes" (1968, p. 76).

Had Maslow chosen to view the peak experience as simply an unusual state of consciousness, he would already have hit upon a psychological phenomenon of some degree of interest. However, he went further: his hunch was that the peak experience had important metaphysical implications because it revealed aspects of reality that are normally hidden or overlooked. For him it constituted what religiously oriented people regard as a genuine revelation. Such a view of the peak experience was entirely consistent with his discovery that his self-actualizing subjects tended to have a more realistic and discriminating perception of life than did other people:

> The philosophical implications here are tremendous. If, for the sake of argument, we accept the thesis that in peak-experience the nature of reality itself *may* be seen more clearly and its essence penetrated more profoundly, then this is almost the same as saying what so many philosophers and theologians have affirmed, that the whole of Being, when seen at its best and from an Olympian point of view, is only neutral or good, and that evil or pain or threat is only a partial phenomenon, a product of not seeing the world whole and unified, and of seeing it from a self-centered or from too low a point of view. (Of course this is not a denial of evil or pain or death but rather a reconciliation with it, an understanding of its necessity) (1968, pp. 81–82).

As Lowry points out (1973, p. 57), the same term—"reconciliation"— was used by William James sixty years earlier to describe the central dimension that he had encountered in his own personal forays into mystical states, which had been induced by his inhalation of nitrous oxide: "The keynote of it is invariably a reconciliation. It is as if the opposites of the world, whose contradictoriness and conflict make all our difficulties and troubles, were melted into unity" (James, 1902, p. 388). In a similar vein, we shall discover in Chapter 6 that for some humanistic psychologists, mystical, or "cosmic," states of consciousness reveal to us the underlying unity of the entire universe.

It is to Maslow's credit that he, more than any other personality theorist, left room in his framework for a possible correspondence between reality as it is perceived during mystical or beatific experiences and reality as it "really is." For him the peak experience (in which stereotyped perceptions were pushed aside and the world again seen with a child's freshness) was able to join together the artist, the theologian, and the scientist, since each attempts to describe the world as it actually *is* (albeit through different means), and each tends to experience, at the moment of revelation or creative insight, extreme emotion, and at times, ecstasy. Indeed, the moment of discovery, whether esthetic, religious, or scientific, has much in common with the peak experience and might even be regarded as one kind of peak experience.

Might it then be that art and science, and religion and science, traditionally seen as antitheses, would prove to be but other instances of reconcilable polarities? If so, the psychologist's own subjectivity and peak experiences, rather than being feared as potential sources of error, could be seen as helping him to gain a better understanding of how man comes to fully "grasp," on both cognitive and emotional levels, his world. Certainly this was to be the approach of those "third force" psychologists who wanted to find a place within scientific psychology for an understanding of the relations among mysticism, higher states of consciousness, and creative insight into the true nature of the world.

Thomas Szasz: The Politics of Adjustment

Szasz, a Hungarian-born psychoanalyst teaching at the Upstate Medical Center of the State University of New York, has developed an approach to the problem of personality and adjustment that is far more sociological and political than Maslow's. Yet one essential point that the two theorists hold in common is their questioning of traditional notions of emotional adjustment. In his study of self-actualization, Maslow had found that people who succeeded in realizing themselves were usually able to transcend their culture. Therefore, because they tended to be less conforming and conventional than their peers, and less concerned with adhering to standards of appropriate behavior, they might often *appear* to be less adjusted. However, when he encountered the so-called "normal," and seemingly untroubled, person, Maslow found a dulled acceptance of life on its most pedestrian and uninspiring terms, and therefore concluded that the so-called average person was seriously arrested in his emotional development. In a similar vein, Szasz wonders if psychiatry and the general society have not been naively uncritical in their equation of social deviance with emotional illness, and conformity with mental health.

"THE MYTH OF MENTAL ILLNESS"

As we have seen, existential and humanistic themes render paramount a person's ability to liberate himself from the social pressures impinging on him. While all the other theorists whom we consider in this book make their primary focus the lone person and his struggle for autonomy, Szasz reverses this, relegating the psychology of the individual to the background and concentrating instead on the society that threatens his freedom.

For Szasz, the interests of the individual and of society are never identical, and there is always potential conflict between them. He is concerned with how society uses the institution of psychiatry (and the mental health professions in general) as a means of social control, and with how psychiatrists are frequently unaware that they are so used. Sensitive psychotherapists must ask themselves if they are working for the genuine liberation of their patients, or for their patients' submission to the social codes of their culture. Szasz's conception of how psychotherapy can best respect the personal liberty of the patient is spelled out in his book *The Ethics of Psychoanalysis* (1965).

By even attempting to define who is healthy and who is ill, psychiatry gives a seemingly rational and scientific guise to what are essentially moral and ethical decisions, for the criteria governing mental health are far more arbitrary and ambiguous than those governing physical health:

> In medical practice, when we speak of physical disturbances we mean either signs (for example, fever) or symptoms (for example, pain). We speak of mental symptoms, on the other hand, when we refer to a patient's communications about himself, others, and the world about him. He might state that he is Napoleon or that he is being persecuted by the Communists. These would be considered mental symptoms *only* if the observer believed that the patient was *not* Napoleon or that he was *not* being persecuted by the Communists. This makes it apparent that the statement "X is a mental symptom" involves rendering a judgment. The judgment entails, moreover, a covert comparison or matching of the patient's ideas, concepts, or beliefs with those of the observer and the society in which they live. The notion of mental symptom is therefore inextricably tied to the *social,* and particularly the *ethical,* context in which it is made, just as the notion of bodily symptom is tied to an *anatomical* and *genetic* context.[1]

Szasz's point is that there is much more unanimity both within a single society and among diverse societies as to what constitutes the proper structure and functioning of the body and its various organs, than there is concerning what constitutes appropriate social behavior. For example, do hypersexuality and aggressive outbursts offer instances of "disturbed" personality functioning? Moreover, even if one was able to secure agreement as to what constitutes a mental symptom, these symptoms cannot be correlated with clearly observable defects within the person, whereas in medicine most physical symptoms can be— e.g. the coughing up of blood is attributed to the clear-cut, visible presence of bacilli within the mucous membranes of the lungs. The defects

[1] Thomas S. Szasz, M.D., *Law, Liberty and Psychiatry* (New York: Macmillan, Copyright © 1963 by Thomas S. Szasz, M.D.), p. 13.

of the "mind" are less concrete and less locatable than are the defects of the body. In the absence of clearly specifiable defects within the person, his mental symptoms are instead attributed to an entirely conjectural illness, this time a "mental" illness (for is not every symptom traceable to an illness?). But Szasz is careful to remind us that the very defining of statistically deviant behavior as *symptomatic* is an essentially arbitrary act. For while it can be demonstrated that physical symptoms threaten the ease and eventual survival of the body, so-called mental symptoms (e.g. verbal assaultiveness or frequent divorce), albeit perhaps disquieting to others and disruptive of the social fabric, need not especially pain the person himself or in any way threaten his chances for survival. Hence for Szasz the entire notion of mental and emotional illness has but mythical status. It represents the misapplication of a concept, illness, that is appropriate in one context—physical medicine—to one in which it is inappropriate—interpersonal behavior. As such, it offers a misleading and potentially dangerous metaphor.

Even to claim that the patient, cited by Szasz above, is *not* Napoleon is to introduce arbitrary definitions of personal identity that are not universally held. If our present-day Napoleon shares with the earlier Napoleon strong feelings of omnipotence, who is to say that his Napoleonic identity is not as fundamental as is the identity that we arbitrarily refer to as "John Jones"? Is not one's personal identity, after all, primarily a *psychological,* and therefore highly private and emotion-laden, affair? But society, ever jealous lest the prevailing order be disturbed (John Jones is John Jones and Napoleon is Napoleon) is quick to ferret out deviant behavior, and psychiatry cooperates by defining such behavior as sick. Given the powerful institution of medical psychiatry, Szasz fears for the freedom of those creative, rebellious, and slightly "odd" people whose eccentricities sometimes strike us as puzzling and irritating. As Keen puts it:

> To call a behavior pattern "annoying" describes primarily the reaction of the observer, while to call it a "symptom" pretends to be "objective" and free of "subjective bias" or "evaluative judgments"— as if personal reactions and evaluative judgments were not part of what is going on. This pretense of non-evaluative objectivity and scientific attitude is not only intellectually dishonest; when translated into social patterns, it becomes coercive and repugnant (1972, p. 42).

THE CASE OF MRS. ISOLA WARE CURRY

In order to illustrate the degree to which social values and expectations play a role in psychiatric judgments, Szasz cites the example of Mrs. Isola Ware Curry, a black woman who had in 1958 attacked

Martin Luther King with a knife and stabbed him. Attempted murder in the first degree was the charge placed against Mrs. Curry in the original indictment. She was never brought to trial, however, and instead she received a pretrial psychiatric examination. On the basis of this examination she was deemed to be incompetent to stand trial and was subsequently sent to Mattawean State Hospital (in Beacon, New York) for the criminally insane (as of this writing, approximately twenty years later, it is still impossible to know if she was ever released, for we, along with Szasz, have written to Mattawean State inquiring into Mrs. Curry's status, only to receive no answer).

> Probably no one was surprised by this sequence of events. An unprovoked attack on an antisegregationist leader by a Negro woman must have seemed to the proverbial man on the street as "just about as crazy as you can get." Consequently, in the public eye, Mrs. Curry was committable. Suppose, however, that the attack had been made on a segregationist leader. Would she still have been committable in the public eye, or would her act have been interpreted as a political crime based on revenge? Suppose Mr. King had been assaulted by a member of the Ku Klux Klan. Would the public have labeled the attacker as mentally ill? Or would his act have been regarded as a political crime? (1963, pp. 193–94).

Szasz had no direct knowledge of the findings that emerged in the psychiatric examination of Mrs. Curry. However, he reasons that whatever their nature, "they could not, *in themselves,* justify her commitment to a state hospital. Psychiatric findings of schizophrenia or psychosis can be demonstrated in millions of people who are not hospitalized" (1963, p. 194). He concludes that all of us conspired to help her evade trial:

> Her trial and conviction could be circumvented in one way only— by raising the issue of insanity. Thus, psychiatrists were hired, ostensibly to examine her psychiatrically, but tacitly to find her unfit to stand trial. If psychiatrists declared an offender "unable to understand the charges against him or to assist counsel in his own defense," he may be committed without trial. . . (p. 194).

In this instance psychiatrists allowed themselves to be used as "social tranquilizers" (Szasz, 1963 p. 196); this is not their legitimate function, and when they act in this way they are serving as agents of the state. (According to Szasz, the one legitimate function that the psychiatrist or psychologist does have is as an individual's therapist, but then he is an agent of the person who hires him, and he must adamantly defend his client's interests against those of the state, to the point of accepting imprisonment rather than being forced to reveal in court confidences made to him by a patient in the course of treatment.)

Why the collusion whereby Mrs. Curry was not allowed to stand trial? Because, says Szasz, we would rather create the substitute problem of Mrs. Curry's sanity than have to face the real issues of the case, which involve race hatred and racial discrimination. One consequence of discrimination is the well-known phenomenon of "identification with the aggressor," wherein the member of a persecuted group adopts the attitudes and values of his persecutors (A. Freud, 1946). For example, studies of concentration camp victims during World War II revealed that inmates frequently emulated the behavior of their guards, to the point of acting in a sadistic fashion to fellow inmates (Bettelheim, 1960). Hence the fact that a black person kills an avowed champion of the black masses is perhaps not so puzzling as it might initially appear, but we would rather look the other way than acknowledge the extent to which discrimination has injured the self-esteem and self-respect of many blacks.

Perhaps, speculates Szasz, there were more rational, ideological reasons motivating Mrs. Curry. She may have sympathized with the Black Muslim concept of absolute segregation. Or she might have agreed with the position of white supremacists. He writes:

> If this was the case, should her color cancel her right to share this view? . . . By affixing a psychiatric diagnosis to Mrs. Curry, her act was branded as crazy and therefore as incomprehensible, except to experts. Thus, the questions raised here were comfortably settled. That she should have a *choice* about the problem of segregation was expressly disallowed. In other words, disposing of Mrs. Curry's case by means of psychiatric, rather than legal, intervention achieved two major objectives. First, it deprived her, and by implication other Negroes, of the *right* to commit a crime against a *prominent* member of their own race. . . . Second, it enabled society—the public— to disguise and evade the moral and sociopsychological dilemmas inherent in her act. It thus injured values which a humanistic democracy is expected to foster (1963, p. 196).

The patients whom we today deem psychotic or seriously neurotic were at one time burned as witches. Therefore we have progressed to some degree, since it is more civilized to institutionalize people than to kill them. Yet, Szasz asks, is it not possible that our categories of well versus sick, which initially seemed scientific and enlightened when they replaced such theologically tinged classifications as good versus evil, might still somehow be turning out to be a modern-day version of those who, in the eyes of God, deserve to be saved versus those who do not?

For invidious distinctions still are made: The sick are often seen as less than human, and because of this they are given second-class citizenship. For instance, some states allow a person suspected of having a mental illness to be detained without a mandatory court hearing for as long as forty-five days; where there is to be a hearing, not all states guarantee the person's right to legal counsel; and when a lawyer is appointed, he or she is sometimes not assigned to the case until the very day of the hearing (Scott, 1976). Furthermore, how much genuine psychotherapy, as opposed to chemotherapy and electroshock, do institutionalized patients receive? And how many have long since stopped receiving any treatment whatever? (Szasz, as we shall see below, goes still further, and questions whether meaningful psychotherapy can take place under conditions that smack in any way of coercion). In other words, despite our professed interest in the welfare of the patient, to what degree are we really attempting to serve the interests of the *state* by segregating out those who are obstreperous, unpredictable, and different?

THE CASE OF DONALDSON VS. O'CONNOR

A significant decision rendered by the United States Supreme Court in 1975 would seem to have been partly set in motion by Szasz's writings, and by the widespread attention they have received. In *Donaldson* vs. *O'Connor*, a patient who had been committed by his parents to a mental hospital in Florida and held there against his will for fourteen-and-a-half years, sued his hospital physician (O'Connor) for damages, claiming that his civil liberties had been deliberately and seriously violated. While the issue of whether O'Connor should be judged personally liable for damages was remanded to a lower Appeals court for adjudication, the Supreme Court arrived at clear-cut findings to the effect that:

> a person does have a right to liberty if he is (1) civilly committed, (2) not dangerous to himself or others, (3) receiving only custodial care, and (4) capable of surviving safely in freedom either on his own or with help that is available in the community (Scallett, 1976, p. 10).

The Court further indicated that state hospital officials are to be held legally accountable for any official acts that injure a patient's constitutional rights. Congruent with this philosophy was the subsequent decision of the lower Appeals court, which acted to award Donaldson $20,000 in damages from the estate of Dr. O'Connor (who had died prior to the Supreme Court decision). Hence there can be little doubt that since the landmark *Donaldson* case "state hospital officials are on notice that deprivation of a patient's right to liberty exposes them to personal liability" (Scallett, 1976, p. 10).

Szasz has mixed feelings about the Donaldson decision, and wrote a book, *Psychiatric Slavery*, analyzing it in close detail (Szasz, 1977). In his view the Supreme Court's verdict partly (and correctly) helps to weaken the institution of involuntary commitment by indicating that such commitment is no longer beyond the purview of the courts and the Constitution. Unfortunately, writes Szasz, the Court's decision at the same time *strengthens* involuntary commitment procedures by implying that they are justifiable and legitimate so long as certain conditions, like the provision of adequate treatment, are met. For Szasz, any treatment procedure that occurs within the context of the patient's physical confinement is essentially involuntary, and any legal verdict that fails to eradicate unequivocally the practice of involuntary institutionalization does not go far enough.

A frequently cited basis for involuntary commitment is a person's dangerousness, either to himself or others. However, Szasz is not at pains to protect an individual against literal self-destruction since he regards suicide as constituting an extremely personal, and potentially responsible, decision which should not be interfered with. And dangerousness to others, says Szasz, can only be properly inferred from one's having actually committed a violent and illegal act upon another. Once this is the case, the perpetrator of the crime can be arrested, tried, and convicted; once convicted, he should be jailed, rather than hospitalized.

It might *appear* as though we are opting for humane values when we insist that people adjudged to be insane not have to stand trial, or that if they do, the charge against them be reduced; in this way we minimize the likelihood of a severe sentence and help to ensure that they will be sent to a hospital for the criminally insane and not to prison. Szasz's point, however, is that we demean the dignity of accused persons when we refuse to recognize their constitutionally guaranteed right to a trial by a jury of their peers. We may eventually, through the trial process, judge their choices to have been wrong and therefore deserving of punishment, but we are nonetheless respecting their right to choose by acknowledging their responsibility in having so chosen. Moreover, while commitment to a hospital for the criminally insane may seem humane, the actual conditions in these places are usually no better than are those in the average prison. Szasz takes an extreme position on these matters, but it is consonant with fundamental postulates of existential thought that champion freedom and make individuals ultimately accountable for their own acts.

A "PROBLEMS IN LIVING" MODEL

Szasz suggests that we replace the traditional medical model with a "problems in living" model (Szasz, 1961). As he sees it, all interpersonal situations, given human ambivalence and the dilemma of choice, are fraught with some potential for conflict and anguish. Hence none of us is without problems in living. It is not to cure an imaginary illness that a person seeks therapy, but to clarify what his actual problems in living are and how he can better solve them.

By abandoning a medical model, Szasz helps place the psychotherapy relationship within a more human and less authoritarian context. But for the patient to experience the relationship in a truly democratic and noncoercive way, he must seek therapy voluntarily and must trust that the therapist will in no way intervene in his outside living. Instead of an expert-apprentice relationship, we now have two people who are more equal than they are unequal, since both suffer and both must tolerate the inevitable ambiguities involved in having to make decisions in a state of human finitude. The two agree to collaborate on the problems of one of them, and the one so designated becomes the client. And it is the client who, at least in the initial stages of therapy, is more "expert" than the therapist in the sense of possessing a much greater knowledge of all that he feels, thinks, and imagines; the first phase of therapy involves his informing the therapist as to just what his emotional life is like. In theory, there is no inherent reason why, given sufficient pain and willingness on the part of the therapist, and sufficient training and understanding on the part of the client, the two partners could not reverse their contract, switch roles, and begin to confer on the problems of the therapist, who now becomes the client. As you might expect, humanistic approaches to psychotherapy, which are presented in the following chapter, tend to view the therapist-patient relationship in this light.

Ronald Laing: The Politics of Madness

Laing is a Scottish-born psychiatrist who presently lives and practices in England. While probably best known to his professional audience for his existential-phenomenological approach to schizophrenia, he is the single humanistic theorist who has attracted the widest general audience in both the United States and Great Britain. Within this broader population he has had particular appeal for the counterculture. Indeed, according to some (e.g., see Boyers and Orrill, 1971), Laing has become a kind of prophet for the counterculture, mostly because he takes a position vis-à-vis society similar to theirs: (1) he questions some of the most basic assumptions of Western culture (e.g., the "self" or "ego" as an indivisible core element in all psychological experience); (2) he is warily skeptical of almost all social institutions, including the family; and (3) he strongly implies that the only means of salvation available to the individual in an increasingly oppressive culture lies in the attainment of mystical states of consciousness, whether through drugs, through religious ecstasy, or through madness.

AN ONTOLOGICAL APPROACH
TO SCHIZOPHRENIA

On the basis of intensive studies of schizophrenic patients and their family backgrounds, Laing eventually formulated what he termed an "ontological" (i.e., existential-phenomenological) theory of schizophrenia. This theory was presented in his first book, *The Divided Self* (1959), which he wrote at the remarkably young age of twenty-eight; it challenged the traditional distinction between sanity and insanity and placed great emphasis on looking at the world through the schizophrenic's eyes. While not questioning the conventional assumption that patients diagnosed as schizophrenic experienced the world in highly unique ways that set them apart from others, Laing wondered if these experiences, and the peculiar symptoms they gave rise to, were necessarily as crazy or deranged as they were typically seen to be. His claim was that if we sympathetically feel our way into the patient's world we will find that his emotions and his behavior constitute rather natural responses to close-to-impossible, existentially precarious situations.

Most of us are, according to the usual definitions of normality, adjudged to be sane. We are fortunate enough to have grown up with what Laing calls a sense of "ontological security," and therefore, despite the emotional strains of our particular childhood (and the neurotic difficulties we consequently face as adults), never sense what it is like to live in an existentially precarious environment for an extended period of time. Ontological security involves a feeling of one's having a distinct psychological identity, or "self," that is confirmed by the reactions of those around him or her:

> Under usual circumstances, the physical birth of a new living organism into the world inaugurates rapidly ongoing processes whereby within an amazingly short time the infant *feels* real and alive and has a *sense* of being an entity, with continuity in time and a location in space. In short, physical birth and biological aliveness are followed by the baby becoming existentially born as real and alive (1965, p. 41).

On the other hand, the person who is later to become schizophrenic has tended, from his earliest beginnings, to suffer a profound unsureness as to his basic sense of self. For a variety of reasons, his early family matrix has not permitted him to develop the sense that he is a unique being who is distinct from, and yet a part of, this world. "He may lack the experience of his own temporal continuity. He may not possess an over-riding sense of personal consistency or cohesiveness" (1965, p. 42). Perhaps his parents do so much for him, appropriate so many of the physical functions that would normally become his own, like feeding and elimination, that he is never quite certain that he has a body separate from theirs, subject to his own control. Perhaps he is treated in such contradictory ways that it is difficult for him to experience himself as the same person on different occasions; it is as though he were two or three persons rather than one. Or perhaps, like Peter, a patient presented in *The Divided Self* (1965, pp. 120–33), he is regarded as a nonperson: "His parents were never openly unkind to him and he seemed to be with them all the time and yet they simply treated him as though he wasn't there" (p. 120).

Laing is not discussing here the subtle identity issues faced by the adolescent, who may be trying to discover just how submissive, or intelligent, or attractive he is. Nor is he even discussing the problem of the homosexual, or of the ambivalent heterosexual, who may experience serious confusion over the question of his or her *sexual* identity. He is grappling with a more fundamental identity issue involving the degree to which one feels oneself to be a human, distinct person, born to two other, specific human persons. This kind of identity has little to do with experiences one has after the first year of life; it comes so early that it seems almost "conferred on one" at birth (Laing, 1961, p. 84), and it depends heavily on a sense of who one's actual parents are:

> When the child grows up without a knowledge of who his real parents are, or if he grows up later to discover that the people he thought were his "real" parents are not so in fact, he is equally involved in a crisis which at base is to do with his own sense of his identity.... *The need to know who one is appears to be one of the most deep-rooted in our humanity* (Laing, 1961, p. 84; italics ours). [2]

The quest for this earliest sense of identity is what often motivates the adopted child to search so earnestly for his actual parents, and it is what caused Brian, one of the patients studied by Laing, to experience the crisis that precipitated his breakdown. As a young child, Brian had been told his father was dead. He remembered only his mother, and

---

[2] R. D. Laing, *Self and Others* (New York: Pantheon Books, a Division of Random House, Inc., © 1961), p. 84.

it was she who traveled a long distance with him when he was four years old and who then left him with a strange couple. This man and woman informed him that they were his mother and father, and he was never to see his real mother again.

His two "parents" had two children of their own, a son, Jack, and a daughter, Betty, eighteen and sixteen years older than he, respectively. He was brought up as their younger brother; he remembered that his brother tried to be friends with him, but he was too much enclosed in his own confusion to respond. When he was a little older, this brother went to Canada (1961, p. 78).

Brian at this point lost whatever sense of identity he had had as his mother's son. In attempting to explain for himself why his mother had abandoned him, he figured that he had somehow been a "bad" son and had needed to be punished; he further determined that if he was to be defined as bad he should indeed behave badly, and he began to misbehave. At a later point Brian accidentally happened upon the papers that had legally permitted his "parents" to adopt him. He was contemptuous of their apparent belief that he naively accepted their claim to be his mother and father. In his perception they had adopted him out of loneliness, had never loved him, and actually enjoyed his mischievousness. To frustrate them he then decided to become "good."

This newer identity seemed to feel right to him, and things began to go better in his life. Brian eventually married and had a son of his own. His wife was good to him, and he found himself more accepting of his confused childhood and less bitter toward life. His crisis occurred when he confided some of this happiness to his adoptive sister, adding that one remaining source of unhappiness was the fact that he could never know the identity of his real father. His sister was surprised that her parents had not told him that her brother Jack had been his father:

Jack, the "brother" who had made a special effort to be "friends" with him when his mother had left him with the family, had recently died in Canada. This last revelation was too much for him. It was just "beyond a joke." All the dynamic of his life had been based on the conviction that he was not "one of them." His most prized secret possession had been that he *knew*. Now the structure and fabric of his whole life was once again torn to shreds. He had been fooled; completely unsuspectingly, he had grown up where in fact he had belonged. The stupidity, the senselessness of it was too much. He reverted to the one certainty which he felt no one could take from him. . . . It seems to me that he decided in effect not to trust "reality" any more, but to act upon his most basic phantasy. He was wicked. He, therefore, went to his wife and flogged her and drank himself stupid until she left him and he had to be taken away (Laing, 1961, p. 81).

The person whose basic sense of identity has not been conferred, or confirmed, by his early interpersonal experience is deficient in one of the crucial ontological premises of living—namely, that he is a separate, alive, *human* person with a legitimate right to autonomous selfhood. He resembles Brian, who, uncertain as to his true family membership and his fundamental goodness or badness, was vulnerable to having "the rug pulled from under him" at any moment. This is what is meant by an existentially precarious position, and the person who lives in such an environment operates on the basis of wholly different ontological principles. The most superficial of interpersonal exchanges may cause him profound disquiet, and personal confrontations that most people can face with some degree of assurance might for him threaten his very existence. Life becomes a matter not so much of gratifying oneself as of preserving oneself. This is what Laing refers to as the situation of "the ontologically insecure person."

Such a person may try to deal with life by becoming a nonperson. One way in which he can attempt to do so is through timidity, another is through withdrawal, and yet another is through the adoption of forms of communication that are egocentric and unsocialized. For example, he may claim that he is "unreal" or that he is dead. It is at this point that he begins to exhibit behavior that others frequently describe as "schizophrenic." Yet in so labeling him, they begin to regard him as not quite human and to thereby rob him of his full measure of dignity.

If we begin to meet the patient so diagnosed just halfway, we will find that his description of himself as unreal is not so strange as it initially appears. Because the ontologically insecure man is not sure that he is a person to begin with, or that he has a right to his feelings, it is a relatively short step for him to become confused about his real feelings, or to want to hide them from people whom he experiences as more human, and as therefore more powerful, than he. He may smile when he feels sad, and frown when he feels happy. Since, as a consequence, he rarely behaves in ways that feel authentic to him, he begins to describe himself as "unreal." In a similar vein, he claims that he is dead because he *experiences* himself as dead.

The ontologically insecure person employs words to describe himself that directly and primitively reflect his most personal sense of things. "A truth about his 'existential position' is lived out. What is 'existentially' true is lived as 'really' true" (Laing, 1959, p. 37). Therefore he states that he is actually unreal, when he simply *feels* unreal. However, consensually validated canons of logical thought and discourse demand that the determination of whether one is real or unreal, alive or dead, be made on a biological and physical, not psychological, basis. The patient who fails to label his statement about being dead as a clear-cut metaphor, and who seems to regard it as literally true, violates well-established standards of logic, fails to engage in socialized forms of communication, is perhaps deluded into thinking he is really dead, and is ultimately diagnosed as psychotic. Indeed, the tendency to deal literally with metaphors and to have difficulty in grasping metaphorical language are often mentioned as key features of schizophrenic thought disorder (Page, 1975).

On the other hand, asks Laing, is the failure to label one's metaphors such a serious deviation? Is not psychological death equal to physical death for the person experiencing it? The message inherent in the single statement "I am dead" is poetically rendered and beautifully clear, just as is the message of the enraged and potentially violent patient who tells his therapist that he has swallowed a time bomb and that it is soon to explode. In a similar vein, Laing does not find the central delusion of his patient, Peter, quite so mystifying (1959, pp. 120–33). Peter's parents had consistently refused to acknowledge his physical presence, to the point of openly engaging in sexual intercourse while he was in the room. Peter's fantasy, that he gave off an extremely foul and offensive odor, was his one means of assuring himself that he was noticed by others and that he could therefore assume his existence to be real. Again, the communications of the patient labeled as schizophrenic, while somewhat different, need not appear as undecipherable or bizarre once they are viewed less judgmentally and more empathetically.

For the ontologically insecure patient, the politics of the clinical-diagnostic situation all too often are reminiscent of the politics of his original family life. In his view, total power is now in the clinician's hands, as once it was in those of his parents, and once again he, the patient, will be shown to be a fool. Laing cites as an illustration of this point a situation involving Kraepelin, the well-known diagnostician and classifier of mental disease who lived at the turn of this century. In describing a catatonic schizophrenic patient whom he had interviewed in front of a large lecture class for demonstration purposes, Kraepelin wrote: "His talk was . . . only a series of disconnected sentences having no relation whatever to the general situation" (1905, pp. 79–80).

Reconstructing the situation from the point of view of the patient's probable rage and humiliation at being exposed to the potential ridicule of a large group of students, Laing sees what Kraepelin viewed as a monologue on the patient's part as a *dialogue* in which the patient first reenacts the role of Kraepelin, the interviewer, in parodied form, and then answers in terms of his own angry, rebellious self. (As Laing points out, part of the patient's anger doubtless results from his difficulty in discerning just what the demonstration has to do with the problems that are torturing him.) Hence the patient's seemingly nonsensical comment in the interview—"How can you be so impudent? I'm coming! I'll show you! You don't whore for me" (Kraepelin, p. 79)—is actually the patient's attempt to impersonate Kraepelin and what he imagines to be Kraepelin's attitude toward himself. In other words, as the patient perceives it, Kraepelin is furious with him for not being coherent and cooperative—i.e., for not being willing "*to prostitute himself*" in front of the class (Laing, 1959, p. 30; italics mine). Hence the patient's remarks about whoring.

Why does the patient obscure his meaning in a tangled web of seemingly nonsensical communication? There may be more "method" to the patient's "madness" than is initially evident, for the seeming incongruity of his speech helps him evade what he experiences as an extremely uncomfortable and potentially humiliating situation. He is very much "on the spot"; however, by not acknowledging his own identity (e.g., the patient claims he is Christ), or refusing to recognize the interviewer's identity (he insists that he is a king, and the interviewer one of his subjects), the patient attempts to mock and deny a situation that threatens to reveal him as the tentative, worthless nonperson whom he experiences himself to be (Bateson *et al.*, 1956). According to Laing, the clinician's treatment of the schizophrenic patient often encourages and justifies these pessimistic expectations, for the clinician, anxious in the face of the patient's seeming differentness, and fearful for his own sense of sanity and wholeness in an insane world, reassures himself by emphasizing the patient's craziness and incomprehensibility. Like Kraepelin, he tends to perceive the patient as an interesting "case" to be demonstrated, forgetting that the patient, like himself, has feelings of self-consciousness and a capacity, however dormant, for genuine pride. In reminding the mental health professional that he is more like the patient than he is different from him, Laing follows the tradition of the American psychoanalyst, Harry Stack Sullivan, and the latter's widely quoted comment that "everyone and anyone is much more simply human than otherwise" (Sullivan, 1962, frontispiece).

WHO IS MAD? WHO IS SANE?

Having begun by questioning the extent to which the ontologically insecure person deserves to be called mad, Laing proceeds to question the intactness of those of us who are supposedly sane. As he reviews the record of Western civilization, especially its recent past, he is appalled:

> In the past fifty years, we human beings have slaughtered by our own hands coming on for one hundred million of our own species. We all live under constant threat of our total annihilation. We seem

to seek death and destruction as much as life and happiness. We are as driven to kill and be killed as we are to let live and live. Only by the most outrageous violation of ourselves have we achieved our capacity to live in relative adjustment to a civilization apparently driven to its own destruction (1968, p. 76).

Reminding us that the psychotic is usually hospitalized because of his supposed potential for uncontrolled violence, Laing wonders who is more dangerous, the seventeen-year-old girl who claims that an atom bomb sits within her, or the nuclear strategist who helps the Pentagon find efficient means of destroying, within minutes, one hundred million people. The girl is diagnosed as schizophrenic and is institutionalized, whereas the Pentagon consultant is wined, dined, fawned over, and paid extremely handsome fees. We grow accustomed to these absurdities, to a point where we can read about the My Lai atrocities in the morning, suffer brief pangs of shock and guilt, and then return our attention to the day's activities. And we do all this while managing to sustain the conviction that we really care about the plight of our fellow man. Each person tolerates these contradictions only, says Laing, by splitting and compartmentalizing his awareness to a degree that must take on schizoid proportions.

On the other hand, the ontologically insecure person takes these absurdities very seriously and tries desperately to resolve them. He knows that the fact of death is all around him and is plagued by images of destruction; yet he sees most people acting as though death did not exist. He realizes that the opportunities for fulfilling and complete relationships are limited in today's fragmented, technological society; yet he sees others behaving as though their relationships are committed and deep. He is aware that he has profound difficulties in relating to others, but is unable to deny his longing for meaningful contact. With this kind of integrity informing his anguished perceptions, his departure from the world of everyday experience may betoken a crucial and courageous healing step toward eventual reintegration and wholeness.

Indeed, as Laing sees it, what we tend to call psychosis actually involves a transcendental or spiritual experience in which a person is, because of a dramatically altered perception of reality, shaken and transformed. This altered state of consciousness often yields valid (though difficult to articulate) perceptions that are not easily available in the world of ordinary, prosaic experience. Therefore the schizophrenic state resembles Maslow's peak experience and the mystical experience as it was described by William James. Like Maslow and James, Laing sees the dissolution of the self-world polarity as one of the cardinal features of such an experience. Once we relax our distinction between "inner" reality (that which we fear can be easily "falsified" through imagination) and "outer" reality (what supposedly is "actually" there, as determined by our senses), we can become less afraid of the experiential and the subjective.

If schizophrenia constitutes an important step in a gradual process of reintegration, forcing the schizophrenic to return to the world of normally alienated experience (via coercive treatments like chemotherapy and electroshock) is not what Laing considers to be a liberating form of psychotherapy. In fact, the milieu of the typical mental hospital often makes the patient worse, so that the most bizarre and regressed of his symptoms (such as assaultive behavior) are not natural consequences of his state of mind, but instead result from the humiliating constraints to which he is exposed. As Laing writes:

> Let no one suppose that we meet "true" madness any more than we are truly sane. The madness that we encounter in "patients" is a gross travesty, a mockery, a grotesque caricature of what the natural healing of that estranged integration we call sanity might be (1968, p. 144).

The natural healing process envisaged by Laing requires a supportive guide who, understanding and respecting the schizophrenic experience, knows how to facilitate it. Such a person need not have received formal schooling in psychotherapy. Indeed, given the suppressive tendencies of most therapists, such training would be more of a liability than an asset. More relevant, though not absolutely essential, is the guide's own personal experience with psychosis. Laing's approach to treating schizophrenia gradually came to be called Radical Therapy (Ruitenbeck, 1972).

LAING'S RADICAL THERAPY

In 1965, as head of the Philadelphia Association, an English organization devoted to the amelioration of mental illness, Laing leased a structure called Kingsley Hall, which had initially been built as a settlement house. His main objective was to establish an environment in which "the voyage within the self" that he saw schizophrenia to be would be allowed to unfold without impediment. If the person could go deep into his psychosis, in his own way and at his own tempo, without any pressure to hasten or modify it, he would eventually emerge from his regression more whole. In Kingsley Hall, hierarchical distinctions were to be minimized, with the result that no one was to be designated as either patient or staff; and while anyone could question or challenge another person's behavior, no rules or prohibitions would be established.

The story of Mary Barnes (Barnes and Berke, 1972), who eventually came to live at Kingsley Hall, illustrates how radical therapy was practiced there. Mary, a middle-aged nurse of Roman Catholic background, had once spent a year in a mental hospital, diagnosed as schizophrenic. After this she worked in a general hospital, functioning adequately but feeling much anxiety and perceiving herself as essentially cold and brittle. Ten years after her initial hospitalization she went to see Laing and requested help because she sensed herself to be on the edge of another breakdown, "but this time, instead of the padded cells and shock therapy of the mental hospital, she wanted to 'go back to before I was born and come up again' " (Gordon, 1972, p. 92). It would seem that Mary had simply existed during this ten-year interval, but had not experienced herself as fulfilled in any fundamental way. Looked at from a Laingian perspective, this second regression may well have been her way of attempting to break through to a more basic connection with her origins and her feeling self. Crucial for the outcome of the regression, and for Mary's eventual sense of well-being, would be the way in which it was handled. Kingsley Hall, and the plans for it, were described to Mary by Laing, but it was not yet ready for occupancy. Sustained by occasional visits to Laing, she managed to function during the one-and-a-half year's waiting period that then ensued.

Like her eventual emergence from it, Mary's regression was gradual. During the first few weeks after she moved into Kingsley Hall she continued at her job. In the evenings, however, she would become more primitive, lying naked in her bed, being incontinent, and smearing the walls with her excrement. After she resigned her position at the hospital, she regressed even more. At one point she would eat no solids, and took milk from a bottle instead, usually being fed by her therapist, a medical school graduate named Joe Berke. She spent most of her time in bed, talking not at all and hardly moving. At a later point Mary refused to eat altogether. The Kingsley Hall residents decided that this situation could not be permitted to continue and that Mary would have to be fed intravenously. When they told her of their decision she gradually resumed eating.

The period of total immobilization seemed to have been the point of deepest regression. After that there was a gradual reversal, with Mary engaging in activities that had not been permitted her as a child, like dancing and playing ball. At a later point she began to draw pictures of the building's interior walls. These were almost always oral in content. At first they were fragmented and involved images of black breasts; later there was a picture of a baby at her mother's bosom.

The drawing and painting continued and then intensified to a point where it seemed to come pouring out of her:

> On the walls of my room I painted moving figures, on my door twining stems and leaves, and on the table an orange bird appeared. Finding odd lengths of wallpaper I made picture stories. Then on strips of wallpaper backing, and on the walls of the house, I painted big, very big, at high speed. Through the spring of 1966 my work poured out, all my insides were loose, the painting, like lightning, was streaking from the storm of me. Joe suggested "paint the Crucifixion"; I did, again and again; hungry for life I wanted the cross (Gordon, pp. 93–94).

It seemed that Mary's art work provided her with a potent means of expressing and reliving her childhood conflicts, at the same time that it earned her genuine recognition. This probably would not have been possible had it not been for her regression, which symbolized an extreme degree of freedom and which also enabled her to get in touch with important feelings.

Mary's relationship to her therapist, Joe, was an extremely close one. Since both lived in Kingsley Hall, their relationship transcended the limits that almost all schools of psychotherapy (to be described in the following chapter) place on the therapist-patient relationship. They would spend several hours together on a typical day, talking, shopping, and relaxing. Not that the relationship was always easy; at times there were crises of trust, and the symbiotic aspects of their closeness at times made Mary uncertain as to where she stopped and Joe began. Joe can be viewed as having given Mary a second chance at development, this time with a healthier and more accepting parent figure. This symbolic rebirth was an important element in Mary's striking improvement. While something akin to it can occur in conventional psychotherapy, the context of radical therapy intensifies it, first because of the greater amount of time spent together by patient and therapist, and then because of the more profound regression experienced in radical therapy. Whereas in conventional psychotherapy the patient might experience himself *as though* fed by the therapist (in terms of attention and caring), the patient in radical therapy may be literally fed, as was Mary by Joe.

Mary remained at Kingsley Hall until its closing several years later. She never resumed her work as a nurse (which had never proved satisfying), continued to paint and to write children's books, and for some of the other residents provided the same support that Joe Berke had for her:

> There, according to other members of the community, she was a highly valued therapist. Having gone so deeply down and come out, she is unafraid of others' madness. A terrified girl would speak with

no one else but came to Mary, slept in her room for days, and drank the mixture of warm milk and honey that Mary prepared for her. When Mary was "down," Joe had given it to her (Gordon, p. 95).

Laing's argument, then, is that the patient's regression is self-limiting and reparative, if only the therapist tending it can learn to respect it and not fear it. While the shift in such a patient's experience of the self-world polarity may be sufficiently unsettling and intense to be termed psychotic, what makes it often appear to be classical schizophrenia is the reaction of the surrounding milieu, which assumes the function of forcing, or prodding, the patient out of his emotional state. This kind of treatment usually makes him appear sicker than he actually is and diverts us from an appreciation of the healing force contained within altered and regressive states of consciousness.

Recapitulation

A brief review of the theories of Maslow, Szasz, and Laing reveals both similarities and differences. All three question conventional notions of adjustment that emphasize the necessity of conforming to social norms. Instead, they see the lone individual, however idiosyncratic or rebellious, as sacred; and they look upon most definitions of normality, of success, and of "the good life" with a jaundiced eye.

Yet there are differences too. Both Szasz and Laing are considerably more skeptical than is Maslow of society's ability to deal humanely with nonconformity. They include in their indictment the mental health professions, which often suppress extreme behavior. Laing's pessimism in particular, makes him much less hopeful than Maslow about the possibilities for self-actualization in today's fragmented world.

If we compare Szasz with Laing, we find that Szasz is the more consistently political and sociological, whereas Laing, although willing to criticize both society in general and the psychiatric establishment in particular, always retains an explicitly clinical and existential focus.

Lastly, a comparison of Laing with Maslow and Szasz reveals that Laing is the only one of the three to concern himself specifically with schizophrenia. In Laing's hands, however, schizophrenia is transformed from a clinical entity into a metaphor for modern alienation and despair.

Humanistic Approaches
to Psychotherapy

chapter four

Psychotherapy can be defined as a relationship between two people who meet with an agreed-upon goal of ameliorating the psychological difficulties and symptoms of one of them. The person who has come to be helped is usually defined as a "patient" or "client," and the helper is traditionally an expert who has been trained in one of the mental health professions—psychology, psychiatry, or social work. All schools of psychotherapy agree that the therapist-patient relationship plays some role in the helping process, and all tend to utilize, to one degree or another, the verbal interchange between patient and therapist as an important means of communication and help. Naturally, however, schools vary in the ways in which they conceptualize and employ these two sources of influence. In the present chapter we will be describing psychotherapies that are exclusively psychological in the sense that they minimally depend on any directly physiologic or chemical means of helping the patient.

If we are to appreciate the innovations and revisions that humanism introduces into the field of psychotherapy, we need to have a firmer grasp of two fundamental orientations to psychotherapy within psychology that do not fall within the humanistic classification and against which humanistic approaches are usually contrasted: behavior therapy and psychoanalysis. In order to facilitate a more concrete understanding of both these therapies, as well as of the humanistic psychotherapies to be enumerated below, we shall present a case study of an actual patient and then take a closer look at how each of these various schools of treatment might approach his problem.

An Illustrative Case Study

The patient, whom we shall call Bill, was reported by Kushner (1965) in his account of an effective application of behavior modification techniques:

> This is a case study of the successful treatment of a fetish of approximately twenty-one years' duration. The patient was a thirty-three-year-old male whose alcoholic father deserted the family when he was a child and who, from the age of about four or five, experienced a series of placements in relatives' homes, orphanages, day camps, and so forth. He described his mother as probably being a schizophrenic who blamed the Communists for her difficulties and who felt everyone had a double, good and bad. He was the middle child of three boys. He places the onset of his fetishistic behavior at about twelve years of age. This consisted of his masturbating while wearing women's panties. He was a shy, retiring child and as he grew older he became more aware of the abnormal nature of his behavior, felt increasingly inadequate and unmasculine, and resorted to body-building and boxing as a means of proving his virility. After a brief period in the Marine Corps and two failures at attempted intercourse, wherein he found himself impotent, the patient consciously set forth to prove his virility by joining a tough gang, drinking, brawling, and earning the reputation of being a "cop fighter." As a result of assaulting a policeman he was sentenced to a reformatory for twenty-six months. A few years later, while slightly intoxicated and influenced by a friend of his from the reformatory, he broke into a hotel room, stole some luggage, was apprehended, and sentenced to six years in prison. While incarcerated he was removed from the exciting stimuli and the fetishistic attraction was considerably reduced. He rejected the overtures of the prison "wolves" but wondered why he was so often singled out as their homosexual target. Following this sentence he asked for treatment for his perversion. He recognized that while the fetishism did not directly get him involved with the law, it was nevertheless responsible for his antisocial behavior as a compensatory mechanism. When he began treatment he was tense, tormented and obsessed by the impulses, and increasingly guilt-ridden and self-depreciative following the act. He was

bright and very well motivated for treatment. He had had no previous treatment (p. 239).[1]

THE BEHAVIOR THERAPIST'S APPROACH TO BILL

The treatment orientation decided on by Kushner involved two behavior modification procedures, aversive conditioning and desensitization. In aversive conditioning procedures, the patient's attraction to inappropriate sexual stimuli is deconditioned, or "extinguished," through the presentation of "aversive," or painful, stimuli (in this case the administration to Bill of electric shocks). In Bill's case, Kushner was at pains to distinguish between normal and abnormal sexual stimuli and to make sure that Bill, too, as a consequence of the aversive conditioning, would make similar discriminations. In other words, in an ideal therapy outcome, Bill would still be excited by the stimulus of either an actual woman or the fantasy image of a woman, but not by either the idea of wearing panties or of masturbating while fantasizing about panties. The therapist also was careful to point out to Bill that no effort would be made to deal with his masturbatory behavior itself (which was considered entirely acceptable) but only with the fetishistic fantasies and activities accompanying this behavior.

As is typical in an aversive conditioning procedure, the first two therapy sessions were devoted to a recording of the patient's history:

> The patient recalled that the onset of the disturbing behavior occurred when he became curious and sexually excited watching girls sliding down a slidingboard with their panties exposed. It was at this same period in time that he was introduced to masturbation and he soon recognized experiencing similar sensations as when he watched the girls. His fantasies during masturbation quickly were centered about the girls and their panties and shortly this association was firmly made. This explanation for the development of such a fetish is certainly more parsimonious than the "dynamic" explanations involving castration threat, symbolism, and so forth. The above explanation for his behavior was briefly explained to the patient as well as the general approach and rationale that were to be used. He understood the method and was strongly motivated to undertake the treatment regimen (p. 240).

Hence, while psychoanalysis tends to highlight the *internal* and enduring personality predispositions that best account for Bill's behavior (for example, the concept of castration anxiety, which Kushner avoids, would

---

[1] From Malcolm Kushner, "The Reduction of Long-Standing Fetish by Means of Aversive Conditioning," in *Case Studies in Behavior Modification,* eds. Leonard P. Ullmann and Leonard Krasner, © 1965. Reprinted by permission of Holt, Rinehart & Winston.

figure in most psychoanalytically oriented explanations of Bill's symptom), behavioral theory investigates those specific and *external* stimuli in the patient's environment that initially elicit the problematic behavior (in this case, the girls with exposed panties). Since Bill's reactions to these stimuli constitute a learned response, they can be unlearned, this time through a planned, aversive procedure.

The aversive conditioning utilized in the present case went as follows:

> On the third session, the patient was connected to a Grayson-Stadler PGR apparatus by means of two fingertip electrodes. A conditioning circuit was used to establish a baseline for this shock. Adjustments in the circuit had to be made that still did not deliver as strong a shock as desired, but since it was uncomfortable it was decided to proceed. Approximately three and one-half milliampers were delivered.
>
> At each session, anywhere from four to six different stimuli were presented, immediately followed by shock. The patient was instructed to tolerate the shock until it became so uncomfortable that he wanted it stopped. He was then to signal for termination of the shock by saying "Stop." Twelve such stimuli were presented each session in random order. Approximately one minute elapsed between the sensation of the shock and the presentation of the next stimulus. The stimuli consisted of a magazine-size picture of the rear view of a woman from the middle of the back to the knees wearing panties; an actual pair of panties which was placed in his hand; and imaginal situations in which the patient was asked to imagine himself wearing panties, imagining a clothesline with panties on it, and imagining himself standing in front of a lingerie shop window. The picture and the panties were always used, with the imaginal situations varying at each session depending upon his reports of particular areas of sensitivity. Discussion was limited as much as possible to the patient's response to the shock and his reaction to the fetish between visits. Each session lasted between twenty and thirty minutes. He was seen three times a week (p. 240).

At the point where Bill no longer suffered from the fetishistic symptoms (the fifteenth week of therapy), the aversive procedures were initially terminated. Approximately a month later a much less severe episode of fetishistic behavior occurred. This spontaneous reemergence of a learned response, after its initial disappearance or removal, is a fairly regular occurrence in behavior modification procedures and is often anticipated by the therapist. It was dealt with by arranging for additional sessions in which the various pictured and imagined sexual stimuli were once again paired with shock.

The following phases of psychotherapy successfully addressed themselves to Bill's sexual impotence, this time via the behavioral procedure of desensitization. Kushner describes it as follows:

In brief, this approach considers the sexual difficulties to be related to high anxiety states that the patient associates with this activity. In order to reduce this anxiety he is instructed to engage in sex-play and stimulation with his partner but is told that he is under no circumstances to attempt to engage in sexual intercourse. This immediately results in a lessening of anxiety since it precludes failure. After a few such contacts the patient is further relaxed and as a result is more sexually responsive. He is told that only when he has both very strong erection and an overwhelming desire to have intercourse is he to do so and then he is to enter immediately and let himself go, disregarding efforts to prolong the act or to try to please his partner. If instructions are followed expressly, success is readily achieved that allows for a continued development of satisfactory coital expression. As can be recognized, this approach requires the full cooperation and understanding of the female partner (p. 241).

A later follow-up on this patient revealed a quite adequate heterosexual adjustment. The patient was married, had begun a family, and stated that he felt his life to be going well. While he might at times have vaguely fetishistic thoughts, these no longer had the preoccupying force that they had previously had.

Several behavior modification techniques exist in addition to aversive conditioning and desensitization. They include other kinds of desensitization (involving more elaborate procedures applied within the therapy sessions themselves), modeling, assertive training, operant methods of self-control, and so on (see Rimm and Masters, 1974). No matter what technique is to be used in any one case, all behavioral procedures tend to reflect the following three principles, each of which is interrelated with the other and at variance with the fundamental assumptions of psychoanalysis: (1) Psychotherapy should address itself to specifically targeted symptoms and complaints rather than to a reconstruction of the entire personality. Behavior theory rejects both "psychodynamic" and "medical" models of psychopathology, wherein symptoms are regarded as manifestations of deep-seated and unresolved emotional problems. The behavior therapist challenges the analyst's contention that without the alleviation of a patient's long-standing psychological complexes, the removal of one set of symptoms will only result in their eventual replacement by another. (2) Behavior tends to reflect sets of responses that are situation specific. Hence behavioral therapies orienting themselves toward the elimination of a patient's inappropriate response to a particular stimulus will be more effective and more efficient than will psychodynamic (and usually longer-term) therapies addressing themselves to the resolution of hypothetical internal states like "complexes" and "conflicts," that are of doubtful theoretical validity and that lack clearcut empirical correlates. (3) Therapy should concern itself with a patient's past only to the extent of investigating the stimulus history of a specific response. For example, in Bill's case the origin of his fetish in various adolescent experiences and fantasies was explored. Earlier childhood experiences were not deemed relevant, since there is little hard scientific evidence that a specific constellation of childhood events is correlated with the later emergence of fetishistic symptoms. The exploration of the infantile past, as is encouraged in psychoanalytic methods, only complicates and lengthens therapy without necessarily ameliorating the problems that brought the patient into treatment in the first place.

A SEGMENT FROM A BEHAVIORAL
SESSION WITH BILL

As we learned above, the case of Bill was successfully resolved through the application of behavior therapy procedures involving aversive conditioning and desensitization. However, it is entirely possible that a later follow-up of Bill's adjustment might have revealed that Bill, while functioning adequately sexually, was experiencing marital conflict along with some psychosomatic symptomatology (e.g., we may imagine that a physician has diagnosed his recent stomach distress as an incipient ulcer). If such is the case, his therapist might well then decide upon a course of assertiveness training.

This is Bill's second session upon his return to therapy. About five minutes have passed and Bill is describing some of his physical discomfort.

BILL: It's a very definite sensation, and the doctor said that it sounds just like what most of his ulcer patients report. I hate to admit it, but I can't help noticing that they seem to get worse right after a bad situation at home, like when Helen starts picking on me.

TH: And can you think of any time when you let Helen know how mad you feel when she suddenly picks on you like that?

BILL: No.

TH: No wonder you have stomach pains. Bill, your anger has to come out somewhere. If not in an oversecretion of your gastric juices, then in high blood pressure, or irritability at work, or nightmares—but it does have to come out. Your feelings must have some sort of outlet.

BILL: But with Helen pregnant and feeling so lousy, it seems like a bad time to upset her—wow! If I came out with some of the feelings I sometimes have—like wanting to hurt her, and how changed and ugly and bloated she sometimes looks to me—well, that would start off an even bigger explosion.

TH: No, Bill, making those kinds of statements wouldn't do any good. Helen would just feel slugged, like you feel, and would look to counter-retaliate. But you have every right to let her know how angry her demands make you feel.

BILL: I sometimes try that. But then she reminds me of demands I make on her, and I see that she does have a point.

TH: You have to stand on your feelings, Bill; whether they're right or wrong, Helen can't deny them. The fact is that she does make you damn angry, and you're going to have to start apprizing her of that fact if you want to feel better about yourself.

BILL: I really want to—particularly after I've left the situation. But just thinking about it makes me nervous. I don't like to fight.

TH: I know you don't Bill, but you have to start some place. Why don't you start by keeping a record of all the times Helen made you angry this week? And I think it would be a great idea if you tried even if it's only once, to let her know just what your feelings are.

BILL (*somewhat dubiously*):   Well, I could try, I guess. . . .

TH: Look, Bill, you're not necessarily going to succeed in an ideal way the first time, but that takes practice. Start with something minor that doesn't represent the biggest issue between you, like it sounds like getting the baby's room ready *is* a big issue.

BILL: Like what?

TH: Like anything, so long as it's something that irritates you. Can you think of something like that, something less than full anger?

BILL: Well, I know it'll sound silly, but usually the first thing she does when I come home is to complain. Right off, just like that, she doesn't even *think* to ask how I am or what kind of day I've had.

TH: And what if you said that to her?—just like you said it a second ago to me.

BILL: Are you kidding? On top of her already being in a bad mood? And besides, she really does have a heck of a lot to complain about compared to me. Things have been going very well for me at work lately.

TH: That doesn't mean you don't have a right to your feelings, Bill. I tell you what. Why don't we try it here, just to get a sense of what it would feel like to talk directly to Helen—even if it feels strained and artificial at first. You be Helen, and complain. I'll be you just home from the office.

BILL (*awkward at first*):   Thank god you're home. I didn't think I could stand on my feet another minute. What a day—do you know that three things went wrong with the house at once? Plus your darling daughter, who seems to get more and more pleasure out of misbehaving.

TH (*as Bill*):   You know, Helen, I appreciate the fact that you had a lousy day but it irritates me that you never ask me how *I* am. I guess I'd feel more important if you once expressed some concern about how *my* day went.

BILL: I don't know—it sounds pretty good and pretty OK when it comes from you.

TH: After a while it may sound pretty good to you when it comes from *you*.

Commentary. The therapist encourages Bill to engage in expression that is appropriate to the situation. Letting Helen know that he is angry is helpful, whereas attacking her character, or hurling at her the same kinds of accusations that she throws at him, would tend to make matters worse. The therapist supportively reminds Bill, again and again, that unexpressed feelings are bound to have unfortunate consequences, and that he has a right, not only to his feelings, but to an expression of them. Feelings are facts, and in this sense there is no right or wrong to them. Bill is also encouraged to keep a diary of the kinds of interactions with Helen that leave him feeling outraged, so that he and the therapist can go over them in the next session.

The therapist suggests role-playing in the session itself, hoping that the kinds of things that he says in the role of Bill will serve as a model, and that repeated rehearsal in the safety of the office will gradually help diminish Bill's anxiety in the actual situation with Helen. Indeed, the therapist does not encourage Bill to assert himself with Helen over the really big issues immediately, but to work instead on less sensitive and charged situations in which his probability of success will be higher. Then, with this kind of reinforcement behind him, Bill can begin to tackle the more important issues.

THE PSYCHOANALYTIC APPROACH TO BILL

In behavioral approaches, the maintenance of rapport and trust between patient and therapist is important if the goals of treatment are to be reached. Yet it is the behavioral reconditioning of the patient that is primary, while the patient-therapist relationship is secondary to whatever reconditioning takes place. On the other hand, in psychoanalytic psychotherapy the patient-analyst alliance is the single most important aspect of treatment. Not only is it important that the patient begin to regard the analyst as a highly significant figure in his life, and eventually to trust him as completely as one can ever trust another human being, but that he verbalize these feelings toward the analyst as he is experiencing them.

The theoretical framework of psychoanalysis conceptualizes the patient-therapist relationship in terms of "transference" (the patient's neurotic response to the therapist) and "countertransference" (the therapist's neurotic response to the patient). No therapy can be considered psychoanalytic unless it first facilitates a regression in the patient to a point where he relives in relation to the analyst those fantasies and frustrations that he originally experienced at the hands of his parents. These attitudes will include intense negative emotions such as envy and hatred. The transference experience helps to bring directly into the therapeutic relationship the problems that bedevil the patient in his outside living, thereby turning what might be somewhat cerebral narration into a deeply felt experience. Transference also helps the patient remember and reexperience, in an emotionally powerful way, those childhood events that have been significant in the formation of his neurosis.

Countertransference represents those unresolved aspects of the therapist's personality that are set in motion by the impact of the patient's intense transference. While most analysts will find themselves having fewer countertransference difficulties as they become more experienced, there is no analyst who is without them. The analyst must be sensitive to his countertransferential reactions if he is to be effective with his patients, and an indispensable step in helping him do this is his own psychoanalysis (for this reason personal therapy is one of the requirements a candidate must meet in order to complete a training program in psychoanalysis). A potentially positive aspect of countertransference is that it might at times, through its emotional intensity, alert the analyst to traits within the patient of which he had been unaware.

Transference and countertransference inevitably result from the basic conditions of psychoanalysis, conditions that usually create a fairly serious degree of emotional regression in the patient. Among these conditions are: (1) the anonymity and detachment of the analyst, which encourage regression in the patient, first because they frustrate his unavoidable wishes for a closer or more gratifying relationship, and second because the absence of details as to the therapist's actual person and life situation enlarges the role played by the more childlike and fantasy-oriented part of the patient's personality; (2) the patient's use of free association, in which he abandons logical and reality-oriented modes of communication and instead reports to the analyst all the thoughts, feelings, and images that happen to cross his mind, however seemingly foolish or tangential; this mode of communication also facilitates more infantile and fantasy-oriented ways of relating; (3) the frustration produced by the fact that the content of the sessions often bears little overt relationship to the patient's current life problems and their amelioration; the patient may be very slowly gaining some insight into the nature of his unconscious psychodynamics, but these insights, especially during the initial stages of treatment, may not relieve him of his painful depression, anxiety, or acting-out behavior; and (4) the use of a couch on which the patient reclines as he free associates; placing him in a relatively relaxed and passive position and turning him away from the direct reality of the analyst's person will probably stimulate further the fantasy dimension that is desired.

Each of these four factors becomes emotionally intensified by the frequency of sessions, which may range anywhere from one to five times a week. Classical psychoanalysis, as it was originally outlined, placed great emphasis on both the use of the couch and on the maximum frequency of sessions, with the result that the first psychoanalysts often saw their patients as frequently as six or seven times per week. Today this degree of frequency is very rarely encountered, and the use of the couch is sometimes bypassed. Consequently, psychoanalysis proper, which usually requires a minimum of three sessions per week and the patient's reclining on the couch, shades imperceptibly into what is often called psychoanalytic therapy. In psychoanalytic therapy, the patient might be seated face-to-face with the therapist and he might have but one session each week. However, such a therapy, so long as it paid careful attention to the phenomena of transference and resistance (to be discussed below), would still be considered psychoanalytic in its fundamental orientation.

Now let us take a closer look at some of the concrete implications that a psychoanalytic approach would hold for Bill's therapy. The neutrality of Bill's analyst would be reflected in his nondirective stance toward Bill's fetishistic acting out. To direct Bill toward certain specific life behaviors (as when the therapist either prescribes or proscribes certain sexual practices) would contaminate the transference situation since the analyst, by actually taking over parental and authoritarian functions, would be making into a reality what should remain only a transference wish or fantasy. It would also help strengthen the patient's dependency on others. On the other hand, should Bill continue to overtly express his fetishistic interests, the analyst might well investigate why he persists in the very behavior he says he wants to stop, thereby directing Bill's attention toward his *resistance* to change. Resistance is another basic psychoanalytic concept and is manifested in a variety of ways, including the patient's coming late to his appointments or his forgetting about them entirely. What these resistance manifestations have in common is the patient's attempt to sabotage therapy and to stubbornly hold on to his neurotic *status quo,* thereby forestalling the need to look deeper into his anxieties and his repressed memories.

A second set of implications posed by a psychoanalytic approach to this case involves the analyst's view of the psychodynamics behind Bill's symptoms. As had been implied earlier, he would perceive Bill's fetishes as a surface manifestation of a long-standing character disturbance that originated in the earliest years of his childhood. This disturbance would, as in all neurotic people, revolve around the patient's efforts to obtain gratification and comfort from his parents (especially his mother) that at its deepest levels is erotic, although this sexuality is more diffuse than is the genital heterosexuality that most people associate with the concepts of sex and sexuality. An unusual degree of instability in Bill's early parenting would doubtless have rendered him vulnerable in developmental areas extending beyond, and earlier than, the emergence of masculine sexuality. For instance, the establishment of a sense of basic trust in the world (which analysts see as a crucial outcome of the oral stage of psychosexual development) would have been seriously compromised, as would the development of autonomy and self-control (which constitutes the ideal outcome of the anal stage of psychosexual development; see Erikson, 1964).

Therefore, in a psychoanalytic framework, Bill's fetishistic inclinations represent far more than a chance conditioning to random stimulus events (namely, that he just happened to be around when some girls were sliding in a playground with their panties exposed). Without crucial predisposing personality structures, these particular stimulus events would never have had the impact that they subsequently proved to have. With these particular personality predispositions, some variety of symptoms would have been inevitable, whatever the nature of Bill's adolescent introduction to sex and whatever overt form his symptoms may eventually have taken. Furthermore, in the viewpoint of psychoanalysis, one is not merely a victim of stimulus conditions but is also to some extent their author, since one often manages to see what one wants to see (albeit not necessarily with conscious intent). In other words, Bill's initial viewing of the girls in their underwear may well have been a function of voyeuristic and already neurotic inclinations, inclinations that had in turn been fostered by previous developmental experiences.

The psychoanalyst's concern with Bill's overall personality adjustment is bound to have implications for his treatment goals. In his view, Bill's overt symptoms might conceivably be removed (Bill might renounce his fetishes, marry, and have children) without any fundamental alteration in the damaged self-esteem and the passivity that lies at the root of his symptomatology. These character problems would continue to manifest themselves in subtle and not so subtle ways, e.g., in Bill's vocational functioning, his relationships to his wife and children, in his overall sense of identity and wholeness. Whereas behavior therapy stops with the remission of Bill's symptoms, a psychoanalytic therapy, provided that Bill were sufficiently motivated, would attend to the full range of feeling and behavior increasingly revealed by Bill's free associational activity and by his intensifying trust in both the therapist and the therapeutic process. This might well include the emergence of his deep distrust of women, his longing for the absent father, and his preoccupation with homosexuality. These dynamics would be interrelated and would be concretely experienced, first via the gradual emergence of transference feelings toward the analyst, and subsequently via the remembrance of specific childhood events in a personally meaningful way. The ultimate goal of psychoanalytic therapy is reconstitution of the patient's personality.

A SEGMENT FROM A PSYCHOANALYTIC SESSION WITH BILL

This is the forty-third session in Bill's psychoanalytic therapy, and we are roughly fifteen minutes into a fifty-minute hour. Bill, associating to a dream that involved successful sexual intercourse, comments that the woman in the dream reminded him of the woman neighbor on whom he had centered most of his adolescent sexual fantasies. There then follows a three- or four-minute silence.

TH: What are you thinking about?

BILL: I was just thinking of how I had forgotten to pay the last bill you sent me, which was about two weeks ago. Normally I'm more prompt in paying, and I wondered if you had noticed it and were a bit irritated about it.

TH: I wonder what would make you think about that now.

BILL: I have no idea. (*Silence.*) But I imagine that *you* do.

TH: I do what?

BILL: Have an idea as to why I suddenly thought of the bill.

(*There is another minute or so of silence.*)

BILL: Don't you get bored with these sessions? A lot of the time I just dry up and don't have much to say.

TH: Just like you dry up sexually?

BILL: You're just like the analyst who appears in cartoons—always bringing the subject back to sex.

TH: You started with sex today when you told about your dream, but you quickly dropped the subject.

BILL: I didn't know what else to say. The woman next door was very nice to me. This was during the period that I lived with my aunt. This woman—Thelma was her name—seemed to take pity on me; she would invite me over a lot, and she seemed to hope I would play with her son, who was sick a lot and often hung around the house, but he was too much younger than me and we didn't have that much in common. (*Short silence.*) I guess my main thought when I was with her, since she was so nice and decent to me, giving me lunch and snacks and all, was: If she only knew about my sexual fantasies, and my masturbating, and my putting on panties. I knew she would be revolted and shocked.

(*A few minutes of silence.*)

And so I would fight going over. My embarrassment, and also my sense that her husband didn't like my coming over. He never said anything, but he didn't spend that much time with us if he was home. He was usually fixing something or puttering around the garden. He didn't spend much time with his kid either—but I always figured he didn't like me.

TH: Just like you figured a few minutes ago that I was irritated about your not being completely up to date on your payments.

BILL: And these things have to be connected, right?

TH: (*Pauses.*) They might be.

Commentary. Bill's associations to his sexual dream have what the psychoanalyst would consider to be "Oedipal" implications, for his fantasized sexual partner is a woman who was in actuality a mothering figure for him. The wandering of Bill's thoughts to the issue of the unpaid bill technically constitutes a resistance to thinking about the dream and analyzing it, yet Bill's thoughts continue to express an Oedipal theme, for he is now talking about possible disapproval from an older male, the analyst, who tends to represent a father figure for him. The two main elements of the Oedipal triangle are now present in the session: love for the mother and rivalrous feelings toward the father. Bill's associations around the husband and his belief that he was not liked or welcomed by this man tend to bear out the Oedipal hypothesis. However, the analyst does not explicitly make this interpretation, thinking that Bill is not yet ready to accept it. He does, however, pave the way for it (in a subsequent session) by pointing out an apparent connection between Bill's perception of the male neighbor as not liking him and his perception of the analyst as possibly irritated with him.

Humanism in Psychotherapy: Three Representative Schools

The following section presents three distinct psychotherapeutic approaches, each of which deviates from both psychoanalytic and behavioral traditions and each of which emphasizes one or more themes that have become prominently associated with humanism.

EXISTENTIAL-EXPERIENTIAL PSYCHOTHERAPY

Existential-experiential psychotherapy evolved through two relatively distinct stages. The first phase, called existential psychoanalysis, originated in Switzerland during the 1930s through the work of two psychoanalysts, Ludwig Binswanger and Medard Boss; these men had been strongly impressed by Heidegger and wanted to systematically apply ontological concepts to the dynamic psychology of Freud. The second phase involved the contributions of two American psychotherapists, Carl Whitaker and Thomas Malone (1953), who formulated what came to be known as experiential psychotherapy. While Whitaker and Malone's theoretical framework made a less direct use of either psychoanalytic or ontological concepts than did that developed by Binswanger and Boss, and made a more clear-cut attempt to acknowledge and *legitimize* what was irrational in both the patient and the therapist, it had enough in common with existential psychoanalysis to justify my incorporation of it within a single approach that we call existential-experiential psychotherapy (see Shaffer and Galinsky, 1974; and Gendlin, 1973). What we present below, then, is a synthesis of European existential psychoanalysis and the experiential contributions of Whitaker and Malone.

Existential-experiential psychotherapy, when contrasted with the other two humanistic approaches to psychotherapy that follow, does not involve a radical departure from classical psychoanalysis. For this reason, an observer, even a relatively sophisticated one, might find it hard to state with certainty which of two therapy sessions was conducted by a therapist identifying himself as psychoanalytic, and which by a therapist identifying himself as existential-experiential. In both sessions the therapist would encourage the patient to give as detailed a report of his consciousness as possible, would occasionally ask questions, would listen silently during large portions of the hour, and when he did respond would do so in nonjudgmental terms. However, certain points of theoretical divergence do exist between these two approaches and these differences have practical implications for how the therapist will respond in particular instances.

Divergencies from psychoanalysis. Four consistent and interrelated features characterize the existential-experiential school of psychotherapy: (1) an interest in maximizing the autonomous, being aspects of the patient; (2) a strong emphasis on the immediate here-and-now experience of both patient and therapist; (3) the belief that part of a person's inherent motivational make-up involves cognitive, as well as strictly instinctual, needs; hence for some patients an existential quest or struggle for meaning in life is as genuinely problematic as is the satisfaction or sublimation of sexual and aggressive drives; and (4) a focus on the real, as well as on the distorted and "as if," aspects of the patient-therapist relationship ("as if" in the sense that the patient reacts to the therapist *as though* the latter were actually someone else, usually a person significant in his earlier life).

One fundamental means by which the existential-experiential therapist can enhance the patient's freedom is to "let him be" (Keen, 1970). This means to accept the patient just as he is, fully acknowledging his right to hold on to his symptoms and to resist all efforts of the therapist and the therapy. No comments and interventions of the therapist can move the patient unless the latter freely chooses to open himself to the analyst's influence, and the patient's willingness to do so is not directly under the therapist's control. Indeed, the idea that the patient will remain in treatment if only the therapist is sufficiently skillful in analyzing his resistance probably helps to perpetuate what is least autonomous in the patient—namely, his sense of himself as an object (who, given a brilliant enough analyst, cannot help but change). There is little in Freud's original writings to directly contradict the patient's right to resist the treatment, but there somehow crept into the writing of Freud's followers (especially as they began to stress the specifically technical aspects of handling resistance) the notion that interpretations of a resistance—if well-timed, correct, and repeated often enough—automatically dissolved that particular resistance (see Durkin, 1965). It was against this conception that the existentialist's emphasis on "letting the patient be" was directed.

Does the patient's freedom to use the therapist and the therapy for good or ill mean that he is in no way subject to the therapist's influence? This question focuses directly on the free will versus determinism issue that partly differentiates the existential school of psychotherapy from the classical psychoanalytic school, with the existentialist insisting that the patient is more free than determined. Of course the therapist has potential influence; otherwise there would be no point to the therapy. Somewhat paradoxically, the therapist's catalytic role is to remind the patient of his freedom; the patient (freely) decides whether or not he will allow himself to be so influenced.

Another way in which the existential-experiential therapist attempts to maximize the patient's freedom and autonomy (one that is consistent with his phenomenological orientation) is for the therapist to remind him that there is no absolute truth or value outside himself. The patient's task is to find his own meaning and his own truth, and to realize that this is his "freedom." Feeling himself powerless and bankrupt, the patient may try to get the therapist to decide how, and in what direction, he should change. If so, the therapist's task is to confront the patient with his freedom and with the fact that any attempt to uncritically adopt the values or life style of the therapist is a neurotic evasion of this freedom. Indeed, the therapist in no way conveys to the patient the idea that he *should* change, even when it comes to the symptomatic behavior that brought him to treatment in the first place. For instance, Bill is in therapy because Bill himself initially wanted to become less deeply entrenched in his fetishistic preoccupations. It is Bill (as subject of himself) who wants to change, not the therapist who wants to change him (Bill as object of the therapist's intentions; see Chapter 2 for the distinction between self-as-subject and self-as-object). Still another means by which Bill's autonomy can be enhanced is for the therapist to consistently point out that the fetishistic behavior, which the patient experiences as forced upon him by alien impulses, is nonetheless initiated by Bill himself, whether or not he "owns" this behavior. Bill creates his own hell by managing to confine sexual pleasure to masturbatory activities that leave him feeling isolated and ashamed. In this way the therapist tries to replace a self-as-object experience (wherein Bill feels himself a victim of impulses that he experiences as originating outside himself) with a self-as-subject experience" (in which Bill takes responsibility for his impulses).

The existential-experiential therapist tries to stick as closely as possible to the patient's immediate experience and to accept it on its own terms, rather than to make abstract inferences about the unconscious dynamics that might underlie it. If we again take the case of Bill as our example, we see that the Freudian analyst might well regard Bill's fetishistic inclinations as disguised expressions of his incestuous longings for his mother, and he would probably, once Bill has been prepared for it, make an interpretation along these lines. However, as the existentialist sees it, this kind of reductionistic thinking can put a harmful distance between the patient and the analyst, as the latter inevitably begins to view Bill as a concrete embodiment of universal psychological laws, and to experience himself as more knowledgable about Bill's psychological nature than is Bill himself. Once Bill is seen as somewhat predictable and not wholly unique, the subject aspects of his existence are diminished, however subtly, and his object aspects augmented. This eschewing of theory, and of an overinvolvement in theory, on the part of the existential therapist is not merely a *technique* whereby a patient is encouraged to take responsibility for discovering himself; it constitutes a firmly held conviction, for the existential-experiential therapist believes that the over-application of any personality theory will blind him to nuances of the patient's psychological life that deviate from what is supposed, on a theoretical basis, to occur. This point of view is well stated by Singer, who writes (1970):

> What strikes me as more important than the question of the correctness or the shortcomings of a particular theoretical orientation is the

dangerous possibility that he who is the originator or the vociferous proponent of a given approach becomes the captive of his own creation and is in danger of subsequently not fully hearing his patient, for he may become wittingly or unwittingly more interested in proving himself right and in proving the value of his creation than in genuinely listening and hearing the other person (pp. 388–89).

In staying with, and accepting, the patient's conscious experience of himself, the existential-experiential therapist remains true to his phenomenological heritage. An empathic listening to Bill, for example, might gradually reveal to the therapist the sense of pleasurable excitement that Bill's sexual fantasies introduce into what normally is for him a rather shabby and barren world. The search for a lustful, self-oriented relief from what is otherwise experienced as a depressive and moribund life is one of the main existential themes of Bill's current living; in the light of how dead he feels most of the time, it might eventually emerge that he feels most alive when he is masturbating. This constitutes the phenomenology of his symptom; these feelings are within the border of consciousness, and the job of the therapist is to grasp and reflect them. There is no need for him to speculate to himself about possible unconscious meanings of Bill's masturbation; indeed, this will tend to lessen the emotional rapport between them. Similarly, it is unnecessary for him to query Bill about any past history around masturbation or masturbation fantasies; such questions might well prove intrusive. All he needs to know is the essence of Bill's psychic reality *now*. What may lie just beyond it is for Bill to discover as he continues to explore his awareness.

The feature of classical psychoanalysis that is most challenged by the introduction of an existential dimension involves traditional definitions of transference and countertransference, and of the analyst-patient relationship. Whereas the concepts of transference and countertransference imply that the emotionally meaningful aspects of the treatment relationship always derive from the past, existential analysts tend to have an I-Thou definition of the relationship (see Chapter 2), which leaves room for here-and-now caring, respect, and even love between analyst and patient. Not all reactions of the patient to the analyst need involve a neurotic reliving of his childhood experiences, for many of his perceptions of the therapist are grounded in reality. Similarly, not all the therapist's deep feelings for his client need entail reactions based on his own infantile history. Indeed, strong positive feelings for the patient probably inhere within any genuinely therapeutic relationship. Some existential therapists indicate that the patient, if he does not sense himself in some way cared for by the therapist, will not have the ultimately transforming experience of feeling himself to be reborn, more whole and acceptable (although he may gain some symptomatic relief from the treatment). The patient is at last able to love himself because he has experienced complete acceptance from the therapist; here the emphasis is not so much on rational insight on the patient's part (as in classical psychoanalysis), but on profoundly emotional relearnings going beyond what can be expressed via words or concepts.

Because of the emphasis on a genuine encounter within the therapy relationship, the existential-experientialist is willing to share with the patient more about his own feelings and his own life than is the Freudian psychoanalyst. In this view, an open and judicious communication of his own experiences by the therapist at certain moments can do much to deepen the therapist-patient relationship and to remind the patient of the therapist's reality as a human, and therefore vulnerable, person. An example of this in Bill's case might occur in the context of Bill's eventual discussion of his homosexual feelings. A male therapist comfortable with a greater degree of openness about himself might well acknowledge that he too has these feelings and that they no longer frighten him.

Divergencies from behavior therapy. Existential psychoanalysis represents a radical departure from behavior therapy and therefore contrasts more sharply with it than with classical psychoanalysis. The behavior therapist is concerned with a symptom's removal instead of its symbolic and subjective connotations. An existential therapist, on the other hand, wants only to explore whatever meaning the symptom may have for the patient; any change that is to occur in the patient's life is up to the patient himself. The behavior therapist brings to the treatment specific methodologies and instrumentation that are designed to induce change, while the existential brings only his being in the largest sense, which will hopefully include the capacity to listen, to empathize, and to care.

Consequently, in the case of Bill, the experiential therapist would question the behaviorist's efforts to normalize Bill's masturbation fantasies (seemingly for normalcy's sake) by eliminating from them any focus on panties or images of panties. More to his interest would be the conscious *meaning* of Bill's fetishistic fantasies for Bill. Do they say anything about a need to experience himself as in some way perverse and different, or his sense of himself as more feminine than masculine? And why would he prefer not to have these fantasies? (In concentrating on the patient's reasons for wanting to change behavior that others usually define as symptomatic, the existential therapist shifts the emphasis away from external social norms and toward the patient's being, which may or may not subscribe to these norms.) All final decisions—whether or not to use his sessions to discuss the fantasies, or to change to a point where he can have satisfying sexual relationships with women and thereby find these fantasies less essential—rest with Bill.

For the behavior therapist, freedom is an illusion. The existential-experiential therapist, on the other hand, believes in the patient's freedom to change; and for him the behavior therapist's elaborate programs for change, however much they may be explained to the patient, emphasize to an extreme degree the patient as an object to be done to and done for. This criticism would apply to the brief example of assertiveness training that we included in our segment from a behavior therapy session above, for here the therapist was quite explicit in advising the patient not only to express anger toward his wife, Helen, but to do so in a specific way. According to the existential therapist, these programs may work in the sense of successfully removing overt symptoms, but the being aspects of the patient, which may involve profound feelings of helplessness and impoverishment, will either remain as they are or become exacerbated. As Wheelis puts it (1974):

> We are in no position to comment on the efficacy of behavior therapy as generally practiced, but in principle we know it works. People may indeed be treated as objects and may be profoundly affected thereby. Kick a dog often enough and he will become cowardly or vicious. People who are kicked undergo similar changes; their view of the world and of themselves is transformed. . . .
>
> Behavior therapy is not, therefore, being contrasted to self-transcendence in terms of efficacy; the contrast is in terms of freedom. If one's destiny is shaped by manipulation, one has become more of an object, less of a subject, has lost freedom. It matters little whether or not the manipulation is known to the person upon whom it acts. For even if one himself designs and provides for those experiences which are then to affect him, he is nevertheless treating himself as an object —and to some extent, therefore, *becomes* an object.
>
> If, however, one's destiny is shaped from within then one has become more of a creator, has gained freedom. This is self-transcendence, a process of change that originates in one's heart and expands outward, always within the purview and direction of a knowing consciousness, begins with a vision of freedom, with an "I want to become. . . ," with a sense of the potentiality to become what one is not. One gropes toward this vision in the dark, with no guide, no map, and no guarantee. Here one acts as subject, author, creator (pp. 104–5).

A SEGMENT FROM AN EXISTENTIAL-EXPERIENTIAL
SESSION WITH BILL

As with the illustrative psychoanalytic session with Bill above, we are again witnessing part of the forty-third session and are about fifteen minutes into the session. Bill has been complaining about his loneliness and his frequent spells of depression.

BILL: I know I'm supposed to do something about it—probably get off my ass and start phoning people, but I'm feeling so tired at that point that I just lie in bed—like it would be too much effort to even lift the phone off the receiver. (*Short silence.*) And who would I call? There are about four or five acquaintances I could call—but it seems like a meaningless act, there's no one of them I really want to call. Deciding which one to phone would be like drawing lots.

TH: So it's as though you know intellectually, in your head, that only you can save yourself—only you can make that contact, no one can do it for you—yet emotionally you feel totally incapacitated and inert.

BILL: Yeah, like I wish someone would do it for me, arrange a dinner date, introduce me to someone, invite me over, something.

TH: Who would you like to do it for you?

BILL: I don't know. I guess that's just the point I'm making, I don't even have a friend who I can imagine doing that. (*Pauses.*) Unless, of course, you—but that's ridiculous. That's not where you're here for.

TH: That doesn't mean you can't have a fantasy like that.

BILL: Yeah, but I can't expect you to do that for me, introduce me to people, arrange for me to be invited to parties and all.

TH: No, that isn't something that I would actually want to do, but the interesting thing is that when you were first talking about how awful you feel that was just the notion I impulsively had—to give you the number of another patient I have, so that you could have someone to talk to. And then I thought—what are you doing to me that I would want to take that much responsibility for you, that I'd want to push you off your ass when, as you put it, that's something you can only do for yourself.

BILL: I guess you were just feeling sympathetic—there's nothing wrong with that!

TH: No, it was more than that. I was feeling sorry for you—and that's something different from my feeling your loneliness or your pain.

BILL: Feeling sorry for—that's what we were talking about last time.

TH: What do you remember?

BILL: Well, my telling you about Thelma, my aunt's neighbor, and how she seemed to take pity on me, invite me over for dinner, and things like that. (*Pause.*) And I remember, at the end of the hour, I said that she didn't have that much to feel sorry about, at least as far as she could tell. My aunt would give me dinner and was pretty affectionate with me, and I even had kids to play with then.

TH: Well, I don't know how you did it Bill—I only knew that for a little while today you were very successful in getting me to feel the same way.

Commentary. The existential therapist's willingness to openly discuss some of the experiences that he has while listening to the patient permits him to be candid about his feeling sorry for Bill and his momentary fantasy of supplying Bill with the name of another lonely patient. He differentiates these feelings from genuine compassion; in being "sorry for" Bill he experiences Bill as a helpless person who can do nothing for himself and who therefore needs others to do for him. Such promptings, if acted upon, would reinstate Bill as an object of others' intentions and actions. By wondering out loud how Bill succeeds in getting other people to pity him, the therapist focuses on Bill as subject—as one who actively "intends" the things that happen to him, whether or not he is fully aware of these intentions (see the discussion of "Intentionality" in Chapter 2).

The therapist tries to be nonintrusive and is therefore content to remain in the present; he does not direct Bill to relate the theme of pity to the past. It is Bill who spontaneously connects the theme of pity to his memories of Thelma and to the discussion of Thelma during the preceding session.

CLIENT-CENTERED THERAPY

The founder of client-centered therapy, Carl Rogers, is an American psychologist who has had an enormous influence on the fields of counseling, psychotherapy, and education. The theories of personality and of psychotherapy that he eventually developed drew heavily on a phenomenological analysis of the person's experience of both himself and the world; yet they did not make a pronounced use of the formal theoretical concepts offered by the European phenomenologists or existentialists. What Rogers wanted to avoid was a conceptual structure that might become, through the introduction of many complex and hypothetical variables, cumbersome and overly abstract. Instead, he employed a common-sensical approach to the phenomenology of day-to-day existence that rested largely on his experience with clients and on his own struggles in living.

In acknowledging his intellectual forebears, Rogers cited such influences as the psychoanalytic theory of Otto Rank and the phenomenological theory of self developed by two American psychologists, Snygg and Combs. In general, the tone and quality of Rogers's writings—his abiding, democratic respect for the ultimate decency of the person and for his or her right to individuality—partook heavily of the American pragmatic tradition as it had been embodied in William James and John Dewey. However, Rogers's interest in contact with actual clients was more acute than his interest in theory *per se,* and whatever concepts he developed tended to emerge from his practice, rather than his practice from his theory.

Central to Rogers's thinking is the concept of an organismic self that is present at birth (in however rudimentary a form), that has inherent strivings of its own, and that is healthy and nondestructive in its aims so long as it remains uncontaminated by the false values and perfectionistic demands of others, particularly one's parents. Rogers's emphasis on the human being's inborn capacity for self-repair and growth had much in common with Maslow's personality theory, which we reviewed in the previous chapter. These approaches share a Rousseauian belief in the natural goodness of the child, or if not in his goodness, his ethical neutrality (i.e., the child is inherently neither good nor evil). Such a view is at variance with Freud's contention that the child, on an instinctual, biological basis, is at times driven to exploitive, sadistic, and antisocial behavior. In the Freudian view, the child, unless pressured from without and given a specific capacity for guilt and self-doubt, will develop in an amoral direction. In the humanistic view epitomized by Rogers and Maslow, there is a natural valuing process in the child that will always, so long as it is not distorted by the values of the parents, tend in the direction of freedom, communality, and a healthy respect for the feelings of other people. The child encounters difficulties at the point where, out of a need for unconditional approval from others, he begins to accept his parents' viewpoints as his own.

What most differentiated Rogers from Maslow was his pervasive interest in psychotherapy. Indeed, Rogers's theory of personality cannot really be divorced from his approach to the therapeutic or counseling process. A distinct advantage of his personality theory for students is its simplicity; Rogers's personality theory does not posit specific defense mechanisms or uniform stages through which all normal children will develop. In this way, Rogers's personality theory helps the therapist avoid a preoccupation with theoretical minutiae that could result in a defensive and distancing intellectualization. No therapist can attend fully to two things at the same time. Therefore, if he begins to conceptualize the client's experience in terms or concepts unfamiliar to the client, or to connect the client's current feelings with hypothetical childhood events far from the client's immediate awareness and perhaps at no point available to his recall, he will remove himself from his client's experience rather than enter it more deeply.

Rogers's aim was to experience the client and the client's world in much the same way as did the client himself. In order to accomplish this, intellectual or theoretical knowledge were not nearly as important as were warmth and emotional responsiveness. In this respect, his phenomenological orientation had much in common with that of the existential experientialist. However, Rogers went even further than the existential therapist in his extreme reluctance to ask questions (which, in requesting new information, took the client away from his or her immediate experience) or to offer a comment that in any way seemed "interpretive" (in the sense of pointing out possible meanings and connections hidden within the patient's communication, rather than simply reflecting the overt, feeling content of the communication).

Because the therapist's aim was to mirror the client's phenomenology as faithfully as possible, he would not disagree with the client, he would not point out apparent contradictions, and he would not suggest that the client might in some way be responding somewhat defensively or exaggerating his feelings. A totally empathic therapeutic environment gave the client an opportunity to gain a deeper awareness of what his perceptions of himself and of life actually were. Aspects of his feelings that he had too quickly cut off because of countering responses from others or because of his own defensiveness gradually unfolded and gained access to awareness.

The candid self-exploration Rogers aimed for could only occur in the context of a close and trusting relationship. Rogers devoted careful study to the nature of this kind of helping relationship and gradually defined what he considered to be its three most essential ingredients:

1. **Congruence.** In Rogers's view this is perhaps the single most important variable in doing therapy. It refers to the therapist's ability to be completely himself, to be "transparent" in the sense of letting the client see through him. He is congruent to the degree to which he is without facade and does not pretend to be anything he doesn't feel himself to be.

Congruence need not involve a counselor's continual *expression* of his personal responses. Instead it relates mostly to his being aware of them and comfortable with them. Where negative feelings emerge, like boredom or transient dislike, Rogers believes that the courageous therapist will share them with the client. He can do this more easily if he remembers that he is describing his own subjective feelings and not stating objective "facts" about the client; the therapist's boredom does not mean that the client is a boring person. In this way, the therapist can happen upon significant aspects of the therapist-client relationship; for instance, it might turn out that the client's subtle shift to increasingly intellectualized statements about himself has resulted in the therapist's feeling more and more distant from him; these feelings of distance or alienation have gradually emerged as boredom on the therapist's part. The therapist who warily communicates his feelings of boredom often finds them beginning to disappear, and he discovers in their place a sense of excited curiosity as to how the client will respond.

2. **Empathy.** Emphasized here is Rogers's interest in grasping, and adhering to, the client's frame of reference as closely as possible. For example, aspects of a client's behavior that the client does not experience as hostile or dependent are never labeled so by the therapist, even though most observers might insist that there are unmistakable hostile or dependent intentions lying outside the client's awareness. The therapist's aim is to refrain from imposing upon the client any of his own perceptions or value preferences. This kind of approach is different from that of the Freudian analyst, who might conceptualize certain material as "oral," which the client does not see in this light. In such an instance the analyst would probably hesitate, at least in the early stages of therapy, to share this perception with the client, since the latter would not be ready to hear it or understand it. In the Rogerian view, however, this withholding would have serious implications for the therapist's congruence, since he would be having distinct reactions to the client that he was not disclosing for a sustained period of time.

According to the theory of client-centered therapy, any client, no matter what the nature of his presenting problems, can improve without being taught by the therapist either a new set of values or a new framework for understanding his experiences. Once he is able to truly accept and respect himself, his own world view will prove adequate to the task of creatively enjoying life. If not, the experience of therapy will enable him on his own to shift and expand his world view to a point where it is more congruent with the way things really are.

3. **Positive regard.** This is the third ingredient in Rogers's conceptualization of the helping relationship, and in describing it I can do no better than to use Rogers's own words:

> I hypothesize that growth and change are more likely to occur the more that the counselor is experiencing a warm, positive, acceptant attitude toward what *is* in the client. It means that he prizes his client, as a person, with somewhat the same quality of feeling that a parent feels for his child, prizing him as a person regardless of his particular

behavior at the moment. It means that he cares for his client in a non-possessive way, as a person with potentialities. It involves an open willingness for the client to be whatever feelings are real in him at the moment—hostility or tenderness, rebellion or submissiveness, assurance or self-depreciation. It means a kind of love for the client as he is, providing we understand the word love as equivalent to the theologian's term *agape*, and not in its usual romantic and possessive meanings. What I am describing is a feeling which is not paternalistic, nor sentimental, nor superficially social and agreeable. It respects the other person as a separate individual and does not possess him. It is a kind of liking which has strength, and which is not demanding. We have termed it positive regard (Rogers and Stevens, 1967, p. 94).

The more this positive regard becomes truly unconditional (and this is not possible in every client-therapist relationship), the more it favors a climate conducive to the client's personal growth. It is this kind of unconditional regard, from parent to child, that is most favorable for the eventual development within the child of an accepting attitude toward himself and others.

A SEGMENT FROM A CLIENT-CENTERED
SESSION WITH BILL

This is the fourth session that Bill is having with his therapist, and about fifteen minutes have gone by. Bill has been discussing his relationship to the aunt who adopted him when he was about thirteen years old.

BILL: I think she tried to do her best by me. She had been trying to track me down for about two years, and when she finally located me in the orphanage she sent for me right away. (*Pause.*) I guess I felt kind of grateful about that.

TH: When you think of what your aunt tried to do for you, you're really touched.

BILL: Yeah—and even when she had to be away at work I felt that she was concerned about me. She would make lunch for me and phone home each day just to see how things were. That was a pretty happy time for me—maybe a very happy time.

TH: It sounds as though that year, after all the various foster homes and orphanages, stands out as a very special time—as kind of an oasis in the middle of the desert.

BILL: Yeah (*pause*), but then she got sick, and everything went downhill. It looked like she would be in the hospital a really long time, and I knew right away that she might die. And my uncle couldn't hack it, he was away most of the time, so there wasn't anything for me anymore.

TH: Do I hear you right, Bill? Are you saying that even here, just when it looked like you were finally going to make it with a family, a family of your own, things didn't work out?

BILL: Yeah, and like I knew it all along. Like all along I had this superstitious feeling of: this is too good to be true; things are finally looking as though they might work out for me—how long will it last?

TH: All along, even when the good things were happening and you had moved in with your aunt and uncle there had been a doubting part of you that looked on and wondered: when is this bubble going to burst?—all the other bubbles have!

BILL: That's it—and it turned out I was right. Soon as my aunt got sick that part of me, the one you called my doubting part, was almost gloating, as if it was saying to me: When are you finally going to wise up?

TH: Almost as though there was a battle going on, between a part of you that wanted to trust, to feel that things could really get good, and another, cynical part, that was afraid to relax and trust and let your guard down. When your aunt got sick the cynical part was all too ready to say: I told you so!

BILL: Yeah—but I think the trusting part of me was just getting to be stronger, cause I remember thinking, just before she got sick: Maybe things are going to work out after all. (*Long pause.*) I thought I had stopped thinking about that time in my life, but I guess I still have some bitter feelings about it.

TH: Like that hurt went very deep, and in a way it's still with you.

BILL: But I can't blame my aunt—she didn't ask to get sick. She seemed to feel real bad about my having to spend so much time alone. (*Pause.*) I don't know why I'm even thinking about blame, but I guess it would be nice if there could be someone specific to blame—somebody besides fate or stupid bad luck.

TH: It would be easier if you could say it was her fault: "She did this to me."

BILL: I guess maybe I'm thinking about that because while I was in the reformatory there was a shrink there who I was supposed to see every now and then, and he kept telling me that I was mad at my aunt, that I resented her, and that it had been like being abandoned by my mother all over again. I remember fighting with him about that, telling him that I liked my aunt, because she was one of the few people who ever seemed to take an interest in me—I mean a *real* interest, nothing phoney.

TH: It was as though he was throwing stones at her, and at your feelings for her, when he said you resented her. And you wanted to defend her, and defend your good feelings for her.

BILL: Well, he was a real pain in the neck in general. Talking about resentment, he was one person I resented for sure, and I wasn't afraid to let him know it!

TH: You sure didn't feel any inhibitions in letting him know your true feelings about him.

BILL: You bet!

Commentary. The client-centered therapist tries to stay with—and reflect—Bill's feelings. He doesn't ask factual questions concerning the specific details of this time in Bill's life, even though there may well be aspects of what Bill presents that are not completely clear to him. For example, what was the nature of the aunt's illness, and at what point did she actually die? Could she have possibly made other arrangements for him, and were there any other children at home? Bill has not mentioned any such children; however, he has not explicitly denied their existence. Any such inquiry would distract Bill from his own spontaneous thoughts and feelings, and since it is a sensitive mirroring of Bill's moment-to-moment experience that is therapeutic, the client-centered therapist is much less involved than either the behavior therapist or the psychoanalyst in a careful reconstruction of the patient's history.

In a similar vein, the client-centered therapist eschews any *interpretation* of Bill's comments. Psychoanalytically oriented therapists might tend to wonder, at first to themselves and later out loud, if Bill's remarks about *not* blaming his aunt did not indeed express some unconscious anger toward her, or if the hostility expressed by Bill for his previous "shrink" in some way stands for some resentment that he is feeling toward his current therapist. The client-centered therapist, on the other hand, trusts that if any such submerged feelings are part of the picture, the atmosphere of acceptance and trust that he has tried to foster will permit them to surface.

Bill's comments show that in *his* perceptual world a person cannot like someone and also resent her. Therapists of a variety of persuasions would be tempted to point out this belief, and to question it ("Are you saying, Bill, that because you had some very good feelings about your aunt, and about what she was able to do for you, you couldn't at the same time harbor some resentment for her?") While the client-centered therapist on a theoretical level has no reservations about the possibility of this kind of emotional ambivalence, he would deem such an intervention in the present context as intrusive—too steeped in the theoretical preconceptions of the therapist and too little grounded in the immediate experience of this particular patient at this particular moment in time.

GESTALT THERAPY

Although it has won many adherents and is widely practiced today (and in this sense has moved well beyond the personality of its originator), Gestalt therapy is still very much identified with the name and the free-wheeling style of the man who founded it, Fritz Perls. Perls was a German-born psychologist who left his native country prior to World War II, first emigrating to South Africa and then to the United States. He established successive bases in New York City, Miami Beach, Cleveland, Los Angeles, and the Esalen Institute, before moving on to Vancouver, British Columbia, where he established a commune devoted to the training of Gestalt therapists. Just as Perls emphasized the theme of personal autonomy when he stated the goals of therapy, his conception of the Gestalt residential community stressed the importance of political autonomy: Rules were established by consensus and authoritarian relationships were nonexistent. It was in 1970, in the midst of continuing involvement with the Vancouver project and giving demonstration-workshops throughout the world, that Perls died.

Gestalt therapy is supremely experiential in that it encourages the patient to focus intensively and specifically on what *is,* and not on what was, will be, should be, or could have been. This "is," rather than being directed toward life problems outside the therapy, is instead concentrated on his moment-to-moment flow of awareness within the therapy situation itself. The therapist's task is to help the patient make as alive and vivid as possible whatever he is experiencing at any particular point in time, to in some way heighten and dramatize it. Hence if the patient is feeling tearful, he might be asked to speak for his tears; if he starts to rock his foot he will be encouraged to exaggerate this movement so that he can begin to experience it more fully. If he states that he is beginning to feel the rise within himself of a not-infrequent irritability which he dislikes, he may be instructed to place this irritability outside himself, in the empty chair next to him, and to address it directly. At a slightly later point he might be directed by the therapist to sit in the empty chair and, now taking the role of his "irritability," to answer himself back (Perls believed that he obtained the best results when the patient became involved with the "let's pretend" theatrical metaphor to the point of literally shifting from one chair to the other). Should a patient find himself preoccupied with an outside problem, he will be encouraged to introduce that situation into the immediate theatre of the therapy. For example, if he finds himself dwelling on a work project that he has not yet begun and that his boss is nagging him about, he will be instructed to have a fantasy dialogue, perhaps with his boss, perhaps with the project itself. The therapist's task is to help him stop talking about his life, and to instead *be* his life in the full immediacy of the here-and-now.

The therapist plays a particularly facilitative role at that point where the patient begins to manifest some of his typical ways of avoiding more direct contact with his experience. For example, if a patient manages, at the first signs of his own tearfulness, to prevent weeping by clenching the muscles in his jaw, the therapist may draw his attention to these motions and may ask him to deliberately intensify the clenching. It probably seems paradoxical for the therapist to ask a patient to *increase* his defensiveness, but such a technique makes sense for two reasons: (1) it is often easier, at least initially, to intensify a habit than to suddenly eliminate it, especially if it is one that reduces tension; and (2) we cannot change something until we have actually experienced it. One of the reasons that Perls paid careful attention to a patient's body movement was because such movement usually symbolizes areas of experience with which the person is not in active contact.

Through these procedures (and others, which will be described below), Gestalt therapy combines several existential-humanistic themes:

1. **Careful attentiveness to the patient's moment-to-moment phenomenology.** More than any other single method of psychotherapy, Gestalt therapy follows closely moment-to-moment changes in a person's awareness. Perls believed that Freud's free-associational technique, by directing a patient to report whatever came to his *mind,* overly focused him on the cognitive, or thought, aspects of his experience. By having the patient carefully concentrate on his "continuum of awareness" (which may include his immediate sense impressions), and by pointing out to him various aspects of his bodily reactions, Perls hoped to contact feeling states within the person that were less accessible to psychoanalytic methods. He tried in this way to extend our definition of awareness beyond what is normally meant by thought and feeling, to sense impressions and to body sensations (which often underlie or accompany what is described in the psychological sphere as "feeling"). Perls was also reminding us that awareness itself can only exist in the present moment (despite the fact that we can, via the *content* of our consciousness, project ourself to the very distant past or future).

It was in this attempt to implement his interest in the patient's immediate phenomenology that Perls hit upon the highly dramatic techniques that we described above and that helped to make him and his approach famous. His method had a strongly theatrical flavor, and to some degree it borrowed from Jacob Moreno's well-known group technique of psychodrama (see Shaffer and Galinsky, 1974), wherein a patient selects from the group several members to role-play—with his help and that of the psychodrama director—significant people and episodes from his life. However, in Gestalt therapy the only actor is the patient himself, and he proceeds to personify not only significant people from his life, but also various feelings, body parts, and long-standing attitudes (like irritability or greediness). As Perls saw it, we often distance ourselves from our immediate experience by talking *about* it in discursive, narrative, and abstract terms. Whatever technique he might use in a particular instance, his consistent objective was to render the patient's feeling experience as immediate as possible by translating it into tangible here-and-now terms.

Some Gestalt therapists practicing today do not go so far as having the patient move from one chair to another (e.g., see Kempler, 1973, p. 253), and they will at times engage with the patient in a relatively straightforward dialogue, like that between patient and therapist in psychoanalytic or existential-experiential therapy. For instance, a patient may describe a fight he had with his wife without having to "speak for" her or to take her role in the session. However, such therapists identify themselves as Gestalt in that they will sometimes ask the patient to attend to, and exaggerate, his body movements, and are willing to be quite active in having him, at certain selected instances, talk directly to significant figures from his past or present, or create a spontaneous fantasy based on a theme suggested by the therapist (e.g., see Polster, 1975).

2. **Encouraging the patient to take maximum responsibility for himself.** According to Gestalt therapy we often word our sentences in such a way as to deny responsibility for our own actions and our own bodies. For example, the Gestalt patient, in attempting to report his immediate experience and to become aware of his nonverbal behavior, might say "My hand is doing this movement" or "The thought comes to me. . . ." One direct way in which Perls encouraged the patient to take responsibility for himself was to have him make "I" statements in which he more fully acknowledged authorship of his own experience and behavior (at least on the verbal level; hopefully what might start out as purely verbal gradually becomes felt at more experiential levels). If we continue with the two illustrations immediately above, instead of saying "My hand is doing this movement," the patient says "I am moving my hand like this" and instead of "The thought comes to me . . . ," he says "I have the thought . . . ," or, even better (in the sense of acknowledging a still greater degree of active authorship), "I *think* the thought. . . ."

Perls believed that many people frequently disown various unacknowledged aspects of themselves by projecting them onto other people or onto the inanimate world. A form of this occurs in what often is construed to be a form of magical thinking in young children, wherein emotions are attributed to natural elements (e.g., "the clouds are angry"), or in the animistic thinking of primitive cultures wherein special powers are attributed to various animal species. All too often similar projections persist into adulthood, and what is projected may involve not only unacceptable feelings (emphasized by Freud in his conception of projection) but also, at least according to Perls, positive strengths and potentials. These disowned potentials (called "holes" or "gaps" by Perls) then emerge in a person's perception of others. Thus a fear of criticism often stems from a projection of one's own unacknowledged power of criticism. Such criticism, albeit sometimes frightening to the person because of its hostile implications, often contains within it elements of strength and mastery, first because it allows one to judge as well as be judged, and second because it may reflect a genuine faculty, like perceptiveness. One technical means by which Perls worked with projection involved what he called "reversal"; for instance, the patient who expressed concern with the therapist's possible criticisms of him is asked to become the *criticizer* and to actively criticize the therapist.

Perls also relied upon the concept of projection in attempting to understand and explain the imagery of our dreams. In his theory, each element within the dream—whether a person, an event, or an object or thing—in some way represented a disowned, or projected, aspect of the dreamer. For instance, a tyrannical parent figure might well embody one's own wish to control either others or oneself. Therefore Perls' main method for dealing with dreams entailed having a patient role-play, and speak for, each of the various symbols within the dream. In encouraging us to reclaim various lost and disowned potentials, Perls was of course sounding one of the keynotes of humanistic psychology. In refusing to take on the role of an authority who interpreted the meaning of the patient's dream, and in insisting instead on the patient's discovery of the dream's meaning himself, Perls highlighted another key theme of humanistic psychotherapy, one that is paralleled in Rogers's extreme care lest he intrude upon the client's frame of reference—i.e., the importance of helping a patient exchange excessive reliance on outside authority (termed "environmental support" by Perls) for a greater degree of trust in his own authoritativeness ("self-support").

3. **Helping the fragmented self to become integrated and whole.** As Perls saw it, most people are encouraged to believe that they have a real "self," which then becomes reified and concretized to a point where it seems to have a definitive, or actual, essence. Perls offered a more "being" definition of self that included all the conflicted, projected, and introjected parts of ourselves ("introjection" refers to a process wherein one identifies with, and incorporates, aspects of significant others). His aim here was to encourage a healing, unifying dialogue among all these diverse selves, many of which are often defined as "not me" and are therefore split off from the person. Therefore the Gestalt technique in which a patient is encouraged to dramatize and to exaggerate two conflicting aspects of himself (e.g., first his controlling,

compulsive aspects, and then his longing for spontaneous play) can be seen as having this related aim—that of blending into a more harmonious integration our various selves.

Perls claimed that the strongly rationalized and seemingly logical categories of Western thought, wherein the person is either one thing or the other (male or female, extroverted or introverted), encouraged the person to view himself in either-or terms. Gestalt therapy offers a more inclusive definition of oneself in which one is many different things. Within this scheme, one's self is defined not in terms of fixed characteristics but in here-and-now terms: The self is equated with whatever one is feeling or wishing at any one point in a continuum of constantly flowing experience. Perls hoped that we would broaden our ego boundaries to a point where we would tolerate within us many different moods and voices. Must we have but one self simply because we have only one body and tend to be viewed by the culture as one particular, continuous person? According to Perls, each of us is in actuality many different people, and he was optimistic about our ability to integrate them.

4. **The importance of self-acceptance.** Somewhat paradoxically, Perls believed that the only way the person could do something about those of his traits that he wished to change was to first accept them. Not that we must heartily like or unequivocally approve the things about ourselves that we wish were different (how could we?), but that we must *accept* them. In other words, while the *content* of our complaints about ourselves might be valid and realistic, all too often their tone and style reveal an internalized, perfectionistic parent-introject (called "top-dog" by Perls) that, by telling us what we "should" and "should not" be like, *demands* change. Since the tyrannical demands of our top-dog stimulate a spiteful counterreaction from our "under-dog" (representing what remains within us of a sometimes rebellious child), this struggle is always doomed to failure. Hence we cannot regulate and govern change within ourselves in the same way that we can manipulate various mechanical objects, like cars and faucets, despite the fact that our technological society often encourages to believe that we can. The person can, however, facilitate processes of change within himself by focusing on what he actually *is* now.

Thus Perls, as much as Rogers, emphasized the tremendous importance of self-acceptance, although the technical ways in which he attempted to implement this goal, as with earlier ones, involved exaggeration and dramatic action. For instance, if a patient claimed that he must stop being a bully, Perls encouraged him to express this aspect of himself as fully as possible within the immediate therapy session. "Go ahead!" he might say, "be as big a bully as you can—boss me around and tell me what to do." Whereas the patient is stating that he hopes to be able to suppress this side of himself, the Gestalt therapist is forcing him to "own" it and to acknowledge it to the point of exaggeration. The therapist also hopes to heal a top-dog/under-dog split by bringing into a more integrated relationship the bullying and nonbullying parts of the patient's personality. Up until now we have had an ironic situation in which the patient's top-dog, by insisting that he *not* be a bully, is bullying the other parts of his personality.

A SEGMENT FROM A GESTALT SESSION WITH BILL

This is the very first session that the Gestalt therapist is having with Bill. Unlike the behavioral, psychoanalytic, or existential therapist, he does not encourage Bill to describe the nature of his problem or his history. Instead he immediately focuses on Bill's here-and-now experience.

TH: Try to describe just what you are aware of at each moment as fully as possible. For instance, what are you aware of now?

BILL: I'm aware of wanting to tell you about my problem, and also a sense of shame—Yes, I feel very ashamed right now.

TH: OK, I would like you to develop a dialogue with your feeling of shame. Put your shame in the empty chair, over here (*indicates chair*), and talk to it.

BILL: Are you serious? I haven't even told you about my problem yet.

TH: That can wait—I'm perfectly serious, and I want to know what you have to say to your shame.

BILL (*awkward and hesitant at first, but then becoming looser and more involved*): Shame, I hate you. I wish you would leave me—you drive me crazy, always reminding me that I have a problem, that I'm perverse, different, shameful—even ugly. Why don't you leave me alone?

TH: OK, now go to the empty chair, take the role of shame, and answer yourself back.

BILL (*moves to the empty chair*): I am your constant companion—and I don't *want* to leave you. I would feel lonely without you, and I don't hate you. I pity you, and I pity your attempts to shake me loose, because you are doomed to failure.

TH: OK, now go back to your original chair, and answer back.

BILL (*once again as himself*): How do you know I'm doomed to failure? (*Spontaneously shifts chairs now, no longer needing direction from the therapist; answers himself back, once again in the role of shame.*) I know that you're doomed to failure because *I* want you to fail and because I control your life. You can't make a single move without me. For all you know, you were *born* with me. You can hardly remember a single moment that you were without me, totally unafraid that I would spring up and suddenly remind you of your loathsomeness.

BILL: You're right; so far you *have* controlled my life—I feel constantly embarrassed and awkward. (*His voice grows stronger.*) But that doesn't mean that you'll continue to control my life. That's why I've come here—to find some way of destroying you.

(*Shifts to the "shame" chair.*) Do you think *he* can help you? (*Bill, as Shame, points to the therapist.*) What can he do? He hardly knows you as I know you—besides, he's only going to see you once or twice each week. I am with you every single moment of every day!

TH: Bill, look how one hand keeps rubbing the other when you speak for shame. Could you exaggerate that motion? Who does that remind you of?

BILL (*rubbing his hands together harder and harder*): My mother would do this—yes, whenever she was nervous she would rub her hands harder and harder.

TH: OK, now speak for your mother.

Commentary. According to the Gestalt therapist, the kind of discursive presentation of symptomatic complaints that is encouraged in the usual initial therapy session distances the patient emotionally (both from his immediate feelings and from the interviewer-therapist) and encourages him to escape from the stressfulness of his here-and-now experience through a focusing on the there-and-then (i.e., in this context, a narration of his problem's history). Hence in this opening session the therapist disarms Bill by concentrating on the shame Bill experiences around his problem, rather than on the problem itself. As the session unfolds, material emerges suggesting that Bill's sense of shame is strongly identified with what Gestalt therapists term a "toxic introject," an introject that in turn appears based on Bill's mother and his experiences with his mother. Introjection can occur at any time in life, but is a process characteristic of infancy and early childhood, when the child uncritically takes in—and embodies—aspects of the nurturing person or persons, including aspects that he does not like and that he regards as noxious. When the nurturing person is experienced as more noxious than nourishing, the resulting introject is said to be "toxic."

Hence Bill's sense of shame, while painful, helps him to feel less lonely and also serves the masochistic end of keeping him in a constant state of torment. However, the Gestalt therapist would never in any way attempt to describe or explain such concepts; instead he encourages the patient *to experience,* in a vivid way, these various splits and fragmentations within himself.

Recapitulation

The three representative schools of humanistic psychotherapy reviewed in this chapter—existential-experiential, client-centered, and Gestalt—have differed from one another to some degree. Yet they have by and large shared the following emphases: (1) a strong interest in the patient's moment-to-moment phenomenology without a need to somehow alter or *explain* it; (2) a reluctance to view the therapist as someone who is in a better position to understand or interpret the patient's experience than is the patient himself; (3) a deep respect for the patient's freedom, whether he should use it to change or instead resist change; (4) a readiness to cast aside any a priori, theoretically based preconceptions about the patient, and to regard him as a unique person who must discover his own meaning and his own definition of well-being; (5) an emphasis on the essential equality of patient and therapist to the point where the latter will at times feel free to expose his own feelings and conflicts; and (6) a tendency to see as curative the therapist's fully accepting, and caring, stance toward the patient.

The therapeutic approaches of Rogers and Perls, in particular, were to become important forerunners of the human potential movement. As early as the 1950s, Rogers had begun to apply his client-centered conceptions to groups, and at a later point he referred to these groups as "basic encounter groups." He found that the basic encounter group was well suited for problems of normal alienation and did not need to be long-term in order for individual participants to experience change. In a similar vein, Perls eventually became impressed with the gains that could be made in Gestalt therapy on a short-term basis. Such a discovery was not too surprising, in view of the fact that Perls saw as the patient's primary task a full attendance to the immediacy of his or her here-and-now experience. He also began to concentrate more exclusively on working within a group context. In this way, the work of both Rogers and Perls helped bridge the gap between humanistic approaches to psychotherapy and the human potential movement; once the distinctions between normal and abnormal on the one hand, and between psychotherapy and education on the other, became blurred, it was but a short step from an often lengthy treatment for the neurotic to short-term growth experiences for the healthy person wanting to expand and revitalize his or her life. Chapter 6 will give the history of these developments in more detail.

Humanistic Approaches
to Education

chapter five

The humanistic movement has had serious reservations about the image of man offered by contemporary psychological theory and conventional psychotherapy. American education has not been immune from similar criticism, since schools, along with families, give children their first serious encounter with the issues of learning, authority, and vocation. Starting in 1960, with the publication of Paul Goodman's *Growing Up Absurd* (1960), a series of books began to appear that documented the degree to which American schools at all grade levels encouraged mindless conformism, a deadening of excitement, and a sense of pessimism concerning the possibilities for meaningful work and for creative play in adulthood (for example, see Friedenberg, 1965, and Kozol, 1967).

Humanistic conceptions of education generally try to eliminate the distinction between means and ends, so that learning is experienced as a source of pleasure in its own right, rather than as an instrument for competing with others or for guaranteeing one's social status in the future (here the emphasis is on the importance of present-centeredness;

learning is exhilarating and meaningful *now*). Humanistic approaches also attempt to ensure that a lesson's content is not divorced from its personal meaning for the learner. Therefore, the teacher is encouraged to pay some heed to the pupil's emotional response to what he is learning (here the stress is on the learner's holistic need to integrate feeling with thought). Lastly, humanism casts the teacher into a catalytic, not an authoritarian, role. The more a teacher becomes an authority who determines what the pupil is to learn, why it must be learned, and how well it is to be learned, the more her pedagogical technique falls within a traditional approach. The more the student is viewed as the source and motivator of his own learning, in that his spontaneous curiosity is the driving force behind what he masters and how well he masters it, the more his schooling approaches a humanistic model (here there is a consistent respect for his individuality and his autonomy).

An Example from the Classroom

In order to make our theoretical discussion more concrete, we would like to cite a specific classroom situation, one that seems immediately relevant to our context—the teaching and learning involved in this book. If you were teaching a course in which this book had been assigned, how would you go about presenting its materials in class? In asking this question, we are arbitrarily imposing for purposes of exposition a particular structure on your course—i.e., we assume that your class meets as a group at regular intervals. (Other procedures, in which the class is granted more freedom in determining the basic structure and content of the course, will be examined later).

Suppose, then, we take as a specific instance a classroom session during which you, as the instructor, would like your students to focus on the material covered in the first four chapters of this book. How would you go about this? Can you think of an approach that is consistent with humanistic goals of education, keeping in mind that its two key features are for students to become maximally involved in what they are learning, and for them to freely express their personal reactions to the material? Should you prefer to lecture to your class about humanistic psychology, you can, of course, leave more room for student participation by encouraging the class to ask questions and to make comments. On the other hand, some teachers believe that lecturing reinforces the student's passivity and thus prefer to run the entire class in the form of group discussion; they believe this approach gives students more opportunity to take responsibility for the lesson and to express their reactions to it (Hill, 1969). If a teacher chooses to emphasize discussion, there still remains to be determined how she will introduce, structure, and facilitate it. Try to take a few minutes out from your immediate reading to think the question through. How would *you,* as teacher, organize this particular classroom session? Such an exercise may help to make what follows more personally relevant to you, for now you will have participated directly in it. This kind of participation can, in turn, make for a greater degree of emotional involvement on your part. It is this kind of involvement that humanistic education tries to maximize.

In my own teaching, I sometimes employ group discussion instead of lectures, especially if the class is a small one. Ruth Cohn, a psychotherapist and educator, has developed a technique for leading group discussions that I at times have found helpful; it is called the *theme-centered interactional method.* A value of the theme-centered method is its suitability for leading discussion on a variety of topics, some of which can be fairly intellectual and some of which can be more personal. Another value is that its central principles clearly reflect fundamental humanistic emphases. For example, through its "Be Your Own Chairman" ground rule, to be explained below, the discussion leader reminds the participant of his inherent freedom to either speak up or remain silent; and through the model's holistic thrust, the leader encourages the participants to share their *emotional responses* as well as their more intellectual questions and ideas. Although some theme-centered teachers have found that they are able to lead meaningful classroom discussions among as many as fifty students, the method seems best suited for groups that have no more than twenty-five.

A THEME-CENTERED CLASS DISCUSSION

In the fictitious example to follow, Dr. B. is a college instructor. Her aim is to focus her class on a discussion of the material thus far presented in this book, and the procedure that she uses is Cohn's theme-centered method. Her class consists of twenty-three students and is part of a course entitled "History and Systems of Psychology." Today is their twentieth meeting. Dr. B. begins the class by announcing the theme for that session: My Understanding of Humanistic Psychology Thus Far. She asks the students to wait a few moments before beginning their discussion so that she can pose some tasks for them. First she asks them to think about which aspects of the material they most vividly remember, and a minute later to silently focus on specific questions they have about what they have read. Since she realizes that not all the group members are likely to have read the assignment, she asks those who did not do the reading to reflect on some of the feelings and conflicts that prevented them from doing so. In the final task the participant is asked how he or she *feels* right now, at this point in time in this group. Dr. B. also encourages the participants to pay careful attention to whatever bodily sensations or tensions they are experiencing.

Dr. B. now encourages the students to express themselves. She introduces the discussion as follows:

> Let us now communicate about whatever we want to—the theme, my suggestions to you, your experiences, thoughts, feelings, whatever you want to communicate about. Please be your own chairman and try to get whatever you want to get from the group and to give whatever you want to give. . . . Do interrupt when you are bored, distracted, angry, or anything else which prevents you from full participation (Cohn, 1972, p. 856).

The students speaking at the outset of the discussion make their points cautiously, while the majority remains silent. Dr. B.'s intent is to reduce anxiety and to encourage maximum participation. Therefore when no one else responds to a student's remarks, she, as leader, empathically paraphrases the gist of what has just been said. During the first ten minutes the discussion is primarily theoretical in nature. Toward the end of this initial phase one student, Mark, expresses frustration over his attempts to understand the concept of "being," and he also wonders about the difference between "being" and "being-in-the-world." Another student, Dorothy, explains what she thinks this theoretical distinction refers to. It is at this point that Margie interrupts.

MARGIE: I probably shouldn't say this, but I wonder why Dr. B. doesn't explain what *she* thinks the distinction is—she should know better than anybody else.

LOUIS: I'm not so sure that's true. I read on to Chapter 5, which is about humanistic teaching, and that's what I liked most about it— the idea that the teacher isn't necessarily an expert who knows everything. He's not so much supposed to tell us the answer as to help us find the way to our own answers.

HENRIETTA: I go along with that, and I like to hear from the other people. But what I haven't liked about a lot of the discussions is that so far there are a lot of people who still are silent. It's usually the same ones who do all the talking.

RUTH: But do you have a right to blame them for not talking? My idea of humanistic psychology is that you don't make value judgments, and you try to see things from the other person's point of view. Like maybe some people here are scared to speak, cause we do tend to criticize a bit—somebody's ideas, for example, or Dr. B. just now for not explaining something, or even some students for not speaking more.

At this point there are a few moments of silence; then Dr. B. makes an audible noise by snapping her fingers, and she proceeds to ask each participant to in turn briefly share with the group what was going on in his or her mind at the point when the sound was heard. Students are encouraged to be open about whatever they were thinking or experiencing, whether or not it was related to what had been going on in the group; however, they are free to "pass" if they want to—i.e., to not say anything because they feel that whatever they were thinking was too private, too embarrassing, or whatever.

As each member speaks briefly in turn, it becomes apparent that several of the students who had not been participating actively had been thinking about their own silence during the session. The fourth student to speak, Mike, said that he had been thinking about how the discussion didn't have much meaning for him, probably because he hadn't read the assignment. After each participant has had a chance to briefly respond, the unstructured discussion once again begins.

DR. B.:   I noticed that a lot of you seemed to be wondering, somewhat self-consciously, whether Henrietta had included you among the silent people who tend not to speak up.

KAREN: Yes, and just now I was beginning to relate my tendency to remain silent to some of the things in the book, like the whole idea of "being-in-the-world." Like maybe this is my way of being in the world. Like I want to say something, but I wait for someone to invite me. For instance, just now (*Karen turns to Dr. B.*) I was hoping you would say something about the whole idea of some people not talking— and then somehow that would give me permission to speak up. I don't know why I'm this way, though.

JERRY: So what if you did know the reason?—Like it had something to do with your mother and father. I agree with Perls, it would probably just be intellectual and it wouldn't change anything.

KAREN: Maybe you're right; I know one thing—I'm glad I started talking just now because it's as though the ice has been broken and right now I don't feel that self-conscious talking.

BARBARA: I know I'm changing the subject, but I've been dying to ask Mike how he felt when he admitted that he hadn't read the chapters at all, and I know the hour is going to end soon.

DR. B.:   If you were to change your question into a statement, Barbara, what would it be?

VICKI: You know, Dr. B., you say there's no structure here, but there *is* one. Like this ground rule about how we should talk and how we shouldn't ask questions.

DR. B.: I would never claim there's no structure because there *is* a clear-cut structure: I make assignments, I set a theme, I end the class when the bell rings. They're like the existential limits discussed in the book. What is your margin of freedom within this structure? Just now you used your freedom to sound off about how you experience me as hypocritical and about how that annoys you.

BARBARA: Maybe Vicki wants to answer you, Dr. B., but I have to interrupt because I'm still curious about Mike. My statement is that I admire Mike for being able to admit he didn't do the reading. There are a few times here that I didn't do the reading but I've never had the guts to say anything about it.

MIKE: I don't feel like it took that much guts—I feel free to attend a session without having done the homework. But I do feel irritation, because I think it's inconsistent to give mandatory reading in a class on humanistic psychology—we should be free to not have to do anything here.

JERRY: But you are free to come to class without having done the assignment.

MIKE: And Dr. B. has the freedom to give me a nice low grade because of it.

HENRIETTA: But can you really expect to exercise your freedom without suffering any consequences? That sounds like what the book mentions with Sartre's concept of bad faith. You make a choice, but you don't take any responsibility for it.

BARBARA: I don't know—that sounds pretty human to me, to want to have your cake and eat it too.

During the fifteen minutes that remain, the class focuses for a while on the related concepts of freedom and responsibility and then returns to the question of how their grades will be determined and the extent to which a student's grade ought to be influenced by the amount of his or her participation in class discussion. As the end of the session approaches, Dr. B. gives some direct feedback as to the kinds of criteria she employs in determining final grades.

BASIC PRINCIPLES
OF THE THEME-CENTERED MODEL

The theme-centered interactional method began as a general means of working with groups of all kinds. Ruth Cohn, who originated the method, was initially a psychotherapist who found herself increasingly interested in applying therapeutic methods that proved effective in resolving individual conflicts to the problems of the larger community (Cohn, 1969). Could techniques that facilitated communication, whether in individual or group therapy, also help improve communication within larger organizations such as industries, government agencies, and schools?

All small groups have a task or purpose that brings them together in the first place. For example, the implicit agenda for an English class on one particular day involves a discussion of *Hamlet,* or an organizational committee may meet for the purpose of revising the organization's budget. These agendas constitute the group's overt content, or *theme,* for that particular meeting. One innovation of the theme-centered approach is that it makes this theme explicit by stating it formally at the beginning of the group.

Along with its task or theme, a group also has "process" aspects involving the feelings that members have toward each other, toward the leader, and toward the group's agenda. The group process includes each person's individual emotions, as well as what is normally meant by "group dynamics"—i.e., how cohesive is the group? who are its unofficial leaders? and so on. Most groups, including the classroom, focus overtly on the theme and ignore the process aspects. A second innovation of the theme-centered method is that it makes active room for the emotional aspects of the group interaction and for this reason does not regard the discussion of feelings as inappropriate. From the model's point of view, the teacher-leader who ignores the fact that some of his or her students are bored by the lesson, or that others have not done the homework, is denying a crucial aspect of their immediate reality.

The theme-centered teacher is interested in an *optimum,* rather than maximum, amount of theme-centeredness; and if the group has remained with its theme for a prolonged period of time, he or she will encourage some discussion of personal reactions and interactional dynamics. Should the participants spontaneously bring up these concerns, so much the better. Three important humanistic principles are involved here. The first involves an emphasis on the whole person—on his feelings as well as his thoughts. The second involves the concept of individuation and uniqueness—i.e., what stimulates one student might well put another to sleep. This has always been true; the novel feature here is that students in theme-centered discussions are encouraged to become aware of and express such differences. The teacher, by taking an active interest in the idiosyncracies of each learner, tries to make the classroom situation personally meaningful for each, and thereby to convert what all too often is "dead learning" into "living learning" (Cohn, 1972). A third humanistic principle involves the basic phenomenological observation (first enunciated by Gestalt perceptual psychology and later amplified by Fritz Perls) that one cannot attend to one item of a stimulus configuration (the "figure") too long without having his or her attention

Alexander Lowen   A psychiatrist who developed a human potential technique called Bioenergetic Analysis.

Ruth C. Cohn   A psychoanalyst and group therapist, she devised a humanistic model of education and group-leading called the theme-centered interactional method.

Martin Buber   A Jewish theologian and philosopher who formulated the existential concept of the I-Thou relationship. (Wide World Photos)

Ronald Laing   A British psychiatrist who developed an existential-phenomenological theory of schizophrenia. (Wide World Photos)

Fritz Perls Originally trained as a psychoanalyst, he later founded the school of Gestalt therapy. (Courtesy of Bantam Books)

Michael Murphy He used property that he had inherited to co-found Esalen Institute at Big Sur, California.

Abraham Maslow The titular father of humanistic psychology, he developed what came to be called a holistic-dynamic theory of personality.

A. E. Neill A British educator who founded the Summerhill School in Suffolk, England.

Carl Rogers   A psychologist who founded client-centered therapy and the "freedom to learn" model of humanistic education.

William Schutz   Psychologist trained in psychoanalysis and group dynamics who developed the human potential technique called Open Encounter.

Thomas Szasz   An ardent critic of institutional psychiatry, he became a champion of the mental patient's legal and civil rights. (Photo by Gabor Szilasi)

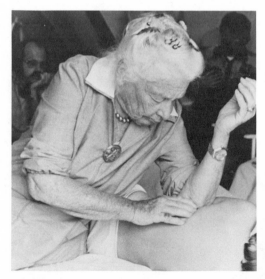

Ida Rolf   She developed the body therapy and human potential technique called Structural Integration. (Copyright David Campbell. Courtesy of Rolf Institute)

wander to another aspect of that same configuration (that which had until this point been "ground" and now becomes a new figure). A major tenet of the theme-centered method holds that a continual focusing on the theme would produce oversaturation and fatigue; the discussion participant can better attend to a theme if it is occasionally allowed to recede into the background.

The content and process aspects of a class's discussion at times may seem quite distinct, as in a class in mathematics, and at other times they may clearly overlap. An example of a overlapping situation would be a lesson on Erik Erikson's concept of Basic Trust versus Mistrust (Erikson, 1964), where the trust theme can be made vivid to the class by focusing on the amount of trustingness that actually exists (or does not exist) in that particular group. The teacher has hit "pay dirt" when he or she can find a point of direct contact between the lesson's theme and an immediate event in the class that illuminates it.

This kind of dovetailing between content and process most easily occurs in curriculum areas involving social science and the humanities. However, teachers of physical science, if they are alert and like theme-centered teaching, may also be able to find points of contact between theme and process. For example, field theory concepts in physics overlap with group-dynamic concepts and therefore can be used to analyze and explain the immediate pattern of a group's interaction. Similarly, the symbiotic interaction between two participants might, at certain key moments, provide a chemistry teacher with an apt analogy for the formation of compounds out of two or more chemical elements. Even when there are no significant points of contact between theme and interaction, a mathematics or science teacher might wish to use the theme-centered method to elucidate just what the pupils are experiencing as they attempt to learn the material and relate to both the teacher and each other.

Setting and introducing the theme. An important element within the theme-centered method is that the leader pay careful attention to the selection and wording of the theme and that he or she announce it at the outset of the group. This is because the theme functions as a kind of directive or "set" for the participants and for their subsequent discussion. In the classroom, the most obvious way to set a theme is in terms of the material that has been assigned. However, the themes for each class need not always relate to the subject matter proper. Should a teacher wish to share some of the responsibility for planning the class with the group at large, she might set as her theme for a particular session: Selecting the Themes for Future Sessions, or Changing the

Class Format. Where possible, the teacher will try to introduce the theme so that the students can relate it both to their personal lives and to the here-and-now of the group. For example, in a theme involving friendship, she might ask the participants to silently relate this theme to their own lives, and a moment later she might ask them to think about which persons in the group they feel most friendly toward.

Ground rules. Ground rules are best understood as guidelines that help to facilitate authentic encounters within the group interaction, and not as arbitrary rules or "laws" that have to be slavishly followed. Sometimes they are introduced at the beginning of the group, and sometimes they aren't mentioned until that point in the interaction where they are specifically appropriate.

1. *Disturbances take precedence.* This ground rule embodies the model's concern with where each student "is at" vis-à-vis the learning situation immediately at hand, and it recognizes that no student can be fully involved in the group discussion so long as he or she is acutely bothered about something. Since the group's purpose is not to resolve personal problems, all that is necessary is for the student to be relieved of his discomfort to a point where he can return his attention to the discussion. Frequently the mere verbalization of his preoccupation, especially if it is responded to supportively by the class, is enough to relieve him. If it is something about the class itself that is bothering the student, the group is of course more able to relate to the disturbance than if it is something outside the class that concerns him; sometimes the group may even be able to directly remedy the problem.

2. *Be your own chairman.* This ground rule attempts to reinforce each student's awareness of his own autonomy—i.e., that he himself is more responsible than anyone else, including the teacher, for what he does or doesn't obtain for himself in the session. This autonomy is an existential given, and as such it is not within the power of the teacher-leader to either grant it or revoke it. What the teacher can do is to consistently remind the participant of the *fact* of this autonomy, and to prod him into a deeper consideration of whether he is exercising it to the fullest. All teachers should also remember that the exercise of a student's autonomy in the discussion will not necessarily result in his speaking more; in fact, if the student is a compulsive talker, the exercise of his freedom may well result in his being able to *listen* more of the time.

3. *Speak per I.* This guideline is directed toward encouraging each participant to state his or her own experience as clearly as possible. This is necessary because participants often mask their statements in such a way as to give the appearance of making generalizations about human behavior. For example: "You find that as you get older. . . .," "One never likes to. . . ," and so on. Some people argue that the tendency in

American culture to begin statements with "You" is merely a habit of syntax, but theme-centered theorists believe that on a deeper psychological level this linguistic convention represents a defensive attempt to project out and to "collectivize," rather than to fully *own*—and assume responsibility for—*my* feeling and *my* convictions.

4. *Give the statement behind your question.* Like ground rules 2 and 3, this ground rule encourages each participant to take as much responsibility for his own actions and feelings as possible. Most questions that one person asks of another hide an unstated concern or tension. For instance, a common tendency to ask a person whom one has recently met what he does for a living may mask more authentic statements like: "I am made uncomfortable by the silence between us" or "I can relate more easily to you if I can 'type' you, and I can 'type' you more readily if I know your occupation." While this kind of defensive hiding may be appropriate to social situations, the aim of theme-centered leading is to facilitate a more authentic level of relating within the group.

APPLYING THE MODEL
TO THE ILLUSTRATIVE SESSION

The fictitious class discussion that was presented above had as its theme My Understanding of Humanistic Psychology Thus Far. The teacher, Dr. B., tried to facilitate the discussion in a variety of ways. One way was to apply the ground rules, as when she asked Barbara what lay behind her question to Mike. Another was to increase the group's cohesiveness; this becomes especially important when the discussion is dominated by just a few participants. This is what Dr. B. tried to do when she snapped her fingers and encouraged each participant to indicate just where he or she "had been at" during that particular moment; in this way each person in the group spoke, however briefly.

In successful theme-centered interaction, points of contact are usually found between the group's theme and what is happening in the group. In our sample session, some participants, with the help of the teacher, were able to apply some of the humanistic concepts encountered in their reading to the class's interaction. This happened when points were brought up involving the limits of each person's freedom, the extent to which the teacher should be viewed as more expert than the student, and the appropriateness of making value judgments about another participant's behavior. The discussion also briefly touched on the definitions of "bad faith" and "being-in-the-world," and Fritz Perls's ideas about how people change.

Students experiencing this kind of discussion in the classroom are often frustrated because they are not being given the "truth" or the "knowledge" that they desire. Their expectation is that this truth resides someplace outside themselves, usually within the teacher. In the theme-centered method, each person speaks from his own subjectivity. What we have is a series of individuals, including the teacher, each expressing his or her unique point of view. The method, in encouraging every student to participate, strongly implies that each is worthy of respect and of being listened to.

To the extent to which a student feels she is not learning, or not getting what she wants, she is responsible for trying to do something about it. If she assumes that it is automatically the teacher's job to increase her learning, she is attempting to deny her autonomy. Similarly, for the teacher to always assume that learning is taking place simply because the students are not overtly complaining, is to evade her capacity for autonomous judgment. If the majority of students believe that the model is not working for them, it is important that the teacher be willing to consider revising her structure. There is no reason why the method has to be used exclusively, or even at all (other humanistic approaches are presented below). In situations where the method is working, it can still be combined with traditional lectures, student presentations, other kinds of discussion, and theme-centered sessions led by the students themselves.

An instructor's skill in teaching the essence of humanism lies as much in her ability to be genuinely humanistic in her style of relating as in her expertise in explicating conceptual material. To the extent to which she retains a firm sense of her own identity at the same time that she has a flexible willingness to allow others to develop differing identities and differing values, she is relating in a humanistic way. Her identity and values are demonstrated in the way in which she structures the classroom, and there is no effective means by which she can evade responsibility for determining that structure. Her respect for the students' integrity is demonstrated in her ability to listen to, and at times accept, their suggestions as they react to the structure and attempt to modify it.

Other Approaches to Humanistic Education

The theme-centered method applies to the handling of specific class discussion and does not have very much to say about how one might go about planning an overall course or class structure. The latter problem is more directly tackled by Carl Rogers in his book *Freedom To Learn* (1969), for Rogers is an educator as well as a therapist, and he has attempted to extend his general ideas regarding man's capacity for growth to the entire process of education.

ROGERS'S "FREEDOM TO LEARN" MODEL

In *Freedom To Learn*, Rogers explores various approaches to organizing classroom and course materials. True to his firm belief in the autonomy of both the teacher and the learner, he does not endorse any one approach as superior to another. Obviously no method can work in the hands of a teacher who is uncomfortable with it, and fundamental to any humanistic approach is the conviction that it makes no sense to discuss a specific method without including some consideration of the attitudes held by the person using it. As Rogers sees it, a humanistic school or college administrator gives the teacher considerable latitude in selecting methods and curricula, just as the teacher similarly tries to maximize the student's freedom to select and pursue learning goals most meaningful to himself or herself. Important elements in an educational transaction between two parties, whether they be administrator and teacher, or teacher and student, are not at all dissimilar from those that ideally exist between a therapist and a patient: they are genuineness, acceptance, empathy, and trust.

Rogers reviews a variety of methods that can help to facilitate the kinds of learning he has in mind, and some of them are reviewed below. While our discussion is primarily oriented toward the college classroom, there is no reason why the approaches discussed cannot be adapted to other grade levels.

The utilization of class time. There is no inherent reason why a class and its instructor need always convene at their appointed time. One way of determining how class time is to be used involves a sign-up sheet. Students wishing to make some sort of presentation, either singly or in groups, can take responsibility for a particular session or for part of a session. The teacher can do the same, either with regard to discussion-oriented sessions or more formal lecture presentations. When she signs up to give a lecture, this may be based upon her own selection of a topic, or upon her response to students' requests; either way, her selection of lecture material will spring from the spontaneous interests of the participants since she herself is one of the participants.

Some teachers, especially those whose conscientiousness does not easily permit them to use class time to pursue their own personal concerns, like to make themselves available for personal appointments with students during those class hours when the class does not convene. Students are invited to sign up for office-hour time as they wish and the content of the session is left up to them. If a student is interested in more personal and experiential learning, he may simply wish to use the time as a way of helping him and the instructor become better acquainted. If he is interested in more academic learning, he can utilize the time to seek clarification around intellectual and didactic issues.

Resources. Here a wide range of materials is made available, and again it is the student's decision as to which of them he or she will take advantage of. Book lists can be optional or mandatory, or a combination of both. Other options open to the student can involve field trips, the use of outside consultants, and the employment of various self-teaching devices, including study guides and audio cassettes. The student's contact with knowledgeable people in the field besides the instructor can help decrease dependency on the instructor as the only source of learning. How the student integrates this material is again up to him or her, although, hopefully, the teacher is available to provide clarification and feedback.

Formal presentations in class are one consistent means by which a student can share his learnings, however tentative, with his fellow students and teacher. He may prefer to emphasize academic material involving a review of basic concepts and theory, a review of various literatures, or the results of original research. Or he may wish to focus on relatively experiential learning in which he discusses some of his personal feelings in relation to his field trips, readings, and so forth. Group presentations involving several students may help the presenting student feel considerably less anxious and self-conscious, and there is no reason why the remainder of the class cannot comment and ask questions. Students who have an understanding of the theme-centered discussion method and of various encounter approaches to group interaction (see Chapter 6) may want to organize a session around these techniques, although here the cautious instructor may well want to actively intervene at times in order to make sure that no procedures are used that will expose another student to unfortunate amounts of group pressure or emotional harrassment.

Contracts. In the kind of unstructured class we have been describing, a student can be confronted by an overwhelming number of choices. If he is especially worried about grades and has received good grades in the past on the basis of his conscientious absorption and retention of material presented by the teacher, he may have much anxiety as to whether, in this novel type of format, he will continue to receive a high grade. Individual contracts specifying the amount and kind of work that he will do during the term, and the grade that he will receive if he completes his contract satisfactorily, are one means by which a student can be given a greater sense of structure and security. While the contract is tentative and open to revision, he at least has some kind of basic ground plan as to the direction in which he is heading. It may be understood that doing the assigned reading and passing the examinations based on this reading will earn him a passing grade, that doing an additional term paper will bring him a higher grade, and that a term paper plus one or more oral presentations in class will earn him a still higher grade. The writing of the contract also provides a contact between student and teacher outside the classroom.

Differential groupings. Like individual contracts, differential groupings can be used to introduce some organization into what can sometimes seem to be too loose a structure. Through different groups, or "tracks," a student can choose which of two or more routes to follow. For instance, in a psychology class he may participate in the more academic group that attends lectures, runs standard experiments, and takes short-answer exams based on them. Or he may instead participate in the more experiential group, in which written papers and class discussions are based on the student's personal reactions to the class, to the readings on the one hand, and to what he has learned about himself through other channels, like field trips and participation in outside activities. Students in the experiential groups might even go so far as to voluntarily take vocational tests and undergo personal counseling as a way of increasing their self-understanding. These groupings can be flexible and allow students in the traditional academic group to attend sessions of the experiential group, and vice versa.

Grades. Although uncomfortable with some of the implications of grades, Rogers, and the other teachers whom he uses as examples, are not prepared to totally eliminate them because: (1) the institutions that they service usually insist on them; and (2) because grades are often in the interest of the student who will need them for admission to still higher levels of education.

In the Rogerian model, the emphasis is on giving students some role in the determination of their grade. The writing of individual contracts, in which student and teacher come to a prior understanding as to what grade will be received for what level of performance, is one approach. Another method personally used by Rogers requires students to grade themselves on the basis of a written and detailed appraisal of their own work. In those instances where Rogers's estimate of a student's work differed markedly from that of the student, conferences were held to resolve this issue. Since the teacher as well as the student has freedom, there is no reason why the teacher *must* include the student in the grading process. And the teacher is always free to grant the student the option of deciding whether he or she would prefer to receive an instructor-determined grade; some students find the responsibility of this decision uncomfortably burdensome and would therefore prefer to give it to someone else.

Despite the arguments that can be cited for the necessity or usefulness of grades, there are some educators who believe that the very fact of evaluation and the categorizations that this implies (smart vs. dumb, hard-working vs. lazy) is inimical to the concept of a humanistic and nonauthoritarian climate. Naturally, one of the teacher's essential freedoms is to refuse to grade the student. Another is to give the individual student the choice of whether or not he wishes to be graded.

THE INQUIRY METHOD OF POSTMAN
AND WEINGARTNER

In *Teaching as a Subversive Activity,* Neil Postman and Charles Weingartner (1969) offer a strong critique of most present-day modes of education. While the authors' orientation can apply to all levels of schooling, their specific emphasis on the primary and secondary grades gives us a chance to look at education below the college level. According to these authors, traditional education assumes a linear model of knowledge in which there is absolute truth and a fixed reality. In such a model, knowledge is often factual and it can be stored, sometimes in books and sometimes in the mind of teachers; at a later point, usually via oral communication, teachers disseminate bits and pieces of it to their pupils. The subject matter to be taught is clearly definable, and it can be divided into well-demarcated categories. Citing anthropological evidence that our language tends to limit our view of reality (see Whorf, 1956) and that the medium through which a message is communicated fundamentally alters the *content* of that communication (see McLuhan, 1964), Postman and Weingartner challenge the linear view of education, claiming that it is wholly inappropriate to a world in which an ever-increasing rate of change demands that children, if they are to develop into adaptive and creative adults, must learn to ask critical questions about any so-called "fact" that is presented to them.

Consequently, Postman and Weingartner repeatedly emphasize helping children ask the right questions and *learn how* to learn. A crucial lesson involves their gradual appreciation of the fact that language invariably abstracts reality and is therefore to some degree always arbitrary and distorting. In this fashion children gain an ever-growing realization that the meaning of anything "out there" is not independent of whatever meaning they choose to give it. While at no point explicitly introducing existential-humanistic philosophy, Postman and Weingartner are clearly positing a complex and always contingent picture of the universe that is wholly consonant with the existential viewpoint presented in Chapter 2. Three lessons of traditional, linear education that they would like to see the children forget or never learn are: (1) that there is only one correct answer to any particular question, (2) that once we have labeled something we have understood it, and (3) that everything in the world (and every person) has an ever-fixed, unchanging identity.

While presenting a philosophic orientation clearly consonant with the humanistic viewpoints in education that we have already looked at, these two authors are more explicitly pedagogical in their focus, for they encourage teachers to use and master "the inquiry method" of education. This procedure has the teacher continually ask questions of the pupil. These inquiries force children to think more deeply about something and show them how to ask questions. Once this inquiring function has been internalized by children, they will no longer need to take anything as "given"—they now have a built-in "crap detector" (pp. 2–3) that enables them to ask probing questions about whatever is presented as "reality."

Let us take a segment from a classroom discussion that the authors present to illustrate their conception and use of the inquiry method:[1]

TEACHER: Well, then, what does "civil rights" mean?

ROD: You're joking.

TEACHER: Me?

ROD: Well, I mean, doesn't it depend on who is defining it? I don't think Stokeley Carmichael and Thurmond would see it in the same way.

TEACHER: Do you mean Strom Thurmond?

ROD: Yes.

LOUIS: That may be true and all that, but what difference does it make? Thurmond or anyone else can't change the facts.

TEACHER: What facts?

LOUIS: Like if a guy wants to buy a house or eat in a store and they won't let him. That's a fact. You can't change it.

LARRY: You can't change what?

LOUIS: The facts, f'crying out loud.

LARRY: Well, what's a fact?

LOUIS: If you don't know what a fact is, well, it's pretty bad.

TEACHER: Wait a second, Lou. What *is* a fact, according to you?

LOUIS: According to me? Well, it isn't according to me. I don't understand this "according to me" stuff about facts. A fact is what happened. Like it's a fact I'm talking to you now. That's what's happening.

TEACHER: Are you angry now?

LOUIS: Of course I'm not angry.

TEACHER: Suppose a historian were writing a history of the events of this class. Would he report that you were angry or maybe a little hostile?

LOUIS: Of course not. He'd be lying.

PHIL: No, he wouldn't. I don't know if you're angry, Louis. But if I were doing it, I'd say you were—upset. Maybe that's not the word.

TEACHER: What word would you use, Chuck?

CHUCK: Dumb.

(Laughter.)

LOUIS: You're a riot.

TEACHER: Madeline?

MADELINE: Seriously. Phil used the right word. Upset. Louis is definitely upset, especially with Chuck.

BOB: Maybe he is now, but he wasn't before. He was just asking some questions.

ROD: He didn't ask any questions. He told everyone what he thought.

LOUIS: I did ask questions.

TEACHER: Well, now here are some interesting problems. Lou says that a fact is what happened. How do you know what happened. Louis says you just look. Is that right, Lou?

LOUIS: Now I'm not sure. If we had a tape recorder, we'd find out if I asked any questions or not.

TEACHER: Would we find out if you were upset, say, two minutes ago?

LOUIS: Well, if you asked me, I could tell you.

TEACHER: But how do we account for the fact that others did think you were upset?

BOB: How do we know it's a fact that others thought that?

CHUCK: Oh, my god!

ROD: Look. There's a point everyone's missing. The thing about "angry" and "upset" is important. What a person *says* happened may not be what happened, but that's all your historian—any history writer —could do anyway. *Say* what happened. I might say Lou was "upset." You—he was happy. Chuck, "dumb."

TEACHER: Are you implying that a fact is not what happened, but a statement about what happened?

ROD: I think so. I mean, who knows what happened? No one can see everything. Or hear. You just say what you think you saw.

TEACHER: Well, in that case, if we couldn't even get agreement on whether or not Lou was angry, wouldn't it be even more difficult to determine when someone's "civil rights" are being violated?

ADAM: It's hard but not impossible.

TEACHER: What do you mean?

ADAM: Well, after all, people do communicate, don't they? And history is communication.

TEACHER: History is communication?

ADAM: Yeah. I like that.

(Laughter.)

TEACHER: Congratulations. But what do you mean by it?

ADAM: Well you know, if history is saying words about things, then it's communication. And if it's communication, there must be some rules to figure out how good someone is communicating. Like take the thing with Lou. Suppose someone wrote that Lou cursed. You would check it out by asking everyone, or by a tape recorder.

TEACHER: Do you remember Lou cursing?

ADAM: No.

TEACHER: I remember he said, "f'crying out loud."

LOUIS: That's not a curse—f'crying out loud.

(Laughter.)

ADAM: I know what you're getting at. Okay. Maybe "curse" is too vague. But suppose a guy wrote that Lou punched someone. You could check that. And everyone would agree. Most everyone, anyway. Because you *(to the teacher)* don't agree with anything.

(Laughter.)

TEACHER: Well, suppose you obtained agreement from everyone but me, how would you handle me?

MADELINE: If everyone agreed except you?

TEACHER: Yes.

MADELINE: I'd want to know why you didn't agree. Maybe you just want to give everyone a hard time.

TEACHER: You mean, you'd question my motives?

MADELINE: Why not? Some people want something to come out the way they want it to come out.

TEACHER: And how would we determine whose statements about something are the most reliable?

CHUCK: You could go to court. *(Laughter.)* No, seriously. Like in court, there are rules about when a guy can be trusted. Like a witness, I mean. Sometimes a judge says, "Rule that statement out."

TEACHER: Are the rules in court the same as the rules for judging historical statements?

CHUCK: That's an interesting question. Are they? (pp. 110–13).

As the authors see it, the "subject matter" of this kind of lesson is no more than "the responses of the learners to the questions they confront" (p. 75). The lesson was no more a lesson in English than it was a lesson in history, or psychology, or communications, or current events. The questions that the pupils, with the teacher's help, raised included the following: (1) Does the definition of "civil rights" change in accordance with the political complexion of the definer? (2) Is it a "fact" that Louis was upset, despite his claim that he was not? (3) If one way of determining a fact is to verify the reliability of the person reporting it, what are the best guidelines for determining his "reliability"? (4) If it is difficult to define a fact, how do we define history? And (5) is there any difference between the guidelines we use to determine a historian's reliability in reporting past events, or "facts," and the guidelines used by a judge to determine the admissibility of a witness's testimony in court? If you find yourself wondering when this class will have a chance to find out the answers to these questions, you are missing the authors' essential point, which is that there are no sure answers, only provisional ones, and these in turn stimulate further questions. Implicit throughout the discussion is the point that it is not always easy to distinguish what is "real" from what is perceived, or what is perceived from the person of the perceiver.

In taking the point of view that there is no such thing as a totally unbiased truth, the Postman and Weingartner inquiry-method teacher is not very different from the theme-centered teacher, whose implicit attitude seemed to be that the student's ideas (e.g., on what the teacher's role in the class discussion should be) were no less valid than her own. What renders the inquiry teacher's approach to leading group discussion somewhat different from Cohn's (and from Rogers's too) is that the inquiry teacher attempts to be more active and cognitive; she forces students to ask themselves key questions about the words that they use. Had an inquiry approach been used in the illustrative theme-centered session above, the students would have been encouraged by the instructor to ask harder questions about the terms they used, like "value judgment," "blame," and "silent." For instance, what do we mean by a silent participant, since the seemingly silent participant does make some sounds, and in some cases he might well communicate more of his feelings than the student who speaks?

Thus we see that both Cohn and Rogers attend somewhat more than do Postman and Weingartner to the personal and interpersonal aspects of the learning experience. They try to help the participant verbalize his feelings, including his degree of trust vis-à-vis his fellow participants and his teacher. Like Cohn and Rogers, Postman and Weingartner doubtless realize that the pupil's motivation is an important element in learning, but their model does not encourage the teacher to make this a specific topic for classroom discussion. When the inquiry method does focus the class's attention on feelings (like those of Louis in the illustration above), this is usually done to make a didactic point (in the instance of Louis, the issue of whether feelings can be regarded as facts).

The choice of which model to employ depends on the goals of the teacher selecting it. The inquiry model seems more appropriate in a context that requires a detailed understanding of the specific content covered. Although the student is encouraged to look at the material in new ways, the interpersonal dimensions of the classroom situation are not focused on for their own sake. On the other hand, the theme-centered method allows the student to explore some of the more deeply personal meanings of the material covered, as well as of the classroom interaction. Such a focus would seem more appropriate for high school and college levels. This does not mean that the theme-centered method is just another form of group therapy; indeed, the model is quite explicit in instructing the leader to run the group in such a way as to avoid a therapeutic focus (see Shaffer and Galinsky, 1974). However, it does strive for an integrative experience in which thought is no longer divorced from feeling, and the uniqueness of each student is expressed to a greater degree than is typical in traditional education.

THE OPEN CLASSROOM

The illustration of the inquiry method presented in the previous section involved students who were just below high school age. A humanistic approach to learning designed for very young school-age children is the "open classroom," or "open corridor," method, which was first practiced in the English infant and primary schools (Weber, 1971), and subsequently received more and more attention from American educators. While regarded as a primarily English innovation, the open classroom has become an increasingly familiar phenomenon in American elementary schools. Frequently these schools are public schools in which the practice has not been adopted wholesale, but has instead been limited to those teachers who are especially sympathetic to, and familiar with, the method. Because the open classroom format permits a child to learn at his own pace (while either by himself or in the company of a relatively small number of peers, as opposed to the entire class), this approach is best practiced where children of more than one intellectual and grade level are grouped together, thereby permitting a comfortable heterogeneity in which the faster reader can help the slower reader, and the relatively mature five-year-old can seek out the immature seven-year-old.

Perhaps the easiest way to convey some sense of what an open classroom is like is to give some concrete examples drawn from actual observations (Plowden Report, 1973). An atmosphere of informality characterizes the entire classroom day. As children arrive before the day's official beginning they are not confined to a playground or central area but instead enter the school building and do as they wish. They might weave, paint, write, or read; they might talk and roam with other children; or they might tend to some of the animals kept in the various classrooms. As the bell sounds, no clear-cut shift in atmosphere takes place, since many of the children continue to be involved in the same activity. Recess time is similarly unstructured; for instance, in a class having nine- through eleven-year-old children, some pupils might listen to one of the faculty play a violin solo during recess, others might use this time to attend a meeting of the Nature Club, and so on.

While in the classroom, children are free to pursue a variety of activities that strike their fancy, either singly or in groups. The children might spontaneously seek some of these activities or they might be encouraged and directed toward some activity by the teacher. Since there may be anywhere from twenty to forty pupils for each teacher, only a small number of children will have direct contact with the teacher at any one point in time, except for those infrequent lessons—e.g., music and physical education—in which the entire class may participate:

> In the large [elementary classroom], too, many different things were going on. Some children were reading quietly to themselves; some were using a recipe to make some buns, and were doubling the quantities since they wanted to make twice the number; a few older children were using commercial structural apparatus to consolidate their knowledge of number relationships; some of the youngest children needed their teacher's help in adding words and phrases to the pictures they painted (Plowden Report, p. 10).

Advocates of this approach argue that although the teacher plays an extremely important role in the education of the child, the child is usually able to learn without the teacher's constant supervision. As an example, let us take a single sequence of activity involving Carlo, as reported by his teacher:

> Carlo (seven) tells me he saw a harp last night ... not quite like the harp I had in my cupboard but the same sort of thing. I ask if he could paint it and show me what he means. He paints this and we discuss the way the strings work. Would he like to try to make one? I find a couple of boxes and some rubber bands of different lengths and thicknesses and he goes away with them. He comes back about ten minutes later—some of the bands make a better noise than others. He then goes away with them again, and comes back a little later with a piece of canvas material tucked in and out of the rubber bands. He says he has turned his harp into a trampoline! He and Michael take it down to the bottom of the steps outside the class and find different things to drop on it. Carlo comes back to tell me (it's his own idea) which things bounce highest and farthest. At my suggestion, they take a ruler and try to measure the differences (Grugeon and Grugeon, 1973, p. 28).

Since we are not familiar with the exact details of Carlo's learning history, we cannot be precisely sure of what new knowledge he has gained in this brief time span. However, through his behavior this particular morning he has possibly added to, or helped consolidate, the following areas of skill and knowledge: (1) perception of subtle differences (between the harp that he saw the night before and the teacher's harp); (2) psychomotor coordination and physical dexterity (making the harp out of boxes and rubber bands and later converting it to a trampoline); (3) an appreciation of how two closely related physical structures, the harp and the trampoline, lend themselves to different functions or purposes; (4) the discovery of some of the correlates of a string's length or thickness (e.g., the sound that it makes when plucked and the degree of its resilience when pushed); (5) how to measure certain physical dimensions and why it is important to make these measurements; and (6) more generally, the value of making observations, and how such observations can, through induction, permit us to infer some basic principles—like the relationship between a string's physical characteristics and the sound it produces. In all likelihood, Carlo is only just beginning to be dimly aware of some of these relationships (e.g., between a string's physical characteristics and the sound it makes); however, the groundwork for the eventual discovery and appreciation of such connections is already being laid.

What is the teacher's role in this educative process? Proponents of the open classroom are quick to point out that it is not nearly so laissez-faire as it may initially appear. Although it is true that the open classroom teacher is generally reluctant to insist that a child embark upon a particular activity, she is willing to make active suggestions and occasionally ask him to finish a particular project by the end of the morning or afternoon session. Her primary task, as she sees it, is to facilitate the child's coming into contact with the right material at the appropriate time. In order to do this, she must make fairly precise observations and written records concerning where each child is with regard to a whole host of areas and functions—e.g., counting, language concepts, visual-motor coordination, and so on. She should be ready to recommend particular activities at times when the child is likely to benefit from them. And she must be prepared to give encouragement, support, and cognitive input at those crucial moments when catalytic and truly pedagogic intervention will help him master more than if he were left to his own devices.

Preparation of a traditional sort, in which lesson plans are made for group-oriented lectures, games, and exercises, becomes less necessary. But preparation involving the laying out of materials and equipment becomes more so, for in individually centered learning, the physical arrangement of the room plays a crucial role in facilitating the child's coming into contact with particular learning tasks and learning contexts. For instance, if we take the example of Carlo mentioned above, the availability of a harp, paints, boxes, canvas, ruler, and rubber bands of different lengths and thicknesses were all needed for Carlo to have the particular experience he had.

Those advocating the open classroom do not tend to describe their orientation as humanistic, and they rarely refer to psychological theory or to existential philosophy. Yet there can be little doubt that their orientation embodies what we earlier in the chapter indicated to be generally humanistic principles of education, for they assume that learning is best facilitated when it is not forced, when it grows out of the child's spontaneous curiosity, when it is geared to his individual history and his natural pace, and when it develops in a relaxed, informal atmosphere.

THE SUMMERHILL MODEL

Any presentation of humanistic education would be incomplete without some mention of A. S. Neill, a British educator whose pedagogical beliefs were implemented and embodied within a school, Summerhill, that he both founded and governed. Summerhill was to become famous throughout the world, and several schools based on it have been established in various countries.

Neill, who died in 1973 at the age of 89, went further than any other well-known figure in advocating almost complete freedom for the child. Indeed, until he had a chance to develop his own school on a private and autonomous basis, without the fear of interference from the surrounding community, he had difficulty because his educational philosophy seemed so radical to others. (And now, over five decades later, there are many who still consider Neill's philosophy too radically permissive.) In 1921 he started Summerhill in Suffolk, England; here he at last had the opportunity to create a school that would conform to his own notions of what education should be. It was his book, also called *Summerhill* (1960), that probably did the most to make his ideas familiar, particularly to American readers. Since the time of the book's publication, the name Summerhill has become synonymous with the concept of a free learning environment in which pupils have an equal voice with staff in determining the school's rules and policies, and where they are not forced to attend any class or do any work they do not wish to.

The principles listed below are central to Neill's philosophy, and none of them seems contradictory to the general humanistic emphases that we have already enumerated in the previous chapters: (1) Children are inherently good; even their aggression is not basic to them but is the result of the way in which a neurotic society tends to thwart their natural needs. Probably the single psychological theorist who comes closest to this unequivocally benevolent view of human nature is Carl Rogers. (2) Education's proper goal is to enable children to work with zest and to involve themselves in life as totally as possible. (3) Children can be trusted to know what is in their interest and what is not. The idea that children *must* learn (and will not want to learn unless they are forced to) is a feature of our moralistic, mistrustful, and compulsive society. (4) Education must relate itself to the emotional as well as the intellectual side of children; it should take into consideration their spontaneous interests and should not expect them to be any better than they are ready to be. (5) The beneficial effects of discipline are to be doubted. However, once a child has expressed an interest in a subject, his teacher should act as a guide and a facilitator who can then help him become his own teacher. (6) Punishment is not at all helpful and is in fact harmful. (7) The relationship between a child and an adult should be one of equality. In his book, Neill frequently cites instances where a child might obey his request—e.g., to keep quiet—not because he feared Neill as an authority, but simply because he liked and respected him enough not to want to disturb him. And (8) physical safety constitutes the one area in which an adult's greater authority should be deferred to, for here the adult is able to perceive dangerous situations that the child cannot; therefore, in these instances setting some limits is in the interest of the child.

While teachers and classes are available at Summerhill, they are not compulsory, and the child who wishes to ignore them for months, or even for years, is free to do so. Neill would rather see a happy ditch-digger than an unhappy professor, and he could not see where any one skill—including reading, grammar, and arithmetic—was absolutely indispensable to a satisfactory adaptation to life. To illustrate his point, he cited various Summerhill graduates. One example was Jack, who never learned to read at Summerhill, yet became an expert and happy toolmaker, and who never learned the formal rules of grammar, yet spoke grammatically. Another instance was Tom, who never attended a single class and never exhibited an interest in being taught reading, yet had taught himself to read by the age of nine.

Neill's ideas are obviously controversial, and one anthology, *Summerhill: For and Against* (Hart, 1960), presents the entire spectrum of opinion concerning them. Our aim here has not been to evaluate or endorse Summerhill, but instead, as with the other models reviewed above, to give some feeling for how various teachers and educational administrators have attempted to concretely apply humanistic principles. Summerhill has given us a chance to view a model in which an entire school, as opposed to particular classrooms, has been developed along humanistic lines.

Recapitulation

In this chapter we have reviewed the criticisms that humanistic educators have made of traditional classroom settings, and have conceptualized the humanistic principles of education in terms of three central emphases: (1) The motivation behind learning should ideally be pleasure and excitement now, rather than some future-oriented concern with what such learning might bring in the way of efficiency, compensation, or status. (2) The personal context in which learning occurs (including the learner's feelings and motivations) must be attended to and not merely the intellectual content of what is being taught. And (3) the teacher's role is most meaningful when it is catalytic and facilitative and not authoritarian.

We then surveyed a variety of settings, ranging from elementary to college classrooms, in which theorists and practitioners have put these principles to work. Cohn's theme-centered method of group discussion involved a technique wherein the teacher imposed some degree of structure in terms of reading assignments and the utilization of class time. However, students were allowed to break into the discussion whenever they wished, to deviate from the topic at hand, and to express any strong feelings that might have been disturbing them. In contrast, Rogers's freedom-to-learn model was a somewhat freer one in which the teacher refused to take responsibility for structuring class time. Instead, decisions regarding what the class was to accomplish and how they would use class time were made by a consensus of the students and the teacher.

The next two models to be considered focused on lower grade levels. Postman and Weingartner's inquiry model, like the theme-centered approach, involved a group-discussion method. However, here the thrust was more cognitive and less emotional, and pupils were encouraged to look critically at every concept and definition they were examining. What was emphasized was the inherent ambiguity of knowledge, with the result that every apparent answer only led to new questions. Very evident was the existential principle that "truth" is as much a matter of perception as of a universally agreed upon reality. The open classroom model was applicable to still younger children (roughly ages five through seven); here the class was not treated as a single unit, but each pupil was encouraged to follow his or her own interest, whether singly or in relatively small groups involving two, three, or four children. Attractive play and learning materials were distributed throughout the room, and children were free to approach whatever they liked.

In the final model surveyed, Summerhill, an entire school had been established along humanistic lines. Here the theme of freedom (though still relative, rather than absolute) seemed to reach its widest expression. Rules and policies of the school are determined at town meetings in which students have an equal voice with the staff, and any child who wishes to absent himself from classes is permitted to do so.

In the following chapter, a survey of the human potential movement, we continue to explore the theme of humanistic education. Only now the overall context ceases to be that of the school, the emotional aspects of learning are much more emphasized than the cognitive ones, and the boundary between education and therapy becomes increasingly blurred.

An Overview of the
Human Potential Movement

chapter six

The human potential movement began and flowered during the 1960s. This movement, and the vast amounts of publicity attending it, helped to consolidate into a distinctive school of humanistic psychology the various strands of existential-phenomenological thought that had already existed in American psychology for roughly twenty-five years. It seems entirely possible that without the movement we would not be witnessing the interest in a transformed consciousness that we perceive today.

Esalen Institute, which was established in Big Sur, California, for the explicit purpose of exploring the human potential, played a formative role in the development and influence of the movement. Of course, something resembling the human potential movement would probably have evolved sooner or later, and an innovative center for human growth might well have emerged somewhere else in the United States. Yet the fact that it was Esalen—developing where it did and when it did— helped give the human potential movement its distinctive cast and flavor. We say *where* because California, as one of the final stopping points of the American frontier, has long been associated in general with anything that is new, open, and bold, and in particular with mystic and Eastern religions (the first prominent guru to live many years in the West, Paramhansa Yogananda, had settled in Los Angeles in 1924, and he was soon to be followed by other Asian "great masters"). We say *when* because America was to experience in the mid-sixties the emergence of a distinctive counterculture which was committed to the exploration of new ways of being and relating. (Some of the relationships between Esalen and the counterculture were explored in Chapter 1.)

The Encounter Group

Although Esalen's program has always featured workshops in a wide variety of human potential techniques and themes—including Gestalt therapy, meditation, yoga, and dance—the single workshop format wtth which it became centrally identified was the encounter group, and it was this group, along with the considerable amount of publicity attending it, that helped make both Esalen and the human potential movement famous. Indeed, for some people the human potential movement *was* encounter, though they were in error, as we shall see below.

The encounter group did not begin at Esalen. What could perhaps be considered its earliest version developed in the early 1900s when a Boston internist, Joseph Pratt, organized into groups tubercular patients who were too poor for in-patient treatment. While the groups were partly instructional in purpose, Pratt appreciated the psychological support that each of his group participants, all of whom shared a common problem, was able to give the others. Pratt's groups turned out to be the forerunners of later psychotherapy groups, where patients continued to meet at regular intervals to discuss shared problems, only this time the problems were emotional and interpersonal, and the patients tended to remain for a longer period of time. The more a group therapist defined himself as either psychoanalytic or existential in his orientation (and these constituted the frameworks within which the majority of group therapists functioned), the more he moved away from Pratt's didacticism and consequently the less willing he became to impose any structure or agenda on the group. What he saw to be more in the interest of the patient's emotional reeducation was a stance wherein the therapist silently waited for the patients themselves to decide how they would proceed and what problems they would discuss.

A therapy group usually continues over a long period of time, with the result that a patient might belong to such a group for several years. A group that is a more direct precursor of the encounter group in that it runs for only a short period of time is the T-group (or "training group"), which was developed in the late 1940s by a team of psychologists headed by the late Kurt Lewin, a social psychologist who had pioneered in the study and theory of group dynamics. The T-group was not a therapy group but was designed instead to help managers and executives within relatively large organizations become sensitive to the interpersonal and group-dynamic aspects of their work settings. Yet there were points in common between the T-group and the therapy group, for the T-group member, rather than being introduced to group-dynamic principles in any kind of didactic manner, experienced them first-hand in a directly personal, sometimes painful, way. To provide an appropriate atmosphere for this kind of learning, the T-group leader (or "trainer," as he came to be called) strove to create within the group a sense of openness, trust, and emotional intensity. Hence an administrator with strong authoritarian tendencies might find out, through feedback from the other group members, just how controlling he could be. The group-dynamics principle that he would hopefully learn in the process is that undemocratic styles of leadership are resented by subordinates (and are thereby inefficient in the long run).

T-groups usually met for one- to two-week periods in a country setting away from the participant's home and work. Change within the group participant himself was but a means toward an end, the end being some sort of beneficial change within his work situation. In other words, the T-group was in its overall philosophy more focused on organizational, and even social, change than on personal growth for its own sake (this is a subtle distinction, to be sure, but nonetheless an important one for understanding the differences between the T-group and the encounter group). For this reason the trainer was at pains to avoid a focus within the group that might be construed as therapeutic. One way in which he was to implement this goal was to have the participants concentrate their attention on the here-and-now events developing within the group. Thus any personal problem that emerged would be focused on in terms of how it manifested itself in the group, rather than in the person's outside living.

A more immediate forerunner of the Esalen encounter group, and one that was closer to it than the T-group in both its name and spirit, was the *basic encounter group* of Carl Rogers (1970). Rogers's initial experience with groups goes back to 1946 in Chicago, when he organized groups to train graduate students in counseling. Later, at the Western Behavioral Science Institute and at the Center for the Whole Person (both located in California), Rogers worked with groups of adults who were not involved in a formal learning program and who, like people attending Esalen workshops, wanted a short-term group experience that would provide an opportunity for personal growth. Rogers's way of conducting such a group, which he came to call the basic encounter workshop, was an outgrowth of his client-centered approach to individual therapy (see Chapter 4); he emphasized a strongly empathic dimension wherein he, as group facilitator, remained as much as possible within the participant's frame of reference. Like the encounter group that was soon to develop at Esalen, Rogers's basic encounter groups at times proved highly therapeutic for the participants, who were in no way discouraged from discussing personal problems or from introducing material relevant to their outside lives. Where Rogers's leadership style did differ from that of Bill Schutz and other Esalen leaders was his reluctance to introduce human potential techniques, like Gestalt therapy or psychodrama, that are sometimes useful in helping a participant work through his or her problem. Rogers preferred instead to let the group interaction proceed in a more spontaneous, natural manner without interference from him.

What, then, is an encounter group? A useful definition was offered by Calvin Tomkins, a journalist writing about Esalen: "A way of achieving personal growth through the exploration of feelings among people gathered together for that purpose" (Tomkins, 1976, p. 30). As the term "encounter" gradually appeared, first through Rogers and then through Schutz, it became clear that the encounter group, unlike the T-group, *could* be openly therapeutic, even though it would run for only a relatively short time and might not be led by a professional therapist. Just how a particular leader was to encourage personal exploration of an intense nature was pretty much up to him. We have already taken a brief look at Rogers's style and noted his preference for a straightforward interaction among participants; Schutz, on the other hand, was to introduce a variety of exercises and techniques specifically designed to heighten whatever participants were feeling. In order to give a better sense of what happens in a group led by Schutz or by someone trained by him, we present below an illustration of what an actual open encounter might be like. Our example is drawn from an earlier book (Shaffer and Galinsky, 1974, pp. 214–19).

ILLUSTRATION OF A TYPICAL SESSION

A total of fifty-two people are in residence at Esalen for a five-day encounter. On Sunday night they assemble for their initial microlab session, which involves the entire membership. Its purpose is to introduce them to the kind of communication games and exercises that they will participate in throughout the week, to prepare them for some intense emotional experiences, and to help them feel more comfortable in physical encounter with one another. The leaders begin by directing the audience in exercises that involve concentrated breathing, careful and quiet attention to their inner bodily and emotional experience, "blind milling" (which requires people to move around the room with their eyes closed and to engage in whatever nonverbal contact they wish with whomever they happen to touch), and "face touching" (here each person selects a partner and attempts, via direct visual and tactile contact with another's face, to form a distinct impression of him) (Schutz, 1971, pp. 160–81). Now the audience is asked to divide itself into ten or so smaller "microgroups" having approximately five people each. The leader guides the smaller groups through a series of exercises designed to help their members get to know each other more deeply. For example, the groups are instructed in a fantasy game in which each person imagines what part of his body he would instinctively try to cover were he to have no clothes on. Later he places this body part in an imagined "empty chair" and, in the manner of Gestalt therapy, engages in a dialogue with it while the rest of the group observes. (For example, a woman might ask her breasts why they are so small. As her breasts, she might reply: "Because you don't deserve any better!" and so on.) Microlabs can also be used to demonstrate encounter techniques and to provide a brief encounter experience in large groups that are meeting for a short period of time like a single afternoon.

Following the microlab, our fifty-two participants are split into five encounter groups, each having ten or so members. One of these groups is to be.led by the leader of the microlab session, and the remaining ones by four other leaders, some of whom are graduates of the Esalen training program for encounter leaders and have been supervised by Schutz himself. The small group now constitutes the primary medium of the participant's encounter experiences, and it will meet throughout the remainder of the week, usually with the leader but sometimes without him. General sessions involving all fifty-two participants, scheduled for the middle of the next four afternoons, will demonstrate particular techniques or methods—e.g., body movement, graphics, Yoga. In one of the afternoon sessions the theme of encountering the world of nature will be introduced via Esalen's famous "Blind Walk" exercise, which requires a blindfolded person to be walked around the grounds by his partner, who will present many natural objects to him through nonverbal means, including touch, taste, and smell. The two will then reverse roles. In this exercise the issue of trust is admixed with a sensory dimension.

Let us follow one of the smaller groups as it meets in its first session with its designated leader, Ted. It is now about ten-thirty in the evening, and the group is composed of eleven people—six men and five women—ranging in age from nineteen to fifty-five. They are seated in an informal circle on the floor of a relatively bare, but carpeted, lodge. The leader begins by reminding the participants that each of them bears the primary responsibility for what happens to him in the session; if he wishes to either go with or resist group pressure, to let himself get injured physically, or to become extremely upset, the decision is basically his. This is stated, in part, to bring home to participants the fact that they have both more responsibility for, and more personal control over, their own behavior than they usually exercise.

The leader now suggests a warm-up exercise in which people give their first impressions of one another. He stops, giving no further directions, while the group is silent for a few moments. Then Alex, a man in his mid-forties who has had some previous encounter experience, leaps up and positions himself in the center of the group. Other participants begin to make spontaneous comments, not necessarily going in order. "He tries to look kind, but I have a sense that he could stab you in the back," says one man. "He's sexy," says a woman. From another woman: "I sense a scared little boy underneath." When almost everyone has been heard from, Alex returns to the circle and is replaced by Meredith, a pretty girl in her early twenties, who stoically seats herself before the group as though grimly steeling herself for the worst. Again the participants offer comments in no particular order. Several participants, most of them male, make some appreciative comments about her attractiveness. Participants replace Meredith in the center of the room in random order; Doris, who follows Meredith, laughingly says that it makes no sense to drag out the anxiety, so she "may as well get it over with." The exercise is over once each participant has taken his turn in the center of the circle. (The encounter leader can start off the session with any one of a number of warm-up exercises, and some leaders prefer to begin in a totally unstructured way, much as in the T-group format. Once the group atmosphere is sufficiently loose, encounter exercises are introduced in a more discriminating and specifically therapeutic way in that the leader will usually introduce them only when he thinks that they will facilitate his work with a particular participant.)

At this point Ted, the leader, asks the participants for their reactions. Alex leads off by saying that he was hurt that more than one person has reacted to him as a frightened little boy. He knows that this is an aspect of himself, but it is one that he has been trying to change both through psychotherapy and previous encounter groups, and he expresses disappointment that this part of him still shows through so strongly. Mike, a husky, vital-looking man in his early thirties, begins to show impatience with Alex and says that the latter, by his whining and self-pitying behavior, is still acting the role of the little boy and subtly asking for the group's sympathy and reassurance. "If you were really a man," says Mike, "you wouldn't need us to tell you you are!"

Alex's initial reaction to Mike's irritation is one of hurt and defensiveness, but as Mike continues to needle him, he becomes increasingly attacking. Finally he lights into what he calls Mike's "cocksureness," and says that Mike has the same self-doubt as does he, Alex, but chooses to cover it with a facade of super-virility. Ted interrupts at this point, and suggests the High Noon exercise (Schutz, 1971, pp. 171–72), which requires the two men to go to two opposite corners of the room and then face each other. Their instructions are to refrain from speaking and to walk toward each other slowly. Once they have approached each other, they are to spontaneously let their bodies lead and to go wherever their impulse leads them. As the two men begin to follow his directions, he reminds them to not plan their actions beforehand, and encourages the group to remain silent as the exercise proceeds.

Once the two men are opposite each other at the room's center, they pause. Alex stands rigidly still, as if determined that it be Mike who makes the first move. The latter seems awkward and uncertain; he reaches out as though to playfully hit Alex on the shoulder, but then impulsively embraces him. Alex seems surprised, then responds by putting his arm around Mike. The latter hugs harder and harder, and then, with his head on Alex's shoulder, begins to weep.,

Ted moves swiftly over to the two men, as Mike begins to sob more loudly, asks him what he is experiencing. Mike, still crying, says that he is thinking of the gulf that has always existed between him and his father. He feels suddenly in touch with the positive aspects of the relationship that existed between them when he was very young, and he is remembering the longing for affection and comradeship that he felt in relation to his father long ago. Ted, attempting to improvise a spontaneous psychodrama, asks Mike to talk to Alex as though the latter were his father, and to try to express some of these feelings. Mike does so and finds himself trying to explain to his father why it seemed that they could never get together. Suddenly he lashes out: "It was Mom who didn't want us to be friends—somehow she kept spoiling it." Ted inter.enes, and asks "How?" Mike responds: "By speaking about him derogatorily to me, and by tearing him down in front of me—and, you—you shmuck" (*here he turns back to Alex*) "you let her!"

Ted asks Mike to select from the group the woman who most reminds him of his mother. He picks Mary, a youthful-looking woman in her mid-fifties. Ted tells Mike to begin to express his feelings toward his mother. He instructs Mary to listen and to begin to respond as she senses Mike's mother might have. Mike begins to upbraid his mother for her behavior toward him and his father; taking his cue, Mary responds in a slightly scared and defensive way. Mike corrects her, and says "No, my mother would counterattack much more forcefully," and for a moment he takes the mother role, in order to show Mary how he perceived his mother to behave. Mary resumes her role-playing in a more forceful way as Mike struggles to get his anger out; perceiving him as too timid, several members of the group spontaneously, without any direction from Ted, assume alter-ego roles and try to shout down his mother. Mike begins to shout too, but in a few minutes turns to Ted in frustration, saying: "I still can't get it out—I'd like to kill her, the bitch!"

Ted suggests that he go to the couch that is against the wall, that he stand next to it with his feet about a foot apart, and that he begin to beat it as hard as possible, all the while shouting at his mother whatever angry words come to mind. Ted cautions Mike that the activity might seem quite artificial at the beginning, but that he proceed in an attempt to see what feelings emerge. Mike begins; as he proceeds to throw his body more and more into the beating, he starts to pound more savagely, his cries become louder, and his curses against his mother more vehement. After several minutes of this, his pounding gets weaker; he turns to Ted, saying that he feels exhausted and "finished," and Ted suggests that he stop.

The group is silent for a few minutes while Mike continues to lie by the couch, breathing heavily. Doris comments that Mary seems to be in great pain. With some encouragement from Doris, Mary begins to talk about some of the feelings that she experienced during her role-playing with Mike, and about how she was reminded of the guilt that she feels in relation to her daughter, Nancy, who died several months ago at the age of thirty. Mary feels that most of the criticisms that her daughter had begun to direct at her during these past few years had been valid ones; she expresses regret that she had not been a better mother, and that Nancy probably had died without realizing how much Mary had loved her.

Ted now encourages Mary to proceed in a Gestalt therapy exercise in which she places Nancy in the empty chair and speaks to her. She begins by describing for Nancy the loneliness she has felt since her death; as Nancy, she directs angry complaints against her mother. Once again in the role of herself, Mary expresses and is surprised by the anger that Nancy's accusations arouse in her; she defends herself and states her love for Nancy. Returning to the role of Nancy, she expresses great wonderment at the extent of her mother's love, which she (i.e., Nancy) had never permitted herself to fully feel before. At this point, as she plays Nancy in the empty chair, Mary is overwhelmed by her feelings and begins to sob uncontrollably. With some encouragement from Ted, a few of the other participants draw slowly to her side, comforting her and tentatively embracing her. Once Mary has regained some composure, Ted insists that she continue the Gestalt therapy dialogue and say Good-bye to Nancy.

At the end of this exercise Mary is softly weeping. Ted quietly gestures toward the other participants who slowly gather around her. Performing the Roll and Rock exercise (Schutz, 1961, p. 178), the group lifts Mary to her feet and forms a circle around her. Ted instructs her to close her eyes and to let herself go completely limp; as she does so, the other participants gather closely around her and pass her around the circle. After a while, they move her to a horizontal position and lift her above their heads; holding her in this position, they rock her back and forth for several minutes while softly singing a lullaby. Then they continue their rocking motion while they slowly lower Mary to the floor.

By now it is two o'clock in the morning. Nothing is said while Mary continues to lie on the floor with her eyes still shut. Her face appears to be in a peaceful repose, while some participants continue to gently touch her or stay close by her side. Other members are off to the side, either singly or in groups of two or three. Most appear to be exhausted; all are silent. Ted says that he is ready to quit for the night, unless anyone has some reaction or feeling that is immediately pressing. Since no one responds, Ted reminds members that they are to reassemble in the same place at ten o'clock that morning, and he bids them good-night.

The format of the small-group sessions does not change during the remaining four-and-a-half days. Now no warm-up exercises are necessary, and the leader waits for members to spontaneously bring up problems and concerns. Many of them do so in response to the previous work of other participants, much as Mary, in her role as Mike's mother, had been moved to speak of her own personal anguish. While the participants are given free rein to talk about the past, they are encouraged, through the use of Gestalt therapy, psychodrama, and other communication games, to connect these concerns to the immediate present, their fellow participants, and their shared group experience. By Friday morning, every participant has revealed something of his own life circumstances through having had a chance—like Mike and Mary—to take "center stage."

CENTRAL EMPHASES

When William Schutz arrived at Esalen, some of Esalen's workshops were centered around a particular technique like Yoga or meditation. Others were thematic in nature and concerned marriage, divorce, loneliness, or intimacy. Still others had no specific focus other than the kind of interpersonal and group exploration engaged in by participants in

Kurt Lewin's T-groups. However, under the aegis of Esalen and its staff, the term T-group was gradually replaced by the word "encounter," and it was the development of Esalen's encounter program, along with the designing of a specific training sequence for people wanting to become encounter leaders, that became Schutz's main responsibility.

Schutz was a social psychologist whose academic background had included a strong grounding in psychoanalysis and also some training for T-group leadership. At a later point he became very interested in the teachings of Alexander Lowen, the founder of Bioenergetic Analysis (see below), a school of psychotherapy emphasizing the essential unity of mind and body. Bioenergetics had been strongly influenced by the theories of Wilhelm Reich, one of the pioneers in the psychoanalytic movement, and it stressed the necessity of reawakening whole areas of a patient's body, often through extremely vigorous exercises involving thrusting and pounding movements of the entire skeletal musculature. Although sympathetic to the psychoanalytic theory of personality development, Schutz began to believe that any purely verbal technique of leading groups that bypassed direct work with the body was bound to be superficial.

Given his background, Schutz was in an ideal position to integrate theoretical strands from Freud, Reich, and Lewin into the unique amalgam that he eventually called the open encounter group. He had a theoretical and intuitive command of group dynamics, but instead of helping the group explicitly observe and understand these dynamics (as is the task of the T-group leader), Schutz preferred to exploit them to build a cohesive, trusting atmosphere in which each participant could start to liberate himself from the enervating effects of his chronic alienation.

The centrality of the body. Following in the tradition of Reich and Lowen, Schutz made the body the single overriding concept in his theory of encounter. While the Gestalt therapy model (see Chapter 4), in its careful attention to body language, had already taken some steps in this direction, Schutz's model was to go even further, for once he was aware of a particular emotional constellation within the participant, Schutz consistently urged him to translate his feelings into a physical activity that would express it in a more primitive and tangible form. For example, if a participant expresses a sense of immobilization and constriction, the leader suggests the Breaking Out exercise, which requires group members to form a tight circle around the particular participant and to forcibly prevent his breaking through it. If the participant expresses mistrust, he is encouraged to engage in the Falling Back exercise, which has him fall back into another member's arms and trust that this person will catch him. In the illustration above, both the High Noon and Roll and Rock exercises comprise attempts to put into physical action emotions that are at that moment the primary focus of the group interaction.

Implicit in Schutz's thesis is the following: Our very earliest experiences originated within our bodies before we had any symbols other than body language with which to code them. The earliest emotions, including feeling good (which probably relates closely to feeling loved and cared for), feeling bad (i.e., deprived), and feeling angry, were body emotions. Therefore, there is no more fundamental way for experiencing ourselves and our being than through bodily sensations. As a result, no amount of verbal communication with the man who wants to break through his self-containment (e.g., as to why he feels so constrained, or what he might do to feel less constrained) will offer a learning experience equivalent to his expressing his problem motorically. Through the Breaking Out exercises there is a much better opportunity for him to experience the full extent of his rage and to become aware of how he sabotages himself through a lack of sustained effort and through premature "giving up." Furthermore, any actual success that he has in escaping out of the group circle will help him to feel more strongly the exhilarating possibility of "breaking out" in the larger emotional sense, again because the body furnishes the most powerful linguistic coding of one's sense of self-expansion and transcendence. In a similar fashion, the risk taken in falling back into the arms of another person, without any chance to check visually just what lies below, provides a direct experience of trust that no amount of conceptual symbolization can parallel.

The facilitative role of fantasy and inner imagery. As we just indicated above, one way to give an emotional conflict more concrete form is to translate it directly into physical activity. Another way is to have it occur at a slightly less immediate, but still relatively concrete, level. According to Schutz, a *fantasy* of physical action still has a greater chance of rendering an issue emotionally alive than does an abstract discussion of the problem to which it relates.

Let us cite a specific example described by Schutz (1971, pp. 322–23). One of the difficulties that Jane was having with her boyfriend was that she, although quite bright, had had considerably less education than he. Schutz, as the group leader, decided to try the Guided Daydream technique in which a leader encourages a participant to engage in spontaneous fantasy as a way of dealing with a particular problem. Sometimes the leader suggests a specific image or symbol that the participant then uses to begin his fantasy, and at subsequent points, where the person fantasizing seems stuck or immobilized, the leader will supply some help.

In her fantasy, Jane visualized herself attempting to crawl through a long tunnel. She became frightened as the tunnel opening became progressively smaller. Schutz viewed this as an analog to the impasse she felt she had reached in her love affair. Therefore, while giving her sufficient encouragement to enable her to continue in the fantasy, he refrained from making any specific suggestions as to how to deal with the tunnel, his reasoning being that the more she used her own resources within the fantasy, the more the experience would carry over into her outside living. Despite some panic, she broke through the tunnel's narrowest opening. Yet when asked to go through the opening again, she balked. Schutz hypothesized at this point that Jane's breakthrough, while real, had not yet been sufficiently consolidated for her to feel confidence in it. As her guide, he urged her to go back through the opening, "using any instrument or people that would make the task easier." She fantasized a magic pick and used it to enlarge the opening. Eventually it was big enough for her to walk through it, back and forth, again and again. She felt joy within the fantasy, and her body actually appeared quite relaxed. At this point the exercise was ended.

Had Schutz wished to introduce a cognitive dimension into the resolution of Jane's difficulty, he could have ventured an interpretation (as would occur in psychoanalytic therapy groups)—e.g., "The obstacle in the tunnel represents the way you feel blocked in your life by your lack of education." Since he wasn't completely certain of the validity of this interpretation and also sensed it to be superfluous, he didn't offer it. His implicit assumption is that in Jane's unconscious her mastery of the fantasy block generalizes to, and eases, areas of her living in which she experiences herself as blocked. The relationship of the fantasy to her psychological dynamics and to her life problems need not be made conscious or explicit. A similar assumption underlies the rationale of Gestalt therapy. For example, if we take Mary's fantasy dialogue with her daughter, Nancy, in the illustrative session presented at beginning of this chapter, it is not necessary for Mary to translate this experience into conscious insight for her to experience some resolution of her conflict. One reason her conflict is eased is that she has been able to express outwardly some of the anger that she had been feeling toward her dead daughter, and to thereby relieve some of her depression. Yet it is not at all clear that Mary has become conscious of this particular dynamic.

The guided daydream, which offers a representative example of how many human potential leaders use fantasy and inner imagery in their work with individual participants, is an alternative to the overt physical activity involved in an encounter game like Breaking Out; here Jane's success in breaking through the tunnel opening is the fantasy equivalent of a participant's actually succeeding in breaking through the group circle. Although the activity is in this instance a fantasy, it is experienced by the fantasizer so vividly as to seem real; for Jane, it was as though she had broken through an actual, physical impediment. According to Schutz and other encounter leaders, this immediacy makes for greater therapeutic effectiveness than would any verbal (and, inevitably, more rational and logical) discussion of the dynamics behind her troubled love affair.

The dissolution of blocks. The examples above can be seen as attempts to resolve one kind of block or another: mistrust, which blocks one's way to closer relationships; devaluation of the body, which blocks one's way to a fuller enjoyment of it; feelings of constriction, which block one's way toward a greater sense of expansiveness; and so on. Schutz seems close to both Maslow and Rogers in assuming that the fundamental human drive is toward growth, with the result that once blocks are removed the organism will resume its temporarily interrupted movement toward greater self-realization. Growth does not necessarily continue uninterruptedly, and the encounter participant is always free to seek out future encounter groups. Indeed, the encounter model tends to see the encounter experience as a psychotherapy for normals that is essentially available on a life-long, periodic basis.

Almost all the body work that Schutz does can be conceptualized within the framework of block-dissolving. Body tensions may be thought of as blocks against feeling; therefore reducing tension in specific body parts can effect emotional release. And certain feelings, like hostility, can serve as blocks against other feelings, like affection. Probably the most basic way to help a person contact body feelings—and feelings in general—is through a relaxation and deepening of his breathing. Hence Schutz's very first exercise in the encounter microlab illustrated above involved breathing. Another technique involves "unlocking," in which people with shallow breathing and cramped, closed-in postures (which usually, according to Schutz, symbolize resistance to interpersonal contact) are encouraged to uncross their arms and legs and breathe deeply. Other related techniques involve screaming, pounding, and pillow-beating.

RATIONALE AND PURPOSE

What are the central purposes of the encounter group? Before attempting to answer this question, we must point out that this kind of conceptual question, in which one wonders how the effects of the participant's encounter experience are transferred to his daily life, is one about which encounter leaders and theorists are deeply ambivalent. The reason for their ambivalence is that this sort of inquiry subordinates raw experience to theory and thought. Such a question also implies that few experiences, even sensory and esthetic ones, are worthwhile for their own sake but are instead important only if they lead to some sort of improvement or change. In other words, in our typically Western linear concern with function and application, we become interested in a phenomenon only if it leads to something else. Once we apply this means-vs.-ends dichotomy to encounter, we start to ask if the encounter experience leads to lasting change for the participant.

It is precisely this kind of "Why?" and "What for?" thinking that the encounter group attempts to bypass. In this respect, its underlying rationale is similar to that of Perls's Gestalt therapy: an experience is an experience, and its possible connections to both the past and the future are of less consequence than is usually realized. Such an attitude toward experience (in which experience is important for its own sake) is in many ways closer to Eastern religions and philosophies than to Western ones. Similarly Eastern in nature is a considerable degree of skepticism concerning the value of concepts involving a "self" or an "ego." Once the "I" or "self" behind the perceiver lose their fundamental importance, then the entire issue of what an experience is *doing* —to and for the "experiencer"—is reduced in significance, and the encounter becomes but one more experience in a stream of life experiences. This attempt to "break down" the participant's ego (and ego concerns leading to a preoccupation with status, achievement, and reputation) is central to other techniques within the human potential movement, as well as to encounter.

In Schutz's view, the overall encounter experience aims for non-programmed personal growth. The individual is free to expand his awareness along any one of an infinite number of dimensions, and the responsibility for choosing these dimensions is his own. Since Schutz believes that contemporary Western man has overdeveloped his intellectual faculties at the expense of his bodily and sensory experience, the major stress is on the latter. Once concentration and contact with one's feelings are sufficiently strengthened, the possibility of achieving experiences that are variously described as "peak," "mystical," and "transcendental" is increased.

We first discussed the concept of the peak experience in our presentation of Maslow in Chapter 3. Peak experiences can occur in a variety of ways, and it is important to remember that they can be seen as important for their own sake, whether or not they lead to more peak experiences in the future. Situations where an encounter participant experiences himself or herself as truly cared for and nurtured by fellow participants can be especially intense. An instance of this is the use of the Roll and Rock exercise in the illustrative session, where the group gave to, and tended, Mary. Such experiences are also likely to occur in moments when the participant allows himself to live fully in the present and feel at one, be it with Nature or with others in the group. According to Schutz, once defenses are penetrated, the similarities among group members become more marked than their differences. The individual and the group reciprocally interact: genuine cartharses on the part of particular members increase the group's cohesion, and increased feelings of group closeness in turn help each participant reach a higher emotional peak and feel more emboldened to reveal himself. The resultant sense of communality helps participants realize that they are more alike than unalike and can give a quasi-mystical feeling of unity to the group experience. It is as though the group has somehow become a single organism instead of a collection of discrete individuals. The more the concept of a forever-separated and individuated ego is questioned, the more seriously one can consider the possibility of units and unities that transcend the individual ego, and this is just what some encounter proponents tend to do.

As we said earlier, the question of encounter's purpose or function is one about which encounter leaders themselves have had mixed feelings. Thus far we have focused on the side of the ambivalence that either denies a central purpose or sees it in extremely general and experiential terms. On the other side of the ambivalence is the natural inclination to acknowldge that encounter sessions, which frequently help a participant feel better, are a form of psychotherapy. While a careful empirical investigation of the degree to which he *continues* to feel better has not been of primary interest to most encounter leaders, they are convinced that in many instances such changes are long-lived. These leaders state that it is up to the participant to use the experience as he wishes; if he is able to employ it in ways that lead to greater personal satisfaction, so much the better for him.

Like Schutz, most open encounter leaders are interested in expanding both personal and cultural freedom. Hence they are wary lest their function be too closely identified with psychotherapy, for to name something is to begin to define it, and to define it is to begin to limit it. On the other hand, in their eagerness to have both the leader and the participant "do their thing," advocates of the open encounter have no anxiety about the fact that much of what happens in the encounter group can be construed as therapeutic. Hence the participant is free to bring up the past and discuss whatever personal problems he wishes. Similarly, the open encounter leader is not at all concerned with the question of whether or not he is professionally "qualified" to do therapy. Since his interest is in liberating the individual from the shackles of an oppressive culture, he is impatient with the concept of "appropriate" role behavior (e.g., who is permitted to function as a therapist? and who is not?) and with the idea that a person's paper credentials (i.e., his license to do psychotherapy) are as important as who he really is (his "being" in the larger, existential sense).

THE ENCOUNTER GROUP IN PERSPECTIVE

The encounter group has always been but one kind of experience offered at Esalen Institute, and many other human potential techniques exist besides encounter (see "Other Paths Toward Growth" below). Yet the encounter group has, in the minds of many professional people and the lay public, come to stand for and epitomize the entire human potential movement. Why the initial popularity, however impermanent, of the encounter group? And why have people tended to equate it with the wider human potential movement, of which it is but a part?

There are several reasons for the prominence of encounter. Probably the most salient one is that encounter, emphasizing as it did open communication and growing intimacy among strangers, was the single human potential method that was most comprehensible to the average person. In actuality an encounter leader (particularly one trained in open encounter by Schutz) might employ, at well-selected moments, specific techniques like Gestalt therapy or Bioenergetics, but as the encounter group was publicized by the mass media, these more esoteric methods were hardly mentioned. Emphasized instead was the fact that the participant was to be honest with the group when it came to presenting his personal problems and expressing his "gut level" reactions to other group members. If there was some discussion of the nonverbal and sensual emphases within encounter, they tended to be the more easily sensationalized ones. Hence publicity was given to Esalen's sulphur baths, sensuous massage, and the nude encounter groups (Bindrum, 1968), which carried to an ultimate extreme the encounter theme of exposing oneself to the group.

In the minds of many people, then, encounter came to stand for an appreciable measure of spontaneous, unstructured interaction among its participants. In this respect, the specific body techniques emphasized by Schutz and by Esalen could be regarded as optional, readily dispensable additions. A free-wheeling group of this kind bore a strong resemblance to Rogers's basic encounter, where the leader was reluctant to intrude upon the group process by suggesting structured exercises or games. Consequently, encounter leaders, unlike specialists in Gestalt therapy, psychodrama, or Bioenergetics, did not have to receive extensive training in any one human potential technique (and even when a leader might want to use such a technique he was free to do so in a somewhat diffuse, eclectic, and unsystematic fashion). This made encounter readily transportable beyond the confines of Esalen or the Center for the Whole Person (which was where Rogers conducted most of his basic encounter groups) to communities throughout the country and to specific institutions within these communities such as schools and churches. There it was a relatively simple matter for teachers, counselors, social workers, and clergymen to adapt the encounter format to workshops and other short-term groups that they might wish to lead. Moreover, since there was little reason why encounter leadership (which required little in the way of intensive professional preparation or specific credentials) could not fall to nonprofessionals, encounter groups sometimes formed in which there was no clearly designated leader, or in which the leadership position was systematically rotated from one person to another at each successive meeting.

Such was the grass-roots and populist flavor of the encounter group which, as it was described by Schutz, grew to have a distinct appeal for many. What Schutz said was that people, by "opening up," by discarding their usual masks and facades, and by stating their truest feelings and yearnings, could feel more joyous and more in touch with life. In this way encounter began to constitute a social movement of sorts; it offered new values for guiding day-to-day existence outside the group as well as within it (be open; trust; try to take risks), and it endeavored in a concrete manner to deal with the alienation that many claimed was endemic to mass culture and technological America. The encounter experience gives the person a chance to immerse himself in an intensive group experience in which he comes as himself, not as a representative of a particular social or vocational role; participants are not categorized as either "sick" or "well," and instead acknowledge their common, albeit sometimes problematic, humanity. Hence the encounter group can result in a sense of mutual concern and of a close-knit community that is increasingly rare in today's fragmented towns and cities, where most people find themselves participating in a wide variety of isolated reference groups—familial, occupational, religious, and civic.

In emphasizing liberation from the pressure to conform, the encounter group was initially identifying in part with the counterculture, yet in a socially acceptable way, for it was, and is, readily available to middle-class people, parents, and older adults. It offers them the possibility of greater freedom without insisting upon their participation in sex, drug-taking or political rebellion. How this freedom is to be realized outside the group is left up to the individual, but within the context of the group it primarily involves a more open expression of one's private feelings and thoughts.

While Schutz's interest in the encounter experience persists, and Esalen continues to sponsor such groups, it would appear that encounter, which reached the height of its prominence during the early 1970s, is no longer in the vanguard of the human potential movement. To some extent it has been replaced by an interest in such techniques as meditation and Erhard's Seminar Training (est), both of which will be discussed directly below.

Other Paths Toward Growth

As we indicated above, the encounter group played an important role in the development of the human potential movement. One reason for this was that it was the single growth group with which the largest number of people, both professional and lay, had direct experience. Another reason for the centrality of the encounter group is that it allowed the leader to combine in whatever way he wished the specific techniques and philosophies comprising the movement in general, such as Gestalt therapy, Bioenergetics, and Sensory Awareness. For example, in the illustrative encounter session presented earlier, the exercise in which Mary had a fantasy dialogue with her daughter constituted an application of Perls's Gestalt therapy, while another, in which Mike relived his angry conflicts with his mother, involved an amalgam of both psychodrama and Bioenergetic Analysis.

In actuality only a small portion of Esalen's program was ever devoted to encounter groups. The majority of workshops take one particular human potential theme or technique and focus on it in depth. When an Esalen growth leader attempts to instruct students in the method or philosophy that is his specialty—e.g., Bioenergetics—he typically does so in a small-group context that at times is similar to that of the encounter group. As in encounter, the atmosphere can be relatively informal, and there is usually an emphasis, no matter what the particular technique, on experiencing and at times communicating present-centered, unencumbered awareness. The more the participants in any such workshop are willing to use the technique being focused upon as a vehicle for expressing personal themes and problems, and the more the leader is willing to at times encourage spontaneous interaction among the participants, the closer the resemblance between the workshop and the encounter group illustrated above. On the other hand, the more the workshop leader emphasizes a theoretical and conceptual understanding of the particular technique, as well as an experiential one, the more he is departing in spirit, however briefly, from the atmosphere and thrust of encounter.

An encyclopedic review of all the myriad techniques formally associated with the human potential movement is beyond the scope and purpose of this book and has already been done. For instance, Peterson's *A Catalog of the Ways People Grow* (1971) lists as many as forty-six distinct entries or topics. What we shall do instead is summarize the methods and orientations that we believe have been most central and encompassing. Inevitably, there is some overlap among them; Sensory Awareness techniques, for example, since they focus on the body, have direct links to Bioenergetics and Structural Integration. In the case of psychodrama, we took a method that has a long but somewhat neglected history and included it because of its pronounced influence on the techniques employed by Schutz in his open encounter model (in addition, psychodrama has been given a prominent place not only in the Esalen catalog but in the catalogs of other growth centers). It is important to note in this regard that any growth-directed effort, to the extent to which it takes seriously the individual, along with his consciousness and his freedom, is in the broad sense humanistic. Hence we shall not try to make fine philosophical or technical distinctions between what is "humanistic" and what is not. Instead, we shall simply review those methods that are frequently employed by human potential leaders.

In a similar vein, there is no inherent reason why individual growth need take place in workshops or groups or through any formal technique whatever; most personal growth doubtless occurs through spontaneous, ongoing living. At the end of the chapter we will mention paths toward "enlightment," or toward newer forms of consciousness, that are geared to a more individualistic context. The prominent association between the human potential movement and *groups* is in part a function of the movement's strong identification with the encounter movement, and in part a function of something far more practical: the human potential movement, despite its therapeutic overtones, is by and large an *educational* effort, and an educator usually communicates with several people (or certainly more than one person) at any particular time. In this sense the techniques surveyed here represent an extension and outgrowth of the pedagogical methods covered in Chapter 5, only now the thrust toward the emotional, the interpersonal, and the experiential is all the more intensified.

BIOENERGETIC ANALYSIS

Like the encounter model, Bioenergetic Analysis emphasizes the inseparability of mind and body. As one Bioenergetics analyst, Stanley Kelemean, puts it: "You don't *have* a body, you *are* your body" (Howard, 1970, p. 193). The brain is part of the body, even though for many people the psyche has become a disembodied controller that puts them out of touch with their deepest feelings and impulses. The attempt to contact and release bodily tensions is the exclusive focus in Bioenergetics, whereas in encounter it represents only one among several diverse growth modalities.

The founder and leading exponent of Bioenergetics is Alexander Lowen. Lowen's theories are to a great extent based upon the concepts of Wilhelm Reich, a psychoanalyst who had been his teacher and personal analyst. Reich is perhaps best known for his concept of *character armor* (Reich, 1949), which postulates that each emotional repression or blockage within us has a specific site of muscular tension associated with it. As a result, various facets of our postures and our movements embody and signal, at least to the sensitive observer, our most characteristic defenses, and psychotherapy that ignores the body is bound to be superficial. Snobbish aloofness can be mirrored in a frozen smile, anger in a hunching of the shoulders, and disgust in a wriggling up of the nose.

In diagnosing aspects of the patient's psychodynamics on the basis of his physique, the therapist uses two yardsticks—the structure of the body and the degree to its rigidity or flexibility. A person whom we term a "pushover" in a figurative sense typically turns out to be one in a literal sense too, because more often than not his body weight lies directly over his heels, rendering him highly vulnerable to a push either forwards or backwards. Consequently, even before we witness his interactions with others, we can detect his lack of self-assertiveness. In general, says Lowen, the extent to which the lower part of the body, and the legs in particular, give strong support for the rest of the body and help it feel securely grounded is one of the most important features of our physical stance.

Bioenergetic therapy that is directly physical usually involves exercises specifically geared to the release of tension; this in turn helps the body come alive again and lose its chronic feeling of deadness. The expression of rage is central, and the therapist will work on those body parts most chronically involved in defending against anger. One typical exercise has the patient lie prone on a mattress and kick down with his feet while also pounding the mattress with his fists. As Lowen sees it, kicking represents protest, and there are few people in our society who have nothing "to kick about." The patient is encouraged to shout whatever words and phrases come to mind, and with as much loudness and fury as possible. This physical position is considered particularly helpful for releasing early and primitive rage because it very much resembles what an angry baby lying in his crib might do. If the patient is to really let himself go, he will kick forcefully with his legs outstretched, and his head will bob up and down loosely with each kick. The therapist is quick to point out if he is not kicking or pounding vigorously enough, if his words and shouts don't match his angry motions, or if he is smiling as he shouts (this would again indicate a holding back, or denial, of his anger).

Since Bioenergetics very much concerns the individual and his body, it can easily be practiced in the context of a one-to-one relationship between a person and his therapist. Yet it is believed that the group setting can be especially facilitative for several reasons: (1) in making a diagnosis of a person's body or posture, the comments of peers, as well as of the therapist, can prove helpful; (2) the patient receives emotional support from several sources as he tries to mobilize his feelings; (3) one member, when he makes a cathartic and moving emotional breakthrough, then serves as a model and inspiration for others; and (4) the physical intimacy of the group can help make the experience of touch more available and more comfortable for each of the participants. Touch helps us become more aware of the tremendous role that physicality plays in our lives, since the touching of one body by another can provide a depth and directness of contact that even the most eloquent of words cannot match. Such contact is particularly important in our culture, where nonsexual touching among adults still has strongly tabooed aspects. In the Bioenergetic workshop, the participant has a unique opportunity to learn that touching can express affection and warmth as well as sexual love, and that physical contact between members of the same sex need not be construed as homosexual.

SENSORY AWARENESS

Sensory Awareness "experiments," in their focus on bodily awareness, overlap to some degree with Bioenergetics. However, in Sensory Awareness there is less emphasis on the motoric and cathartic expression of bodily energy and correspondingly more on the perceptual and sensory aspects of experience.

Charlotte Selver, a German-born woman who initially began as a teacher of rhythms and expressive movement, is the person most frequently credited with the origin of Sensory Awareness, at least as it developed in the United States. One of Selver's goals is to help the workshop participant come to a quiet, open attentiveness—a "concentration that allows things to happen" (Gustaitis, 1969, p. 255). In order to accomplish this, a person must gradually learn to relinquish processes of enculturation that he has subtly absorbed since childhood. This enculturation encourages him to impose judgment upon his experiences (e.g., auditory stimuli might be immediately categorized as to what gave rise to them—a baby's cry, a car's motor, and so on), and to superimpose an attitude of conscious effortfulness on what would otherwise be an organismically regulated pattern of attention (with the result that he often, in his preoccupation with scheduling, interrupts—and shows little respect for—his own natural rhythms of attention and effort expenditure).

There is no end to the procedures that the Sensory Awareness facilitator can use in helping a person find his way toward a more natural and unencumbered awareness of his own sensations. These exercises may involve sensitizing the person to what he takes in visually and auditorily ("Try just listening to the *sound* of each noise you hear without trying to label it or to identify its source"), to his smell, taste, and touch ("Close your eyes and let yourself be touched by the person on each side of you—can you feel the difference in how they touch you?"), and to his kinesthetic sensations and his perception of space ("How much space is there between your shoulders and the floor?"). Another question favored by Selver is: "Could you allow your head to become more a part of you, not something special or separate?" (Gustaitis, pp. 256–57). Compared to Lowen's Bioenergetics and to Rolf's Structural Integration (see below), Selver's is a calmer approach; there is no pounding of one body by another, no kicking, beating, or shouting. And no diagnosis is made of what an individual's body specifically reveals about his emotional background or difficulties.

While Selver led many workshops at Esalen, Bernie Gunther, a former weight lifter and physical culturalist, was the person on Esalen's staff who led the great majority of its early workshops on sensory awakening and relaxation. Gunther was also responsible for the incorporation of massage into Esalen's Sensory Awareness groups and for the creation of workshops that were devoted solely to the teaching of massage.

STRUCTURAL INTEGRATION

Structural Integration involves a penetrating massage of the entire musculature that is often called "Rolfing," after its founder, Ida Rolf. Rolf believes that our bodies are no longer properly aligned, having been partially deformed by faulty body training and body posture in general and by traumatic emotional experiences in particular. In this respect Rolf's concepts have much in common with those of Lowen and his mentor, Wilhelm Reich, for she is stating that emotions and the body are inextricably interrelated; each specific emotional block has its concomitant anatomical blockage, sometimes in the muscles, but equally often in the fascia, which are sheaths of connective tissue surrounding and containing the various organ and muscle systems. In describing the relationship between fascia and muscles, Schutz writes:

> Physically, the fascial envelope, a thin layer over the muscle, will lose its elasticity through lack of exercise, so that when a muscle has become stuck in a tense position, the subsequent relaxing of the muscle is difficult and painful. It is as if someone crawled into a leather sleeping bag and out of fear curled up tightly in the middle for a long time. Then the leather dried and hardened. Now, even if he lost his fear and wanted to stretch out, it would be very difficult because he would now have to soften the leather (1971, p. 10).

Unless the supporting tissue around a muscle is worked with directly, that muscle cannot be properly relaxed.

The Rolfer attempts to alter the fascia's stiffness through a direct mechanical manipulation or massage. These manipulations usually involve a series of ten one-hour sessions in which the person is at times heavily kneaded, and in which the masseur uses his elbows as well as his hands. Gone is the quiet, receptive approach of Sensory Awareness, and one returns to the more thrusting and vigorous emphasis of Bioenergetics, only here the person, rather than doing the pounding himself, is being pounded by another. Rolfing is often very painful, at times excruciatingly so, but Rolf claims that the pain, since it helps release specific emotional blockages, can be extremely therapeutic. Mind-body connections are such that as particular muscles and fascia are penetrated, specific—and frequently traumatic—emotional events are remembered and relived.

The problem that Rolfing seeks to correct is that each deviation in the body's proper alignment with gravity produces all sorts of compensatory shifts and readjustments in various supporting organ segments. What Rolfing ideally permits is a natural realignment of the body, one that Rolfers insist is necessary for an *integrated* (body *and* mind) sense of well-being.

PSYCHODRAMA

Psychodrama is one of the oldest forms of group therapy extant, since its founder, Jacob Moreno, was practicing it as early as 1921, the year he opened his Theatre of Spontaneity in Vienna. Like all forms of group therapy, psychodrama strives to help the individual confront his problems in more adaptive ways. However, unlike conventional group therapy, which usually permits a patient to talk *about* his problems, psychodrama asks him to *dramatize* them just as they happened or happen in real life. In this way, Moreno's action-oriented method had an important influence on how Schutz, in his formulation of encounter technique, helped his group participants communicate their deepest feelings and conflicts. Psychodrama also has become part of the human potential movement in that Esalen Institute, in addition to encounter groups, offers workshops and seminars devoted solely to psychodramatic techniques.

A formal psychodrama session (as opposed to how psychodrama might be informally incorporated into an encounter group) begins with the selection of a protagonist, who then describes something that has been bothering him. With the director's help, he starts to establish a setting where his problem might typically manifest itself. For instance, if the difficulty involves his sense that he fails to stand up to his wife when he feels she is unjustly reprimanding their daughter, the director will ask him to portray a recent situation where this occurred. The protagonist chooses from the group "auxiliary egos" who will play the roles of his wife and daughter, and he instructs them in detail as to how these women usually behave in the crucial situation.

The evolution of the scene itself is a spontaneous event; although the protagonist has set the scene, no detailed scenario is prepared beforehand. The drama develops instead out of the unrehearsed playing of the characters and the feelings that the scene's unfolding generates within them. Later there can be a discussion as to what the participants felt about one another during the enactment. This often helps the protagonist better understand why others react to him as they do. He is then in a good position to replay the scene in the way he *would have liked* to behave in it.

Two psychodramatic techniques that have influenced the way role-playing was subsequently adapted to the encounter group are "doubling" and "role reversal." Doubling is called into play by the director when he senses that a protagonist is finding it difficult to express his feelings or assert himself in general. The director will at this point have either an auxiliary ego or another group participant stand behind the protagonist and state what he thinks the protagonist is experiencing but cannot say. Role reversal has the protagonist and the auxiliary ego switch roles. This reversal sometimes gives the protagonist a more empathic insight into what the other person in his central life conflict is feeling; someone who has appeared to be an "enemy" might suddenly take on a humanness that he had not previously thought possible. And, since an auxiliary ego is now performing the protagonist's role, the protagonist also has a unique chance to observe how he is perceived by others.

GESTALT THERAPY

As we saw in Chapter 4, Gestalt therapy was originally conceived as a variant of standard psychotherapy and, like most forms of psychotherapy, could be practiced on either a long-term or short-term basis. Indeed, the possibility of being conducted on a longer-term, continuing basis applies also to encounter techniques (which can be used by group therapists in their weekly meetings with patient groups), to Bioenergetic Analysis, and to psychodrama. This kind of overlap is to be expected, since one way of characterizing the human potential movement in general is to view it as a psychotherapy for normals. Probably the most practical way of distinguishing between ongoing psychotherapy and human potential techniques is that the latter, unlike the former, do not emphasize the need for a detailed diagnosis of the participant's problems in living (and their developmental origin) or for a prolonged relationship in time between the participant and his human potential leader or facilitator. Gains can be made in a quite brief period of time, without the facilitator's having any detailed biographical knowledge concerning the participant and his past life.

Gestalt therapy was ideally suited to the human-potential format; because it centers on the participant's immediate flow of experience and because it believes that the therapist does not need an extended period of time in which to help dissolve some of the blocks to present-centered awareness, there is no reason why the contact between therapist and participant be prolonged. Consequently, while Perls's Gestalt therapy techniques had existed since he had first begun to develop them in the 1930s, it was their inclusion as a regular feature of the Esalen program that gave them national publicity and a prominence that they had not hitherto received.

Within a human potential context, Gestalt therapy is almost always practiced within a group—as opposed to an individual—context, even though the leader tends to work with one particular participant while the rest of the group looks on. The Gestalt leader's feeling is that the other group members function as a kind of Greek chorus that will resonate and empathize to a point where it vicariously gains, through a process of identification, from the intense experience of the participant being worked with. (For a more thorough introduction to Gestalt theory and technique, see Chapter 4.)

MEDITATION

A dominant theme running through the human potential movement involves the attempt to help an individual contact his experience and the world as directly, and with as little self-consciousness, as possible. What we are describing here is a process in which whatever distorting filters or screens exist between us and the world are eliminated or minimized; gone is our awareness of an "experiencer" behind our experiences, and gone also are the self-centered preoccupations of everyday life, our biases and expectations, and our active, planning, forever anticipative thoughts. Instead there is a calmer, more receptive orientation in which we are "at one" with our experience. In the religious traditions of Sufism and Zen Buddhism, this process is sometimes thought of as "direct perception" (Ornstein, 1972), with the mind existing as a kind of mirror that reflects back only what it receives, with nothing revised or changed. Direct perception, then—or what Ornstein also refers to as an "opening up" of consciousness—is the primary aim of meditation techniques.

The methods of meditation are somewhat diverse, and they depend on the particular religious or cultural tradition from which they are derived—yoga, Buddhism, Sufism, or Christianity. However, in their interest in enabling an individual to experience a different form of consciousness, one that is attuned to the deepest levels of his being, the different kinds of meditation have a definite common denominator. In this sense, they are many diverse means that reach toward a common end. Because meditation is a solitary experience, it lends itself to group approaches less than do most of the other human potential techniques that we have surveyed. However, Esalen Institute does sponsor workshops that focus solely on meditation. Often, along with experiential sessions devoted to the practice of meditation, such workshops offer didactic sessions in which the theory behind meditation is presented.

Most meditative techniques are of the kind termed "concentrative" (Ornstein, 1972, p. 108). Here the person is encouraged to actively withdraw from the stream of everyday life and to engage in a focused, trancelike, undistracted form of consciousness. He is instructed to attend continuously and intensively to either an external stimulus or an internal, cognitive one, and to attend to it again whenever he notices that his attention has strayed. This process isolates the practitioner from his usual activities and markedly reduces the amount of stimulation impinging on him. Sessions typically last about thirty minutes and might occur twice during the day—once in the morning and once in the evening. The basic aim of meditation is to empty the mind of its usual contents. While most concepts of meditation are drawn from what Ornstein refers to as "the traditional esoteric psychologies" (Zen Buddhism, yoga, and Sufism), and therefore make little use of concepts derived from existentialism, it seems clear that the consciousness sought resembles a rather pure state of *being* in which our usual, somewhat externalized and *essentialistic* concerns (with wealth, prestige, and reputation) are exchanged for the most palpable sense possible of what it feels like "to *be*" (see Chapter 2).

External objects can be used to provide a specific point of visual concentration; one might use a candle, a jewel, or a piece of silver. The yogic tradition uses "mandalas," which are visual, symbolic designs that are circular in form and religious in content. Another stimulus for concentration within the yogic tradition, this time more cognitive in nature, is the *koan,* which is a riddle or paradox and therefore has no intellectual solution (one of the best-known koans is "What is the sound of one hand clapping?"). In Zen Buddhism, the meditator might be instructed to focus on his own breathing, which he does by counting each breath from one to ten and then repeating the cycle. Later he is encouraged to direct his "attention to the *process* of breathing itself. He thinks about nothing but the movement of the air within himself, the air reaching his nose, going down into the lungs, remaining in the lungs, and finally going out again" (Ornstein, 1977, p. 160).

In Transcendental Meditation, which is derived from yoga and which has become the most popular form of meditation in this country, the meditator is given a specific "mantram" by his teacher. The mantram is a sound, or a combination of sounds, and is to be repeatedly chanted and concentrated upon by the person meditating. The mantram is particular to him (having been selected because its sound is in some way suited to his temperament) and is to be kept private. An advantage of the Transcendental technique is that it can be practiced almost anywhere, for it does not require a fixed body stance or posture as in some other yogic forms of meditation (where one might be told to stay in the "lotus" position, in which the legs are crossed and the back is to remain perfectly straight). Right now there are a number of Transcendental Meditation centers for the teaching and practice of meditation throughout the United States.

EST

Est is the newest of the techniques that we have reviewed and did not appear on the human potential scene until the 1970s. Devised by an ex-salesman named Werner Erhard, est's initails stand for the Latin word "est," meaning "is," as well as for "Erhard's Seminar Training." For, in the existentially tinged philosophy of Erhard, it is an illusory and damaging "belief system" (involving life as it could be, should be, must be, or was supposed to be) that prevents most of us from accepting life—and each moment within life—as it *is*.

As the person who conceived the idea of est training, Erhard was the first teacher, or "trainer," to conduct the seminars. Since that time he has selected and personally supervised roughly ten additional trainers and has been able to establish est as a large-scale educational corporation that sponsors seminars in major U.S. cities throughout the calendar year (est has also volunteered its services in running experimental programs in various correctional facilities). Consequently, est constitutes a technique that exists within its own autonomous organization and that has become less integrated within the overall human potential movement than have other such human potential methods as Gestalt therapy and encounter. For example, growth centers like Esalen do not sponsor est seminars or weekends, since all est training occurs within the est organization itself.

Formal est training takes place on two consecutive weekends, starting early on Saturday mornings and continuing very late into the night. Hence it comprises as much as fifteen hours per day and sixty hours for the total four days of training. Sessions are usually held in the ballroom of a hotel and can encompass a large number of students, sometimes as many as two hundred. The overall atmosphere is ascetic; trainees often sit on hard, uncomfortable chairs and are required to observe a number of rules involving various kinds of abstinence; for instance, they are told they will not be permitted to leave the room to eat or to go to the bathroom; much later in the day there will be a break for these purposes. Training consists primarily of running comments from the trainer and of remarks from any trainee who wants to share any thoughts or reaction he is having (once he has been recognized by the trainer and given a microphone from which to speak). Part of the trainer's commentary constitutes a verbal assault on the audience; trainees are told that they are "assholes," that their lives are "shit," and that they resort to all sorts of games or "rackets" in order to avoid confronting their forever false promises to themselves and their forever disappointed expectations.

Most est graduates claim that the training has to be experienced in order to be understood. Therefore it is not easy to clearly explain how the est format leads to a breakthrough in consciousness for the trainee. Yet the rules seem designed to show the participant that he is capable of more self-discipline that he had thought. They also, by emphasizing the processes of ingestion and elimination, remind him that he is no more than a tube-like machine, albeit a living one. In this fashion, est training challenges the elaborate belief system that a trainee has often created around a somewhat exalted notion of himself and of the grandiose purposes he likes to think he has been put on earth for.

> Gradually, trainees are forced to give up their "acts" and to focus on their experience of what is happening to them. Many cry, faint or get sick. Then, dialectically, they are shown how to make backaches, headaches and other discomforts induced by the long est sessions dissolve through various exercises in visualization and self-hypnosis. Once trainees realize that consciousness can alter bodily states, they are prepared to accept one of est's cardinal principles: "I am the cause of my own world."
>
> The purpose of est is to make each trainee experience the "satisfaction" of becoming the author of his own subjective universe of sensations, emotions, and ideas. This experience—called "getting it"—typically comes toward the close of the last day of the training. Est trainees are shown how to create an inner "space" into which each of them can retreat and immerse himself in his own consciousness. . . . The culmination of training comes when everyone realizes that he is free to transform experience through the prism of his own consciousness (Woodward, 1976, p. 59).

Toward a Transformation of Consciousness

Central to the diverse techniques encompassed by the human potential movement is the search for a newer, less alienated, and more alive consciousness. Just what this consciousness is like is very difficult to spell out, since we are limited in this book to verbal descriptions; and words, say the advocates of human potential techniques, constitute artificial—and necessarily limiting—constructions of experience evolved by one particular culture and one particular language. Hence it is easier to say what this new consciousness isn't than to say what it is.

An experiment conducted by Jerome Bruner in 1949 (Bruner and Postman, 1949) and cited by Robert Ornstein (1977), a humanistically oriented psychologist, helps us consider what enlightened consciousness is *not*. Bruner's research subjects were told that they would be looking at playing cards via a tachistoscope, an instrument that projects visual stimuli onto a screen for a precisely measured, usually brief, span of time. It turned out that not all the cards shown to the subject were conventional ones. Some showed the suits in reversed colors—for instance, a three of clubs might appear red and a nine of diamonds black. Many subjects perceived such a card not as it actually appeared but in terms of their preconceptions or "biases"—a person shown a card with red spades might perceive no incongruity. Once subjects were enabled to revise their expectations by being told that the suits would not necessarily be colored according to convention or tradition, they made fewer errors of this nature. As Ornstein (1977) puts it, "our 'assumptive world' is conservative. It is quite difficult to alter our assumptions even in the face of compelling new evidence. We pay the price of a certain conservatism and resistance to new information or knowledge in order to gain a measure of stability in personal consciousness" (p. 5).

In enlightened consciousness, presuppositions based on the categories and constructs of our culture (which in turn are derived from our language and from our daily habits of thought and fixed routine) are minimal, and the world is seen freshly, perhaps akin to the experience of the very young child before he has acquired the rudiments of language. In this book we first glimpsed the possibility of this kind of perception when we encountered, in Chapter 3, Maslow's concept of "the peak experience." As we pointed out then, Maslow claimed that the peak experience revealed aspects of reality that are usually concealed or disregarded, and the emotion accompanying such a perception—or revelation—was exultation.

For some close watchers of the human potential movement, the possibility of this kind of peak experience for ever-increasing numbers of people suggests that we might be witnessing, during this last quarter of the twentieth century, a distinctive, qualitatively different—and therefore important—leap forward in man's evolution. Michael Murphy, one of the cofounders of Esalen, argued just this thesis in an interview with Calvin Tomkins, a journalist; Tomkins wrote as follows:

> Carried far enough, the human-potential idea leads to speculation about the transformation of man and society. According to Murphy and others, we are on the verge of tremendous social changes—changes as great as those that accompanied the evolution from hunting and gathering to farming and stock raising in the Neolithic age, or from feudal to modern society during the Industrial Revolution, the difference this time being that evolution has accelerated to such a degree that we can be aware of the changes as they are taking place, and can to some extent prepare ourselves for the post-industrial world that is in the process of being born. What is needed, the transforma-

tionalists say, is new paradigms—new models for looking at the nature of man and the universe.... The myths of antiquity recur; the new journey, one hears, will be inward, into the depths of our conscious and unconscious powers. The new science will be closer to religion than to technology (1976, p. 30).[1]

Murphy's comments are again reminiscent of Maslow, for Maslow, in emphasizing the sense of awe and of epiphany that often goes along with the peak experience, suggested that religious metaphors are as appropriate as scientific ones for understanding such an experience. Hence the point made by many that we seem to be in the midst of a revolution of consciousness, this time a *spiritual* consciousness, not wholly different from the revolution in sexual consciousness prefigured by Freud, the first psychoanalyst, during the last quarter of the nineteenth century.

CENTRAL EMPHASES
OF AN ENLIGHTENED CONSCIOUSNESS

Some of the changes that humanistic psychologists have attempted to bring to contemporary consciousness (like an enlarged awareness of the body and of here-and-now experience) have been mentioned throughout our book. However, there are two additional emphases that deserve highlighting here:

1. **The dissolution of the ego.** Many human potential leaders, more interested in practical techniques than in theory, do not elaborate all of the concepts underlying their work. Yet a close examination of their writings reveals that most of them, while not explicitly committing themselves to this point, regard with considerable skepticism the notion of an experiencing "self," or "ego," that is somehow separate from one's experience. They believe that much of modern man's alienation stems from the split that he feels between himself and his experience, and that many of our ego-related concerns—such as achievement, status, and wealth—arise from a preoccupation with an essentialistic, rather than "being," definition of the self (see Chapter 2).

Alan Watts was a scholar who had studied Zen traditions deeply and who felt that one of the main virtues of the Zen approach to enlightenment was its deemphasis of the ego. According to Watts (1951), man's ability to envision his own future, which implies both anxiety and hope, creates the possibility of distancing himself from his experience. Caught in the chaos and flux of our experience, and our intense dislike of pain, we try to gain some source of leverage and anchorage. One clear-cut

---

[1] Calvin Tomkins, "New Paradigms," *The New Yorker*, January 5, 1976, p. 30. Reprinted by permission; © 1976 The New Yorker Magazine, Inc.

way we find some sense of security and continuity is to develop the notion of an essential, historical "self"—or "I"—that watches, reacts to, and is independent of, our experiences. It is as though we are tempted to gain "an edge" on our experience, to guarantee that it will not be lost to us through death, and to find a meaning that will extend beyond the transitoriness of experience. This is a futile task, writes Watts, because the "I" is an artifact, and our attempts to fix our experience are akin to a child's efforts to make a wrapped package of water—i.e., to capture something that by its very nature cannot be captured:

> If you look at it carefully, you will see that consciousness—the thing you call "I"—is really a stream of experiences, of sensations, thoughts, and feelings in constant motion. But because these experiences include memories, we have the impression that "I" is something solid and still, like a tablet upon which life is writing a record. . . . In truth, "I" is of the same nature as "me." It is part of our whole being, just as the head is part of the body. But if this is not realized, "I" and "me," the head and the body, will feel at odds with each other. "I", not understanding that it too is part of the stream of change, will try to make sense of the world and experience by attempting to *fix* it. We shall then have a war between consciousness and nature, between the desire for permanence and the fact of flux. This war must be utterly futile and frustrating—a vicious circle—because it is a conflict between two parts of the same thing. . . . Struggle as we may, "fixing" will never make sense out of change. The only way to make sense out of change is to plunge into it, move with it, and join the dance (Watts, 1951, pp. 42–43).

In Watts's scheme, death is but another part of life's flux and a sign of the body's weariness with living. Though in the humanistic tradition, he sets himself apart from that wing of humanism that is grounded in European existentialism, because for him the existentialists' emphasis on our ontological aloneness and our *inevitable* dread of death is very much a product of Western thinking. The spiritual traditions of the East represent life and death in terms of a dialectic, a mutually interacting and interpenetrating polarity; in this more cosmic view, man is but an interconnecting unit within a larger patterned whole, and it is not altogether clear that a person's consciousness cannot, should it become increasingly liberated, grasp this more universal design. Then it is possible that death can be more gracefully accepted as part of life's inexorable flow.

2. **The experience of unity.** Anyone describing the kinds of consciousness to which "enlightenment" can lead realizes that consciousness is, in the final analysis, always individual and that it to a large extent

defies verbal description. Bearing this in mind, some human potential advocates have nonetheless attempted to trace some common threads they have discerned running through the verbal descriptions of those who have experienced dramatically altered states of consciousness. One central thread involves an experience sometimes described as cosmic consciousness, an experience of "unity."

The experience of unity refers to a felt sense that one is joined to the world. It is as though a fundamental dualism that some have tried to challenge *conceptually* (the subject-object and being-world dichotomies) is obliterated at a most immediate, phenomenological level, and a person no longer feels separate from other people or from the universe at large. Such an experience is often described as "mystical," though Ornstein (1972), because of the negative connotations that sometimes accompany this word, prefers to call it "mystic" (p. 136). To give some sense of what he means by a mystic experience of unity, of "oneness," Ornstein quotes the well-known phrase from William Blake, "If the doors of perception were cleansed every thing would appear to man as it is, infinite" (Keynes, 1957, p. 154).

It was from this same quotation that Aldous Huxley drew the title for *The Doors of Perception* (1954), a book that describes the dramatically liberating effects of psychedelic drugs, which in the 1960s became prominently associated with consciousness expansion. It was also experience with a specific drug, nitrous oxide, that led to William James's conviction that a central principle of "reconciliation" characterized mystical, or transformed, states of consciousness. We initially outlined James's idea of reconciliation in Chapter 3 in order to demonstrate its similiarity to Maslow's conception of the peak experience, and we repeat it here: "It is as if the opposites of the world, whose contradictoriness and conflict make all our difficulties and troubles, were melted into unity" (James, 1902, p. 388).

While taking drugs is one possible way of experiencing cosmic consciousness, human potential leaders obviously believe that there are other routes toward it; the several techniques reviewed in this chapter reveal some of these paths. In general, the person experiencing something akin to reconciliation describes himself as feeling less isolated and alone, more aware of himself as a sentient being in a universe of sentient beings. When viewed from this more organic perspective, he is but one aspect of a larger design in which each part is linked to every other part. According to Bill Schutz (1971), a sense of unity is a not infrequent outcome of encounter, and there are times during an encounter session when the group acts, and is experienced by many of its members, as a single organism.

Why is the experience of unity so important? Because, say the transformationalists, it can help us grasp dimensions of reality that we usually fail to perceive. As we saw in Chapter 3, it was a similar belief and a similar metaphysical concern that led Maslow to conclude "that in peak experience the nature of reality *may* be seen more clearly and its essence penetrated more profoundly" (1968, p. 81). What this revised view of reality involves is not easy to describe, but it is a strongly holistic view that emphasizes the interconnectedness of all living matter and it casts doubt on the existential view of man as ultimately alone.

It is hardly surprising that we hear more and more about organic unity in a world where the need for interdependence (e.g., nation with nation), simply for physical survival, has become increasingly obvious. One writer, David Bakan (1966), claims that themes involving both individuation (or "agency") and interconnectedness (or "communion") are inherent in the very fabric of life:

> Agency manifests itself in self-protection, self-assertion, and self-expansion; communion manifests itself in the sense of being at one with other organisms. Agency manifests itself in the formation of separations; communion in the lack of separation. Agency manifests itself in isolation, alienation, and aloneness; communion in contact, openness, and union. Agency manifests in the urge to master; communion in noncontractual cooperation. Agency manifests itself in the repression of thought, feeling, and impulse; communion in the lack and removal of repression (p. 15).

Looked at in this way, agency and communion form an inevitable dialectic polarity wherein certain periods of history accentuate one pole (e.g., the rise of the Protestant ethic during the seventeenth century would seem to represent the supremacy of agency), which in turn will be succeeded by the other (e.g., our own era, in which many aspects of the counterculture—"dropping out," an interest in mystical experience, and the creation of communes and intentional communities—reflect a less competitive and less individualistic style of life). Ecological themes emphasizing the extremely delicate symbiotic balance man has struck with the earth's atmosphere bring Bakan's communion motif very much to the fore, and it is because this balance is threatened by an increasingly destructive technology that Mike Murphy and other transformationalists (see Roszak, 1976), see cosmic consciousness as having evolutionary importance. According to them, a more unified view of reality may offer one of the "new paradigms" they are seeking and may yet help to save us from either ecological or thermonuclear disaster.

"THE TRADITIONAL ESOTERIC PSYCHOLOGIES"

While Mike Murphy talks about a need for new paradigms if man is to experience a desired transformation of consciousness, his earlier remarks, from which we quoted, make clear that such paradigms are new in only a relative sense and that they originated in earlier times and within older cultural traditions. What Murphy said in his talk with Calvin Tomkins was: "*The myths of antiquity recur;* the new journey, one hears, will be inward, into the depths of our conscious and unconscious powers" (Tomkins, p. 30; italics ours).

Robert Ornstein resembles Murphy in that he too believes that our newest paradigms represent a necessary return to antiquity. Ornstein likes to contrast modern, rationally oriented, linear consciousness with the kind of consciousness embraced by the three great philosophic and cultural traditions of the East, which he calls "the traditional esoteric psychologies" (1977, p. 114). He writes:

> From modern psychology we learn that our normal, stable consciousness is a somewhat arbitrary personal construction. Although this construction has been a success, it is not the only way in which an external "reality" can be approached. . . . Scientific knowledge is perhaps the highest development of the linear mode, but the linear mode is only *one* mode possible for us. We find that another major mode of consciousness manifests itself culturally, personally, and physiologically. It is a mode of consciousness that is arational, predominantly spatial rather than temporal, and receptive as opposed to active. Such a mode is difficult to encompass within the linear, verbal terms so dominant in our culture, but it is this mode of knowledge that is predominantly cultivated within the esoteric traditions (1977, p. 116).[2]

Western approaches to consciousness tend to be rationalistic and materialistic; something has to be directly evident to our senses to be believed, and to be considered scientifically demonstrated it has to be shown to occur repeatedly under controlled conditions. On the other hand, the ways of knowing encompassed by the traditional esoteric psychologies are, at least as judged by Western standards, more immediate and intuitive. While the scientific experiment epitomizes one way of knowing, or consciousness, the myth, fable, or tale epitomizes the kind of consciousness embraced by the esoteric traditions. While a review of the main tenets of Zen Buddhism, yoga, and Sufism lie beyond the scope

[2] Robert E. Ornstein, *The Psychology of Consciousness,* 2nd ed. Copyright © 1977 by Robert E. Ornstein. Reprinted by permission of Harcourt Brace Jovanovich, Inc.

of this book, we shall take a Sufi tale and indicate how it might, for the serious student of Sufism, serve as a step toward a more enlightened consciousness.

The typical Sufi tale attempts to bypass the conventional constructs through which we look at the world (as in Bruner's experiment, cited above, in which subjects assumed that all club suits would be black, all diamond suits, red). One famous tale, "The Elephant in the Dark," goes as follows (Shah, 1974):

> A number of blind people, or sighted people in a dark house, grope and find an elephant. Each touches only a part; each gives to his friends outside a different account of what he has experienced. Some think that it was a fan (the ears of the animal); another takes the legs for pillars; a third the tail for a rope, and so on (p. 291).

According to Shah, this story at its simplest level mocks scientifically oriented academicians who often like to think that the evidence that they have uncovered concerning a particular phenomenon is the only relevant evidence. On a philosophical level the story says that man is without sight and tries to appraise something (reality) that cannot be properly appraised by his typically limited ways of knowing. On the religious level it seems to say that God is ubiquitous and to be encountered in all things; "man gives different names to what seem to him to be separate things, but which are in fact only parts of some greater whole" (Shah, p. 291).

As Ornstein sees it, the Sufi stories, while seemingly innocent, have several serious purposes:

> They can hold up a moment of action as a template, so that the reader can observe his consciousness more clearly in himself. Often one may read a story, and on later encountering a similar life situation, find oneself prepared for it. In addition, these stories can be considered "word pictures," which can create visual symbolic situations. They embody a most sophisticated use of language to pass beyond intellectual understanding to develop intuition. Indeed, the stories are illustrated to aid in their visualization (1974, p. 274).

However, without some grounding in the overall teachings of Sufism, the uninitiated reader cannot hope to grasp the true significance of such tales. Surely our description here, which has had to rely on the most impersonal of constructs—abstract, *written* language—can do no more than barely suggest some of its meaning. To imply that the story has *one principal* meaning which can in some fashion be logically discerned, or that it has a finite amount of meanings which can be listed or enumerated, is to approach it in the rational-linear mode, rather than in the intuitive-holistic mode that is its proper context. Moreover, in Sufism, as in yoga and Zen, a personal teacher (as well as intense concentration and discipline) is almost always necessary if learning at a profound level (i.e., a genuine transformation of consciousness) is to occur.

CONVERSATIONS WITH DON JUAN

In the summer of 1960, Carlos Castaneda was a graduate student in anthropology at the University of California in Los Angeles. Having an interest in medicinal plants and their role in ancient religions, he set out for Mexico in order to study such plants at closer hand. According to his subsequent account, while there he met a Yaqui Indian by the name of don Juan Matus. Don Juan was a sorcerer, and after a year's slowly developing acquaintanceship between the two men, it was decided that Castaneda would be initiated into sorcery. Castaneda's twelve-year apprenticeship under don Juan is described in a series of four books written by Castaneda (1968, 1971, 1973, and 1974) that have sold widely in this country. The first of these, *The Teachings of Don Juan: A Yaqui Way of Knowledge,* is a published version of Castaneda's doctoral dissertation.

As a potentially public figure, Castaneda has been very elusive and certain biographical details concerning his early life have proved to be inconsistent. Partly for these reasons, some have alleged that Castaneda's apprenticeship and don Juan himself are largely apocryphal. For our purposes, the issue as to whether don Juan actually exists is of little importance, for Castaneda's books, even if read as fiction, describe with considerable power and detail the search for enlightenment. The enormous popularity of Castaneda's writings is but another manifestation of the contemporary interest in altered states of consciousness.

As with the traditional esoteric psychologies, there is in don Juan's spiritual system a need for a teacher and for an extended period of learning, if one is to abandon the constructs through which he typically views the world. And there is a similar emphasis on a more mystical comprehension of the universe in which a person, once he allows himself to grasp the existence of powers outside himself, can control his consciousness (and perhaps, his physiological rhythms) to a degree that he had not thought possible. As with William James, and with many whose first contact with the human potential idea was via the counterculture, drugs often help initiate the learner into his newly experienced sense of reality. In Castaneda's case it was a variety of psychotropic plants, particularly peyote, though by the end of his apprenticeship he could relinquish his usual ways of perceiving the world without the use of medicines. In don Juan's words, Castaneda—the apprentice—had to eventually learn "to see," rather than to merely "look," if he was eventually to be able to experience the world freshly, without interpretation, and drugs would only offer a temporary facilitation of this process. A first step in seeing is the capacity "to stop the world," and one stops the world at any point when he ceases to view it in terms of what he has been told by others the world is like.

Don Juan's teachings helped Castaneda grasp "a separate reality" (Castaneda, 1971), and for a fuller description of it the reader is referred to Castaneda himself. Here we shall limit ourselves to showing how Castaneda's "other" reality reflects the central emphases of an enlightened consciousness. All the quotations that appear below are from Castaneda's third book, *Journey to Ixtlan: The Lessons of Don Juan* (1973).

One major thrust of don Juan's teaching involves what we referred to above as "the dissolution of the ego." For example, the apprentice will be helped to the extent to which he ceases to think of himself as a distinct and special being who is altogether separate from his world. In order to move in this direction, he must try to lose "self-importance" (Castaneda is told, " 'As long as you feel that you are the most important thing . . . you cannot really appreciate the world around you' "; p. 42), and to "erase personal history" (says Don Juan. " 'If we . . . erase personal history, we create a fog around us, a very exciting and mysterious state in which nobody knows where the rabbit will pop out, not even ourselves' "; p. 35).

Another theme found in Castaneda's writings involves what we have called "the experience of unity." According to don Juan, there is a mysterious order in the world which most people—especially those for whom the ego and personal agency are supreme—do not comprehend. At one point, when Castaneda has inadvertently killed a trapped rabbit that he had wanted to free, don Juan reassures him of a larger universal design wherein the rabbit's death has permitted him to live ("He said that the powers that guided men or animals had led that particular rabbit to me, in the same way they will lead me to my own death. He said that the rabbit's death had been a gift for me in exactly the same way my own death will be a gift for something or somebody else"; p. 115). In an *agentive* view of human life (see the discussion of Bakan above), the individual ego and will are all, and the dominant image is essentially one of man *over* Nature; man subdues and harnesses the forces of Nature for his own purposes. In don Juan's *communion*-oriented system of belief, on the other hand, there are autonomous forces (or spirits) outside ourselves more potent than we realize, which some very few people (usually sorcerers) can learn to utilize as "allies" (and as equals); however, this can occur only when a person has become sufficiently humble and sufficiently respectful of his own limitations. Therefore it is as a lesson in humility and in communion that don Juan repeatedly reminds Castaneda that plants are our equals (" 'So, all in all, the plants and ourselves are even,' he said. 'Neither we nor they are more or less important' "; p. 43).

A final theme articulated by don Juan and also emphasized throughout this chapter entails trust in one's body and in the wisdom of one's body. (Says don Juan to Castaneda, " 'When one does something with people . . . the concern should be only with presenting the case to their bodies. That's what I've been doing with you so far, letting your body know. Who cares whether or not *you* understand?' " p. 233).

Recapitulation

In this chapter we have briefly traced the history of the human potential movement. In doing so, we used as our beginning foci Schutz's open encounter group and Esalen Institute, which provided the original setting for Schutz's groups. We tried to make clear that the encounter group was not the only kind of group experience sponsored at Esalen, and that Esalen was not the only growth center offering human potential experiences. However, in the minds of many people both encounter groups and Esalen (partly because of the vast amounts of publicity they have received, and partly because of their influence on the way similar groups were conducted around the country) came to epitomize the human potential movement.

Since 1970 there has been a noticeable decline in the popularity of encounter groups. The once widespread attention to encounter groups seems to have been replaced by an interest in meditation. Along with these latter means of expanding one's potential, we reviewed a variety of other human potential methods: Bioenergetic Analysis, Sensory Awareness, Structural Integration, psychodrama, and Gestalt therapy.

Because some change in consciousness is a goal common to the diverse methods of the human potential movement, we gave some thought at the chapter's conclusion to just what the nature of this expanded, enlightened, or transformed consciousness might be like. In doing so, we mentioned two particular emphases: the dissolution of the ego and the experience of unity. A third emphasis, the awareness of the body, was evident throughout the chapter. To demonstrate how themes concerning a transformation of consciousness have historically emerged in other far older and far more spiritual cultural traditions than our own, we singled out the esoteric psychologies highlighted by Ornstein (Buddhism, yoga, and Sufism) and Castaneda's initiation into sorcery by the Yaqui Indian, don Juan.

Castaneda's description of his experiences, along with Ornstein's analysis of the esoteric traditions of the East, strike us as particularly important in that they remind us that the voyage into another mode of consciousness is long, arduous, and never really complete; neither is it easily integrated into the consciousness of our habitual, ordinary, workaday lives. In this sense they counterbalance the earlier review of the various human potential techniques, for these techniques (and the people writing about them) sometimes imply that the path toward a more enlightened consciousness must follow *one particular* route (be it encounter groups, Bioenergetics, Structural Integration, and so on) and that radical changes in consciousness can occur over a short period of time. When he describes his apprenticeship under don Juan, Castaneda is detailing *his* particular experience; he does not suggest that a person's introduction into another reality can take place only by don Juan's system of sorcery, nor does he offer a specific school of mysticism that a reader can then use in his or her struggles for enlightenment. Ornstein (1976) puts it as follows:

> Castaneda's experience demonstrates primarily that the Western-trained intellectual, even a "seeker," is by his culture almost completely unprepared to understand esoteric traditions.... We do not often realize that such an extended knowledge cannot be instantly transferred or even "given" in one experience, but demands a radical change in our attitude toward our lives, though not necessarily into the external fate of our lives. No hopeful journeys to Central or South America are really necessary, nor voyages to the Middle or Far East, or Africa. We do not attain an extended consciousness by an instant cultural transplant, by a sentimental journey to other cultures, by adopting the habits of an ancient tradition, or the dress of the Indian holy man (p. 81).

However much the human potential movement may emphasize short-term groups and short-term group experience, the road toward a transformed consciousness (whether it be through a teacher, a therapist, a sorcerer, or a Sufi master) is almost always a lonely and lengthy one, and there is no guarantee that the path initially embarked upon will be the right one. The loneliness of this quest is underscored by the fact that each of us, if he is to seek this kind of enlightenment, must *autonomously* choose that particular path that seems best for him.

Toward a Science of Being

chapter seven

Humanistic psychology, which tends to see itself as psychology's "other side," has a unique, and somewhat divergent, point of view concerning psychology's traditional attempt to ground itself in scientifically tested and validated principles of human behavior. It is this latter question, involving humanistic approaches to psychology as a science, that we wish to take up in the present chapter.

Up until this point we have considered humanistic psychology in terms of itself without paying much attention to how it relates to traditional areas of psychology, like perception, measurement, or physiology, or to scientific research in general. This essentially descriptive approach seemed consonant with the spirit of humanism, which questions the positivistic model of science altogether, and which rests on certain philosophical assumptions—like the importance of freedom, dignity, uniqueness, and consciousness in human life—that cannot be directly tested empirically. On the other hand, humanistic psychology, as its name implies, still views itself as being in the domain of psychology, and we therefore need to consider how it fits into the mainstream of modern psychology and where the significant directions of its future growth might lie.

Science is a way of acquiring and verifying knowledge concerning the world and the universe in which we live. Usually we think of a particular theory or belief as being scientifically grounded when we know that it is not a matter of conjecture alone but has been verified by careful observation and measurement. How do we arrive at the various theories, or hypotheses, that we wish to validate? One means is through an inductive process wherein we generalize from concrete, empirically observed events to a general and universal law that encompasses them. For instance, we might tentatively formulate the hypothesis that performance in a learning situation is related to the degree of motivation in the learner, on the basis of our own personal experience (what we have been able to learn easily and well versus what we have been able to learn only with great difficulty) and the observations of experienced teachers.

In order to test our hypothesis, we can now proceed on a *deductive* basis—i.e., we predict observations that we have not yet made but that can be expected to occur if our hypothesized relationship between motivation and performance is valid. If it is, then a group of hungry children who have been promised a candy bar as a reward for memorizing a list of nonsense syllables will perform better than a nonhungry, or food-satiated, group of children. In making this prediction, we are forced to give an *operational* definition to our theoretical concepts—i.e., to give thought to how they relate to actual empirical data and to how they might be measured. In this situation we have chosen to measure motivation in terms of the number of hours since each child last ate a full meal, and to measure performance in terms of the number of nonsense syllables he or she retains.

An important feature of the scientific method is the degree to which it allows us to control the relevant variables. If we use the experimental situation just cited as an illustration, we want to be sure that the differences in learning performance between the two groups (the *dependent variable*) are due to differences in *motivation* (the independent variable). Hence we try to make sure that the full meal last eaten by both groups of subjects is approximately the same for both groups, and that the children in the food-deprived group have had no opportunity for snacking since eating that meal. Similarly we try to insure that the two groups are reasonably equivalent with respect to all other variables (like intelligence) that could conceivably affect the subject's performance. Another significant feature of the scientific method is its *repeatability;* if the same relationship between performance and motivation should hold true of two new groups, each comprising children wholly different from the first two groups, then our initial hypothesis will have received that much more empirical confirmation.

In the more modern approach to the philosophy of science (Hall and Lindzey, 1970), we are encouraged to think in terms of a theory's being either useful or not useful rather than "true" or "false." Without a theory, we would have no framework to help us determine which phenomena are worth observing. Whatever theory we do devise can be considered useful as long as it generates significant research—i.e., enables us to make a series of specific predictions concerning as yet unobserved events that we are then able to put to empirical test. By making these kinds of systematic observations, we slowly find out more and more about the physical, social, and psychological worlds that we inhabit.

One aspect of the scientific method that is very much emphasized is its objectivity. This is especially true in the realm of behavioral science, where there have sometimes been as many versions of a particular interpersonal event as there have been different people watching it. In other words, in science an observer's possible bias or subjectivity is minimized by making sure that what he sees or measures checks out with the observations of another independent observer. It is largely because of this concern with objectivity that consciousness, which is often regarded as "private," is disregarded by the behaviorist in favor of overt, observable, and therefore "public," behavior. Thus a *feeling* of anxiety per se has little meaning for the behaviorist; he would find the person's *verbal report* of feeling anxiety, which is at least observable by others and which can even be recorded on tape, to have more significance. Even better would be a reading of the galvanic skin response, which records the electric potential of sensitive parts of the skin, and which has been discovered by psychologists to provide a reliable and direct measure of anxiety's physiological concomitants.

As we already know, one of the distinguishing characteristics of humanistic psychology is the centrality given to a person's conscious experience. Here the very phenomenon that experimental psychologists view with distrust becomes for the humanist a crucial source of data and concern. This belief in the fundamental importance of a person's experience of the world does not constitute a hypothesis that can be empirically tested or verified in the direct ways mentioned above. Instead (like the behaviorist's belief in a material and knowable world in which the psychological and behavioral characteristics of people can be reliably measured), it constitutes a basic premise on which humanistic theory rests. A similar kind of philosophical "given" in humanism is the assumption that human beings have some measure of freedom within which they can choose and act. These preconceptions have inevitable implications for the kind of research that humanistic psychologists find valuable.

The remainder of the chapter is divided into two sections. In the first, we will look at some of the implications that a humanistic definition of psychology has for the scientific paradigm just outlined. In the second part we will briefly summarize Robert Ornstein's blueprint (1977) for an empirical psychology of consciousness that is at the same time both humanistic and scientific.

A Science of Being: Caveats and Implications

When it comes to empirical investigation, humanistic psychologists question both the *content* (what are the significant problems to be studied?) and the *style* of the research (how is the psychologist to proceed as he goes about collecting and interpreting his data?). We take up the issue of style first, and then in the section called "A Psychology Relevant to Man," return to the question of content.

Humanistic psychologists remind us of the *human* context in which all empirical research, even research with animals, occurs. Any investigation involves a motivated researcher who hopefully feels some degree of passion and commitment toward his endeavor. Where the investigator's object of study is another person, whom we refer to here as a "research subject," this subject may feel cooperative or antagonistic toward the investigator and bored or excited by the investigation. His reasons for participating in the study will be personal and idiosyncratic (in that they differ from those of other subjects), and he is likely to have some fairly active hunches as to the kinds of behavior that the researcher would like him to emit.

THE RESEARCHER'S HUMANNESS

Our image of an objective, impersonal scientific inquiry is sometimes carried to a point where the man behind the research—his drives, longings, and disappointments; his personal world view and his creative leap; his proclivity toward a certain kind of experimental and statistical design—are totally ignored. Ever-mindful of certain polarities that inhere in human life, the existentially rooted humanist reminds us that, just as there is no world without a person to perceive it, there is no discovery without a discoverer. The idea that knowledge is to some extent a function of the imagination and thought categories of the man producing it is not a new one in epistemology. Indeed, it furnished the major part of Mannheim's (1952) sociology of knowledge, though Mannheim was more concerned with the influence of sociocultural factors on thought than with personal-idiosyncratic ones, and it has been echoed more recently in the writings of Polanyi, who has been explicit about the way in which all significant knowledge is essentially "personal knowledge" (Polanyi, 1958). If the researcher's personal outlook can influence *any* inquiry, even one concerning the chemical nature of inorganic matter, then cannot we expect it to play an even stronger role in the social sciences, where he is in a sense studying himself?

Giorgi (1970) gives an explicit account of how the researcher's presence influences the research situation at every step of the way:

> Let us first take a research situation. Everyone agrees that a laboratory situation is an artificial situation. But what does that mean? It means that the laboratory situation exists in a way that is not found naturally in the world. But how did the laboratory situation get that way? Precisely through the activities of the experimenter. He is the one who structured it. He constituted the experimental situation by his selection of equipment, his definition of variables, his selection of stimuli, etc. In other words, the laboratory situation is artificial because it is a *human artifact;* it, more than an everyday situation, is the result of a single human person's intervention. Surely, the experimenter draws upon general principles and accumulated knowledge, but the specific variables that are chosen are still selected by him, the number of subjects are determined by him, the procedures used to analyze the data are determined by him, and so on. In other words, rather than being independent of the researcher, the artificiality of the laboratory situation means that more so than many other situations, it represents the viewpoint of *one* other person using the media and knowledge of a community of persons.
>
> . . . Let us pursue the matter to the stages of data collection, interpretation and writeup. If experiments simply generated objective, independent facts, there would be no need for the organization of the facts, nor for a discussion of them. The simple truth would be there for all to see. However, no published reports ever present merely raw data. The data are always summarized or organized in some fashion, and there is always a discussion of them. The discussion tries to indicate the significance of the facts, and it relates them to relevant theories and points out the hypotheses and interpretations that the data support and oppose whenever this is possible. If there were "objective" facts with univocal implications, none of the above would be necessary. In other words, organization and discussion of data are not just pleasant activities a scientist indulges in, but they are necessary to complete the research. That is, human intervention is once again necessary; there is no "reality-in-itself" that man merely registers. . . .[1]

---

[1] A. Giorgi, *Psychology as a* Human Science (New York: Harper & Row Publishers, Inc., © 1970), p. 167.

The investigator's humanness dynamically interrelates with the humanness of his research subject, for some aspects of the subject's behavior in the experiment will be influenced by the researcher's mood and personality and by the procedures he has decided to use. Consequently, while the researcher's concern with objectivity may tempt him to see himself as an observer only, he is more properly termed what Harry Stack Sullivan (1954) referred to as a "participant-observer"—i.e., an observer who, in his attempt to observe another person, must inevitably *interact* with him, and in doing so unavoidably becomes a participant in the very behavior that he had hoped to passively and "objectively" observe. A tape recorder can provide one means of insuring that the investigator has not falsely remembered or recorded the subject's verbal response; yet the presence of such a machine can have a clear-cut effect on how the subject experiences—and therefore behaves in—the situation.

What is the researcher to do about his humanness? There is little that he can do to eliminate it, although the behavioral-positivistic model of a totally objective psychological science sometimes implies that the ideal research situation would be one in which his presence could be in some way obliterated. The investigator can, if he wishes, become more aware of his inevitable effect on what he observes and begin to explore its implications. On a practical level, he might become more thorough in asking his colleagues how they would design *their* investigation of the same problem, in carrying out his study in accordance with some of their suggestions, and in varying some of his instrumentation—all in an attempt to learn if any of these variations yields appreciably different results.

As for specific biases and expectations, it is best if the investigator writes them out explicitly beforehand and includes them in his formal description of the study. According to Giorgi, a knowledge of the experimenter's preconceptions on the part of the research-consumer helps the latter assess how reliable the experimenter's results are. Once the consumer has evidence that similar results were obtained by another experimenter, one who had no specific expectations, or expectations that were different from those of the first researcher, he can begin to view these findings as reasonably generalizable.

THE RESEARCH SUBJECT'S HUMANNESS

According to the humanistic psychologist, the investigator all too often sees the research subject as a person-to-be-done-to, an "object" who will help confirm his status as a scientist and scholar. Once it is forgotten that the participant is the center of his own world, with a subjectivity and intentionality all his own, he is starting to be treated like a "thing" (in Buber's framework, the researcher and the participant are moving toward an "I-It" relationship; see Chapter 2). One specific way in which the researcher sometimes exploits the subject is to coerce his involvement, as when he includes participation in his research as a requirement of a course that he teaches. Another is to subject him to experimental conditions or inputs that are damaging to his dignity or self-esteem. Yet another is to deceive him about the purpose of the study without revealing to him its true nature. Because of abuses in these areas the American Psychological Association in 1973 revised its earlier code of ethics to more stringently define the ethical standards governing research with human participants.

Deception of human subjects has been a consistent and thorny problem in psychological research. It has been especially widespread in social and personality research simply because the investigator, in order to stimulate within the laboratory the kind of anxiety-arousing social stimuli that exist in the outside world, often has to deliberately misinform the research subject about the precise nature of the experiment. Milgram's (1974) well-known study of obedience, in which the subject (designated as the "teacher" by the experimenter) thought that he was administering electric shock to another subject (designated as the "learner") offers an example of this kind of deception. Subjects did not know that the so-called learner, or "victim," was in fact collaborating with the investigator, and had been hired and trained by the latter to play this role. The naive subject was told that the shocks he was administering were a form of punishment that would help the learner correct his errors in memorizing a list of paired words. At several points the learner interrupted the proceedings by emitting loud groans, by crying that the shocks were producing intolerable pain, and by pleading that he be released from the situation. Had deception not been used and the naive subjects known that the situation was artificial, Milgram's dramatic results (in which over half the subjects, despite overt conflict and repeatedly attempting to have the experiment stopped, complied with the experimenter's demands) could not have been obtained. At the experiment's conclusion, Milgram informed all his subjects of its true nature.

Principles 4 and 8 of the ethical code drafted by the American Psychological Association (1973) indicate that deception in psychological research is generally permissible so long as it is justified by the nature of the problem and the subject is told of the deception at the experiment's end. Formal objections to Milgram's research were made before the Ethics Committee of the APA citing the use of deception and the obvious stressfulness of the situation for the subjects, but Milgram was cleared of all such charges.

Another kind of deception frequently used in psychological experimentation involves information that the research participant is given concerning his own personality, intellectual abilities, or performance within the experiment. Seeman (1969) cites a study in which psychiatric patients were asked to rate themselves on the dimension of hostility; those who had adjudged themselves to be less hostile than the typical person were chosen to serve as subjects. At a subsequent point these subjects were handed "fictitious 'profiles' of themselves indicating that they were *more* hostile than the average person" (Seeman, 1969, p. 1027; italics ours). The participants in this study were never informed of the deception, even though the ethical guidelines of the APA insist that this be done.

However, even when a research subject is extensively debriefed following an experiment and told of a deception, problems may remain; despite the investigator's nullification of the information initially given to the subject, certain doubts may persist in the latter's mind. For example, an incident reported in the APA manual of ethical guidelines (1973) involved a college student who was first told that the study in which he had just participated showed him to have homosexual tendencies, when in fact no such tendencies had been revealed. Despite this subject's subsequent debriefing, he continued to feel threatened by the possibility of latent homosexuality, to the point where he confided in a psychologist, hoping that the latter would help him secure treatment.

If we look at this situation from the perspective of the subject, his doubts need not prove all that surprising. Since he has already been deceived by the investigator, why should he unquestioningly trust what is later told him at the time of his debriefing? Indeed, the research psychologist would seem to be somewhat unsophisticated in assuming that once he tells a subject that he has lied, he is automatically believed a second time. Seeman has this point in mind when he writes: "In view of the frequency with which deception is used in research we may soon be reaching a point where we no longer have naive subjects, but only naive experimenters" (p. 1026), and he goes on to wonder about the social value of a science that encourages a cynical skepticism concerning everything said by the investigator during the experiment.

When it comes to Milgram's experiment, we have another difficulty, for even if the subject who obeyed is not troubled about having been deceived and about what this might imply (either about the investigator's trustworthiness or his own gullibility), he is still left with the problem of knowing that he has been willing to violate one of his own ethical standards in response to pressure from an authority. Despite Milgram's genuine efforts to deal as effectively and as therapeutically as possible with emotional aftereffects in his subjects, the long-term consequences of this kind of self-knowledge on the part of his subjects are difficult to determine.

Deception is not the only ethical issue that scientific research poses for psychology. Two others involve the use of unnecessary coercion in gaining the subject's participation and the confidentiality of his behavior in the experimental situation; the investigator is never free to reveal any information that could identify the subject or his specific behavior in the experimental situation to anyone else. We have chosen to focus on deception because it is the ethical issue that has received the most concerted attention by psychologists and because it has allowed us to raise the kind of question that the humanistic psychologist likes to ask. The latter's anxiety concerning the use of deception in research helps us underscore one of his most central emphases: a belief in the possibility of trusting relationships wherein each of us treats the other in a manner that takes his full humanity into account.

THE SOCIAL PSYCHOLOGY
OF THE EXPERIMENTAL SITUATION

In discussing ethical considerations above, we wondered about the effect that general attitudes of the research participant might have on the data obtained—e.g., his overall skepticism concerning the experimenter's candor. Similar questions have been raised about the effect of more specific anticipations on the part of the participant—namely, his perception of the investigator's expectations and hypotheses. It is rare for the research subject to come to the experiment with no presuppositions whatever; usually he has some hunches, however hazy, as to the kinds of results the experimenter hopes to obtain. If the subject does indeed have some sense of the hypotheses to be tested, he can move in either a positive or negative direction. If motivated to ingratiate himself with the investigator, he might well be subtly influenced to make his behavior conform to what he believes the investigator's hypotheses to be. If he feels antagonistic toward him, he may act in such a way as to disconfirm what he anticipates the hypotheses to be. It is important to note that these inferences of the subject need not be altogether within his awareness.

That this kind of influence does occur was first demonstrated in a remarkable study by Rosenthal and Fode (1961) and was twice replicated with similar results (Rosenthal and Fode, 1963; Fode, 1965). In these experiments undergraduate students were asked to serve as "experimenters" in an investigation in which subjects rated a series of neutral photographs in terms of whether the person photographed had been experiencing success or failure at the moment the picture was taken. Half the experimenters were told that their subjects' ratings would tend toward the success end of the success-failure continuum, while half the experimenters were told the opposite. In all three studies the results were the same: those experimenters expecting success ratings obtained them to a significantly greater degree than did those experimenters who anticipated ratings of failure. Just how these expectations are communicated no one is certain, though Rosenthal, who has written the most comprehensive treatment of "the social psychology of unintentional influence" (Rosenthal, 1966, p. 401), has little doubt that it is primarily through nonverbal channels.

Such a finding is not necessarily surprising, for several psychologists have noted the researcher's extraordinary potential for social influence in the experimental situation. For example, subjects have shown a willingness to cooperate with a seemingly absurd situation in which, after finishing each sheet of arithmetic computations involving addition, they were asked to pick up a card from a pile of cards and comply with whatever directions were on it; each and every card required the subject to destroy the sheet he or she had just completed, and it gradually became clear to the subject that none of the sheets were to be handed in to the experimenter. Nonetheless, subjects continued to conscientiously perform their task (Orne, 1962). A subject's susceptibility to influence on the basis of what he imagines the experimenter to want is but another demonstration of Sullivan's contention that the observer inevitably participates in, and thereby affects to some degree or other, what he is observing. As Rosenthal sees it, this problem need not lead to despair concerning the possibility of obtaining objective data in research on human subjects, but instead challenges the psychologist to devise evermore effective means of either controlling for, or minimizing, such expectancy effects. Among the many ways of doing this that he mentions are: giving greater care to the process of selecting and training psychological experimenters, making more precise observations of their behavior, minimizing the amount of active contact between the experimenter and the subject, and wherever possible, maintaining "blind contact"—i.e., making sure that the experimenter does not know whether the particular participant whose behavior he is observing had originally been placed in the experimental group (which was subjected to the experimental variable being investigated) or the control group (which was not). Since the investigator anticipates that the behavior of subjects initially exposed to the experimental variable will differ from the behavior of those who were not, the blind contact procedure insures that in later rating a subject's behavior his judgment will not be influenced by a foreknowledge of which group the subject was in.

If anything, then, Rosenthal wants to reduce the amount of contact between experimenter and subject. Approaching the same problem from an explicitly humanistic perspective, Sidney Jourard (now deceased) wanted to open up the contact between them and encouraged an "experimenter-subject dialogue" in which both became more fully known to each other (Jourard, 1967):

> We can begin to change the status of the subject from that of an anonymous *object* of our study to that of a *person,* a *collaborator* in our enterprise. We can let him tell the story of his experience in our studies in a variety of idioms. We can let him show what our stimuli have meant to him through his manipulations of our gadgetry, through his responses to questionnaires, with drawings, and with words. We can invite him to reveal his being. We can prepare ourselves so that he will want to produce a multifaceted record of his experiences in our laboratories. We can show him how we have recorded his responses and tell him what we think they mean. We can ask him to examine and then authenticate or revise our recorded version of the meaning of his experience for him. We can let him cross-examine us to get to know and trust us, to find out what we are up to, and to decide whether he wishes to take part (p. 113).

Jourard reported some initial data involving interview situations in which self-disclosure on the part of the interviewer resulted in much greater rapport with interviewees and a significantly greater degree of willingness to reveal themselves. Just what changes might occur when the investigator undertakes such a dialogue in more standard laboratory experiments is of course unclear, since no one has as yet systematically studied the effects of such a procedure. Jourard posed the question when he asked: "What will man prove to be like when he is studied by an investigator who consents to be studied by the subject?" (p. 115).

The differences between Rosenthal's and Jourard's approaches to the problem are instructive. Rosenthal seems to want to render the experimenter more anonymous than ever; indeed, one of his suggestions for reducing the degree of contact between the experimenter and the subject is to provide the latter with televised instructions and to have a machine record his responses. Jourard, on the other hand, recommends that the experimenter eventually level with the subject as to what he has been looking for and how he interprets the subject's responses. Jourard suggests that the subject then be equally candid. Of course, aspects of the subject's expectations (and of the experimenter's too) may well be unconscious and therefore will not be directly reflected in their dialogue; yet it might be possible to infer them. Jourard's approach may well strike the sophisticated experimenter as ingenuous, but as we indicated above, the experimenter's frequent assumption that he has a "naive subject" seems equally naive. Jourard assumes neither sophistication nor naiveté on the part of the subject; instead he wants to find out for himself, from the subject, just how trusting or suspicious he or she has been. Actually the two approaches are not mutually exclusive, since the investigator using Rosenthal's paradigm is theoretically free, once the experiment proper is completed, to interview and be interviewed by the subject, even if neither has until that moment been fully visible to the other.

For the positivistically inclined psychologist, Jourard's approach would be useful only if it led to the collection of more reliable data. The humanist, however, is not so ready to divorce his scientific concerns from his ethical ones; for him, Jourard's dialogue, because it serves as a model of openness and trust, has merit beyond whatever scientific knowledge it produces. From a humanistic point of view, our methods of observations are inextricably bound to the content of what we observe. If we behave as manipulators by regarding one another as things to be used, our data will gradually reveal this to be the "truth" about human nature, for manipulators will be what we, and our research subjects, have become.

THE DISTINCTION BETWEEN PUBLIC
AND PRIVATE EVENTS

As we noted earlier, the behaviorist attempted to bypass the problem of consciousness (which for him was "private" in the sense that one's experience is known only to oneself) by focusing on external, or "public," behavior (which can be known and agreed upon by two or more observers). In this respect a verbal report of anxiety is more public than is an inner *feeling* of anxiety. Phenomenologists, however, point out that the behaviorist engages in a conceptual sleight of hand when he claims that concentrating on a subject's verbal report eliminates the problem of the latter's inner experience. According to the phenomenologist, the behaviorist must assume, however implicitly, some degree of correspondence between the research participant's verbal report and his actual perception. Otherwise, he would be interested only in the subject's spoken words without any regard concerning their truth or falsity. Yet rarely is this the case. For instance, in what are known as psychophysics experiments, subjects are asked by the experimenter to report as precisely as possible the point where they are able to perceive a just-noticeable-difference between two discrete stimuli. Consequently, the subject's spoken words are of interest to the behavioral experimenter not merely as a verbal report but as a reasonably accurate reflection of an inner private experience. If subjects do not act in good faith and give the verbal report "I perceive a difference" when they in fact have no conscious experience of a perceived difference, the experimental results will have no meaning or validity. Koehler, an important figure in the phenomenological movement in psychology, expressed much the same thought when he wrote (1966):

> I must therefore conclude that, in all his observations, the Behaviorist relies on facts that appear in his private experience, the only experience in which he can do any observing. Moreover, when other observers are present, and describe what they have seen during his experiment, their descriptions again refer to occurrences within their private perceptual worlds (pp. 85–86).

Koestenbaum (1966) makes a similar point when he argues that any fact, whether public (e.g., "the subject's galvanic skin response is currently registering at 70") or private ("I feel anxious") essentially begins as a first-hand subjective experience. For instance, as an observer in a scientific experiment, I cannot know that the subject's galvanic skin response registers at 70 unless I consciously perceive this. This is true for the other observers, each of whom also reports a galvanic skin reading of 70. Since the others seem to have had the same (or similar) private experience as mine, I am tempted to regard the galvanic skin response of 70 as a "public fact," forgetting that *my* perception was private and first hand, and that the verbal report of another observer can in no way directly reveal to me *his* conscious experience of the same event. Therefore, as Koestenbaum indicates, to claim "public verification" of my private experience is legitimate only to the degree to which all of us, as philosophers of science and students of human behavior, agree on a fundamental philosophical assumption—namely that if each of our private experiences indicates a particular event to have occurred, we can then conclude that the event has actually taken place. In this sense public verification is what we call a "construct" or "construction"; it has not been so direct or palpable as we would like, but on the basis of the kind of assumptions sketched above, we act *as though* direct verification had occurred.

Why then, asks Koestenbaum, cannot "private" facts—which are similarly first hand—also be granted scientific status?

> However, just as public confirmation of public facts is in the last analysis a construction, so there can be public confirmation of private

facts. . . . It is true that I cannot have the pain or fear of someone else, but I can search within me for experiences that correspond to the evocative words that he utters. . . . I have no access to my colleague's first-person experience of free will; but, likewise, I have no access to his first-hand experience of the result of my chemical experiment. My belief that he has confirmed the existence of the observed results of my experiment is an inference. Similarly, my belief that he has confirmed my description of my sense of free will by comparing that description with his own sense of free will is also an inference. . . . If we condemn first-person or private facts (a typical characterization of phenomenological descriptions) as "too subjective" to have any scientific significance, we pari passu condemn public facts. Conversely, if we accept public facts as bona fide facts, we are equally committed to acknowledge the existence and usefulness of first-person facts (1966, pp. 292–93).

In this way, Koestenbaum attempts to demonstrate that a phenomenological psychology need be no less scientific than a behavioral one.

A PSYCHOLOGY RELEVANT TO MAN

The student of psychology and the intelligent layman often seek a psychology that will be relevant to their immediate concerns, that will help them relate more meaningfully and comfortably to themselves and their world. However, the positivistic model of psychology that still generally prevails wants first to establish quite general laws governing such basic psychological processes as perception and learning (and their underlying physiological correlates) before tackling the kinds of personal and value questions that many people hope psychology will answer. In fact, as we suggested in Chapter 1, questions involving meaningful life goals have traditionally been left to the theologian.

Humanistic psychology, partly because of its existential-phenomenological heritage, takes quite seriously the concerns that consciously plague the proverbial "man-in-the-street." Since the man-in-the-street is alive *now*, just as is the humanistic psychologist, and would like to have his questions answered *now*, just as would the humanistic psychologist (or, if not answered, at least placed within a theoretical framework he can grasp), the humanist is not so sure (as is the logical positivist) that either he himself or the man-in-the-street can afford to wait until a basic science of universal psychological laws has been created. Hence an area of empirical research that has received increasing attention in recent years is the study of the person's entire life cycle, particularly the years of adulthood bearing most on the quest for meaning, creativity, and personal growth. Two psychologists who have tried to look at adulthood in these specifically developmental terms are Erikson (1964) and Buhler (1968). The best-seller status of a book summarizing the results of these kinds of life-cycle studies (Sheehy, 1974) indicates the extent to which many people look to psychological research as a means of understanding their own experience.

This is not to say that any problem that a layman deems worthy of study necessarily is worthy, or that humanistic psychology should proceed with little rigor, conceptual clarity, or appreciation of psychology's intellectual history. The humanist's argument has been that phenomenological analysis can be more precise than most people imagine, and that supposedly "objective" research rests on an epistemological foundation that has to take into account private experience. Child (1973), for example, insists that well-controlled, carefully conceptualized empirical research can be, and has been, carried out that leaves ample room for both man's consciousness and complexity. Among the areas of significant research that Child believes fulfill the two criteria of rigor and relevance are Kohlberg's work (1969) on the evolution of morality in children, Barron's research in creativity (1969), some recent developments in extrasensory perception (Ornstein, 1976), and Festinger's (1962) investigations of cognitive dissonance, which focus on how people think about, and come to terms with, their decisions once they have made them.

A Framework for an Empirical Psychology of Consciousness

Ornstein (1977) has attempted to integrate humanistic concerns and humanistic research into the predominantly scientific model of contemporary psychology. Ornstein's paradigm, which we have already briefly referred to in the previous chapter, postulates a bifunctional brain that encompasses two distinct modes of knowing or consciousness: one linked to the functioning of the left cerebral hemisphere and primarily rational-intellectual in nature (and therefore consonant with a positivistic orientation to science), and the second linked to the functioning of the right cerebral hemisphere and primarily intuitive-holistic in nature (and therefore congruent with humanistic approaches to knowledge). Ornstein's paradigm strikes us as the most useful one to date for an assimilation of humanistic themes into a psychology that, while sympathetic to the more experiential and less rational aspects of man's functioning, retains an interest in careful conceptualization and in systematic empirical investigation.

BIMODAL CONSCIOUSNESS

The first mode of knowing is the one in which most of us are socialized and educated in Western society. Rational-empirical in structure, it encourages us to conceive of the "truth" in terms of what is logical, reasonable, and ultimately based on direct observation. It is synonymous with a positivistic model of science in which hypotheses are induced or deduced according to formal laws of logical inference and in which these hypotheses are then subjected to rigorous empirical tests that will either confirm or disconfirm them.

A central aspect of the rational-intellectual model is its linearity and sequentiality: things are thought of as having a beginning, middle, and end. This is particularly true with regard to our structuring of time, with the result that we tend to have a strongly historical consciousness in which we are acutely aware of both the past and the future. A highly analytic mode of verbal discourse that is prevalent within the culture illustrates the rational-intellectual mode; an object like a table can be thought of in terms of several distinct aspects, and linguistic concepts have been devised for representing them—like height, weight, length, width, color, and texture. While this mode can consider relationships, these are usually one-to-one relationships (e.g., is the table's height greater than its length?), and it is difficult within the mode to represent the simultaneous relationship of everything to everything else.

On the other hand, intuitive-holistic ways of knowing involve experiences that do not readily lend themselves to verbal representation. Less saturated with the linear and conceptual characteristics of language, they are geared toward sensory concreteness (including an awareness of the spatial and the kinesthetic), toward the symbolic, and toward a present-centered simultaneity wherein a pattern is grasped as an entire whole (the table, rather than being described in words, is experienced in terms of its immediate reality).

If one looks at these two modes in terms of some of the existential concepts outlined in Chapter 2, it seems that the concept of "being" embraces the second mode of knowing, while that of "essence," involving as it does an *analysis* (rather than a synthesis) of something's essential attributes, pertains to the first mode. Another way of characterizing the two modes is offered by Deikman (1971), who equates the rational-intellectual approach with an *action* orientation and the intuitive-holistic approach with a *receptive* orientation:

> The action mode is a state organized to manipulate the environment. . . . The principal psychological manifestations of this state are focal attention, object-based logic, heightened boundary perception, and the dominance of formal characteristics over the sensory; shapes

and meanings have a preference over colors and textures. The action mode is a state of striving, oriented toward achieving personal goals that range from nutrition to defense to obtaining social rewards. . . .

In contrast, the receptive mode is a state organized around intake of the environment rather than manipulation. . . . Other attributes of the receptive mode are diffuse attending, paralogical thought processes, decreased boundary perception, and the dominance of the sensory over the formal (p. 481).

Since the positivistic approach of Western science attempts to systematically manipulate various data, usually in a laboratory setting (with an eye toward elaborating and refining a logically inferred theoretical system), it clearly partakes of the rationalistic, action-oriented mode. As we saw in Chapter 6, Ornstein sees the traditional esoteric psychologies —Buddhism, yoga, and Sufism—as characterized by the receptive-intuitive mode. These less secular orientations involve an amalgam of spiritual-philosophic principles on the one hand and specific disciplines or exercises on the other, like meditation and yogic body exercises. According to Ornstein, modern psychologists, once they are curious and flexible enough to look beyond purely rational-linear models of analysis, might have something to learn from these esoteric traditions:

> For the first time in our intellectual history, we are now in a position to begin a serious consideration of a psychology that can encompass a "transcendence" of time as we ordinarily know it; consider arational mentation; use exercises for control of the "autonomic" nervous system; develop techniques for entering a state of "void" or "no mind"; and employ procedures for inducing communication that is "paranormal" to ordinary conceptions of what is possible for man. . . .
> Since these experiences are, by their very mode of operation, not readily accessible to causal explanation or even to linguistic exploration, many psychologists and other students of the mind have been tempted to ignore them or even to deny their existence (1977, pp. 116–117).

The paradox is that we are now in a position to exploit rational-analytic ways of knowing to investigate intuitive-holistic ways of knowing. For example, some experimental psychologists have tried to study the physiological effects of meditation (Wallace and Benson, 1972), the extent to which various yoga practitioners are actually able to control their autonomic nervous functioning (Ornstein, 1972, p. 150), the possibility that various "paranormal" phenomena such as extrasensory perception do exist (Ornstein, 1976, pp. 57–73), and physiological differences between the functioning of the left and right cerebral hemispheres. Below we summarize some of the empirical research on the left-right hemisphere differences, because it was these results that initially led to Ornstein's theory of a bimodal consciousness and a bifunctional brain.

EMPIRICAL EVIDENCE
FOR A BIFUNCTIONAL BRAIN

A number of studies reviewed by Ornstein (1972, pp. 53–64) reveal a sizable body of evidence indicating an association between the left cerebral hemisphere and the rational-intellectual mode, and the right cerebral hemisphere and the intuitive-holistic mode. For instance, patients who have suffered an injury to the left hemisphere often show some degree of language disturbance, such as an inability to speak, whereas an injury to the right hemisphere will have little effect on language capacities but may instead interfere with the person's musical sense, his body awareness, or his ability to orient himself in space. These correlations are most marked in the case of right-handed people, in whom the association between the left hemisphere and the verbal-conceptual mode is most clear-cut. In left-handed people the relationships between a particular mode and a particular hemisphere are more equivocal.

Also relevant are a number of "split-brain" studies conducted by Roger Sperry and his associates (Gazzaniga and Sperry, 1967). In an attempt to develop a more effective treatment for severe cases of epilepsy, Sperry performed surgery that completely severed the corpus callosum, which normally connects the two hemisphere, with the result that each hemisphere in effect operated independently of the other. The daily functioning of such patients proved to be surprisingly unimpaired. Several experimental tests, however, did indicate that some striking differences exist between split-brain patients and those having an intact cerebrum. For example, take a split-brain patient who is right-handed; if we hide a small object from his sight but permit him to touch it with his right hand, he has no difficulty in describing it verbally. However, if we place it in his left hand and ask him to describe it he is unable to do so. The explanation for this finding rests on the fact that in a right-handed person information from the left hand is relayed to the right hemisphere, which is not involved in speech; normally the right hemisphere will then pass on this information to the left, thereby enabling him to articulate what is in his left hand. Once the interconnecting corpus callosum is destroyed, however, this internal communication is no longer possible. Further tests produced similar results: the left hand of a right-handed split-brain patient could perform tasks demanding a utilization of the spatial-relational (intuitive-holistic) mode (such as reproducing a printed geometric design with colored blocks) while the right hand could not, and his right hand could do tasks requiring a utilization of the verbal-conceptual (rational-intellectual) mode (like writing a sentence in English) while the left hand could not.

Situations involving organic damage do not constitute the only evidence for postulating a bifunctional brain. It is important that this be so, since studies involving impaired functioning, while suggestive, cannot provide the firmest foundation for testing hypotheses of normal psychological functioning; it is always possible that where there is injury, one hemisphere has begun to assume functions previously belonging to the other. Ornstein cites two specific experiments that involved intact research subjects, the first done by Dunford and Kimura (1971) and the second by Filbey and Gazzaniga (1969):

> If the right hemisphere operates predominantly in a simultaneous manner, it could integrate diverse input quickly. This mode of information-processing would be advantageous for spatial orientation, when the person must quickly integrate visual, muscular, and kinesthetic cues. In a carefully controlled experiment with normal people, the right hemisphere was found to be superior to the left hemisphere in depth perception.

> When a tachistoscope is used to introduce information to only the right hemisphere and either a nonverbal or a verbal response is required, the nonverbal response comes more quickly than the verbal one. A verbal response requires the information to be sent across the callosum to the left hemisphere, which takes some time. This indicates that the normal brain does indeed make use of the lateral specialization, selecting the appropriate area for differential information-processing (Ornstein, 1977, pp. 31–32).

The two modes of knowing would seem to involve different kinds of information-processing, with the spatial-holistic mode requiring the coordination of information that emanates from several inputs simultaneously, and the intellectual-linear mode proceeding in a more piecemeal, sequential fashion. If so, one would expect the two hemispheres to have different patterns of physiological response, and some degree of incompatibility to exist between them. This is just what the research summarized above, along with other studies indicating a more diffuse organization of the right hemisphere than the left (Semmes, 1968), suggests. Hence the lateral specialization of the cerebral hemispheres that has evolved in man is most likely related to his distinctive ability to communicate via language, and to the uniquely linear mode of functioning that language, as opposed to other cognitive functions, entails.

THE TWO MODES OF KNOWING
AS COMPLEMENTARY

As Ornstein is at pains to point out, the two modes of consciousness need not represent two competing attitudes, one of which is valid and the other invalid, so much as different sets of phenomena or data:

> Suppose there were two completely independent groups of investigators; one group (scientists) works exclusively during the day, the other (the mysterious "esoteric" psychologists) works exclusively at night, neither communicating well with the other. If those who work at night see faint starlight in the sky and concentrate on the movements of the stars, they may produce documents that predict the positions of the stars at any given time, which might be useful for navigation, but these writings would be totally incomprehensible to someone who experiences only daylight. The brilliance of the sun obscures the subtle light of the stars from view (1977, pp. 12–13).

To view these two ways of knowing as completely separate and distinct from one another is to see them in a highly limiting way. Such a view partakes too much of the rational-analytic mode of consciousness wherein boundaries can be too firmly set and interrelationships obscured (it also encourages a dualistic, either-or manner of thinking that humanistically inclined psychologists tend to eschew; see Chapter 1). For instance, both modes are inextricably intertwined when it comes to doing scientific research; while the first mode is crucial when it comes to the statistical analysis and interpretation of one's data, the intuitive-holistic mode is vitally important in the initial stages of the study, where the researcher may find himself getting sudden hunches (occasionally during sleep or during twilight states of consciousness) about how two or more variables might be related to one another, and about the experimental setting that might adroitly reproduce and test these relationships.

In addition, some of the conceptual models and visual paradigms that the scientist devises to explain his theories are as much steeped in the second mode as in the first. Here we encounter that complex border area where the creative leap takes place, whether that leap is taken in the world of science or art. Indeed, any metaphor, whether scientific, religious, or poetic, since it typically relies on highly symbolic, intuitively conceived forms of communication, will always be heavily saturated with the holistic-receptive mode of consciousness (and this includes the analogy, or metaphor, quoted from Ornstein immediately above, in which he contrasts the scientists of the day with those of the night).

Can, then, the procedures of Western science, which have typically been seen as antithetical to traditions characterized as spiritual, magical, or mystical, somehow embrace, verify, and *explain* these more esoteric psychologies? According to Ornstein and Murphy, the answer is Yes. In reporting his interview with Michael Murphy, Tomkins writes as follows:

> Recent developments in scientific research have lent reinforcement to some aspects of the human-potential idea. . . . Through galvanic skin response and other "biofeedback" indicators, it has been shown that man can become aware of his own internal processes, such as blood pressure, nervous tension, and brain-wave patterns, and that by becoming aware of them he can learn to control them—as Indian yogis have been doing for centuries. Experiments of this sort have made it possible for scientists to take an interest in areas of human experience that were formerly considered fit for study only by humanists or divines. In fact, it is beginning to be thought that telepathy, clairvoyance, mystical transports, and other altered states of consciousness may be latent in most, if not all, of us, along with psychic powers and dominions not yet demonstrated. Is some revelation at hand? In a society whose institutions all seem to be crumbling, in a cosmos that has expanded lately to include antimatter and quarks and black holes, it grows easier to conceive that anything is possible.[2]

In Conclusion

In this chapter we took some of the humanistic themes considered earlier in the book—in particular the humanist's interest in individuality and consciousness—and tried to examine their implications for a scientific psychology. The issues that we focused on involved the relevance of private experience in experimental investigation, and the subjectivity of both the researcher and his experimental subject. In concentrating on the investigator and his subject, we stressed their mutual influence on one another, and we also explored some of the methodological and ethical parameters of the experimental situation. For example, how much direct contact should the two of them have, how well should they get to know one another, and how much specific information concerning the experiment should the subject have? To conclude the chapter, we took a look at Ornstein's framework for an empirical psychology of consciousness, in which the rational-linear mode of knowing is utilized as

[2] Calvin Tomkins, "New Paradigms," *The New Yorker,* January 5, 1976, p. 30. Reprinted by permission; © 1976 The New Yorker Magazine, Inc.

a means of empirically investigating, and better understanding, intuitive-holistic ways of knowing. If the material has seemed somewhat piecemeal and fragmented, this is doubtless because some degree of fragmentation still exists between psychology defined as a positivistic science, and psychology defined as a humanistic quest—despite the humanist's aim of wholeness and despite Ornstein's specific attempt at integration. And so we have presented bits and pieces that might shed light on this somewhat thorny issue, realizing that our material tends to raise as many questions as it answers.

We have presented Ornstein's paradigm because of its attempt to find points of contact and reconciliation between positivistic and humanistic ways of knowing. Yet for some, he has not gone far enough, and in trying to integrate the second mode of knowing with the first, he has remained too wedded to the traditions of the first. For instance, in discussing Ornstein's concept of a bifunctional brain, Roszak (1976) writes as follows:

> This cerebral division of labor has been nominated by Ornstein and other split-brain enthusiasts as the definitive explanation of all metaphysical and psychological dualities; it has also been presumptuously offered as "proof" that mysticism, meditation, yoga, and aesthetic perception are *important* and even *valid*. Why? Because research has finally given these "intuitive" forms of experience a neurophysiological location in the brain. Only *now*, therefore, do we know they *really* matter and need be taken seriously (p. 53).

> The very research Ornstein and his colleagues speak from goes on to make clear that (except in brain-damaged individuals or those who have undergone split-brain surgery) all information is continuously exchanged and all behavior coordinated between the brain's hemispheres, in such a way that any so-called dominance of the hemispheral functions has no philosophical meaning (p. 56).

In Roszak's view, Ornstein has not only, in looking to the brain to explain certain qualities of mind, reinforced an old duality that many humanists have struggled to transcend (that of mind-vs.-body), but introduced a new one (that of left-hemisphere thinking-vs.-right-hemisphere thinking); he has also tended toward a reductionistic viewpoint (first mentioned in our introductory chapter), wherein particular properties of consciousness are accounted for in terms of more fundamental causes that might reside in the body (in this case, the brain). In Ornstein's eagerness to use science to better understand some of the "peak" and mystic experiences of interest to the humanist, Roszak detects a subtle condescension wherein science continues to emerge as *the* preferred way of knowing. Again, we have as many questions as we have answers.

As we see it, Ornstein's two modes of consciousness offer a useful framework for viewing the place of humanistic psychology within the overall field of psychology, for no amount of knowledge gained via the rational-intellectual mode (which is conservative in that it looks at its freshest observations in terms of preexisting constructs and what is already known) can ever exhaust the possibilities of the holistic-intuitive mode (which, by the very nature of its creativity, will always have novel ways of regarding the world. Hence, whatever its content at any particular time, there will always be room for a humanistic psychology lying at the boundary between what is known and what is unknown about man, between the human potential that has already been actualized and the potential that remains as yet unfulfilled. Once viewed in this way, the synthesis envisaged by Ornstein between scientific and humanistic modes of knowing emerges as a dynamic dialectic, moving first one way and then the other, never to become either/or.

What will humanistic psychology be like ten or twenty years from now? In keeping with the tenets of humanism, our interest is more in what *is* than in what will be, and if this book has been at all successful in its aims, you will now at its conclusion have a larger sense of what humanistic psychology is *today* than you did at its beginning. Viewed from the perspective of the future, certain aspects of the human potential movement might one day appear somewhat faddish, and the contemporary interest in the occult, short-lived. But, as we stated at the end of the first chapter, there will always be a place for a humanistic orientation in psychology as long as there are theorists emphasizing the importance of both the individual and his consciousness.

References

ALLPORT, F. 1955. *Theories of perception and the concept of structure.* New York: John Wiley and Sons.

AMERICAN ASSOCIATION OF HUMANISTIC PSYCHOLOGY. 1962. *Articles of association.*

AMERICAN PSYCHOLOGICAL ASSOCIATION. 1973. *Ethical principles in the conduct of research with human participants.*

BAKAN, D. 1966. *The duality of human existence: An essay on psychology and religion.* Chicago: Rand McNally and Company.

BARNES, M. and BERKE, J. 1972. *Mary Barnes: two accounts of a journey through madness.* New York: Harcourt Brace Jovanovich.

BARRETT, W. 1962. *Irrational man: a study in existential philosophy.* Garden City, N.Y.: Doubleday and Company.

BARRON, F. 1969. *Creative person and creative process.* New York: Holt, Rinehart & Winston.

BATESON, G., JACKSON, D. D., HALEY, J., and WEAKLAND, J. 1956. Toward a theory of schizophrenia. *Behavioral Science,* 1: 251–64.

BETTELHEIM, B. 1960. *The informed heart: autonomy in a mass age.* Glencoe, Ill.: The Free Press.

BINDRIM, P. 1968. A report on a nude marathon. *Psychotherapy: theory, research, and practice* 5: 180–88.

BLANCK, G. and BLANCK, R. 1974. *Ego psychology: theory and practice.* New York: Columbia University Press.

BOYERS, R. and ORRILL, R., eds. 1971. *R. D. Laing and antipsychiatry.* New York: Harper & Row.

BRUNER, J. and POSTMAN, L. 1949. On the perception of incongruity: a paradigm. *Journal of Personality* 18: 206–23.

BUBER, M. 1970. *I and thou.* New York: Charles Scribner's Sons.

BUGENTAL, JAS. F. T. 1963. *American Psychologist* 18: 563–67.

———, ed. 1967. *Challenges of humanistic psychology.* New York: McGraw-Hill Book Company.

BUHLER, C. and MASSARIK, F., eds. 1968. *The course of human life: a study of goals in the humanistic perspective.* New York: Springer Publishing Company.

CAMERON, N. 1963. *Personality development and psychopathology: a dynamic approach.* Boston: Houghton Mifflin Company.

CAMUS, A. 1955. *The myth of Sisyphus, and other essays.* New York: Alfred A. Knopf.

CASTANEDA, C. 1968. *The teachings of don Juan: a Yaqui way of knowledge.* Berkeley: University of California Press.

———. 1971. *A separate reality: further conversations with don Juan.* New York: Simon and Schuster.

———. 1973. *Journey to Ixtlan: the lessons of don Juan.* New York: Simon and Schuster.

———. 1974. *Tales of power.* New York: Simon and Schuster.

CHILD, I. L. 1973. *Humanistic psychology and the research tradition.* New York: John Wiley and Sons.

COHEN, J. 1958. *Humanistic Psychology.* New York: Collier.

COHN, R. C. 1969. From couch to circle to community: beginnings of the theme-centered interactional method. In *Group therapy today,* ed. H. M. Ruitenbeek. New York: Atherton Press.

———. 1972. Style and spirit of the theme-centered interactional method. In *Progress in group and family therapy,* C. J. Sager and H. S. Kaplan, eds. New York: Brunner/Mazel.

DEIKMAN, A. J. 1971. Bimodal consciousness. *Archives of General Psychiatry* 25: 481–89.

DURKIN, H. 1965. *The group in depth.* New York: International Universities Press.

DURNFORD, M. and KIMURA, D. 1971. Right-hemisphere specialization for depth perception reflected in visual field differences. *Nature* 231: 394–95.

ERIKSON, E. H. 1964. *Childhood and Society.* 2d ed. New York: W. W. Norton and Company.

FESTINGER, L. 1962. *A theory of cognitive dissonance.* New York: Harper & Row.

FILBEY, R. A. and GAZZANIGA, M. S. 1969. Splitting the normal brain with reaction time. *Psychonomic Science* 17: 335–36.

FODE, K. L. 1965. *The effect of experimenters' and subjects' anxiety and social desirability on experimenter outcome-bias.* Unpublished doctoral dissertation, University of North Dakota.

FREUD, A. 1946. *The ego and the mechanisms of defense.* New York: International Universities Press.

FRIEDENBERG, E. Z. 1965. *Coming of age in America: growth and acquiescence.* New York: Random House.

FROMM, E. 1955. *The sane society.* New York: Rinehart.

GAZZANIGA, M. S. and SPERRY, R. W. 1967. Language after section of the cerebral commissures. *Brain,* 90: 131–48.

GENDLIN, E. T. 1973. Experiential psychotherapy. In *Current psychotherapies,* ed. R. Corsini. Itasca, Ill.: F. E. Peacock Publishers.

GIORGI, A. 1970. *Psychology as a human science.* New York: Harper & Row.

GOLDSTEIN, K. 1940. *Human nature in the light of psychopathology.* Cambridge: Harvard University Press.

GOODMAN, P. 1960. *Growing up absurd: problems of youth in the organized system.* New York: Random House.

GORDON, J. S. 1972. Who is mad? who is sane? R. D. Laing in search of a new psychiatry. In *Going crazy: the radical therapy of R. D. Laing and others,* ed. H. M. Ruitenbeek. New York: Bantam Books.

GRUGEON, D. and GRUGEON, E. 1973. One morning in an infant school. In *The open classroom reader,* ed. C. E. Silberman. New York: Vintage Books/Random House.

GUSTAITIS, R. 1969. *Turning on.* New York: Macmillan.

HALL, C. S. and LINDZEY, G. 1970. *Theories of personality.* 2d ed. New York: John Wiley & Sons.

HART, H. H. 1970. *Summerhill: for and against.* New York: Hart Publishing Company.

HEIDEGGER, M. 1962. *Being and time.* New York: Harper & Row.

HENRY, J. 1963. *Culture against man.* New York: Random House.

HILL, W. F. 1969. Learning thru discussion. Beverly Hills, Calif.: Sage Publications.

HOWARD, J. 1970. *Please touch: a guided tour of the human potential movement.* New York: McGraw-Hill Book Company.

HUXLEY, A. 1954. *The doors of perception.* New York: Harper & Row.

JAMES, W. 1902. *The varieties of religious experience.* New York: Longmans, Green and Company.,

JOURARD, S. 1967. Experimenter-subject dialogue: a paradigm for a humanistic science of psychology. In *Challenges of humanistic psychology,* ed. J. F. T. Bugental. New York: McGraw-Hill Book Company.

KEEN, E. 1970. *Three faces of being: toward an existential psychology.* New York: Appleton-Century-Crofts.

————. 1972. *Psychology and the new consciousness.* Monterey, Calif.: Brooks/Cole.

KEMPLER, W. 1973. Gestalt therapy. In *Current psychotherapies,* ed. R. Corsini, Itasca, Ill.: F. E. Peacock Publishers.

KENISTON, K. 1965. *The uncommitted: alienated youth in American society.* New York: Delta Books/Dell Publishing Company.

KEYNES, G. (ed.) 1957. *The complete writings of William Blake.* New York: Random House.

KOEHLER, W. 1966. A task for philosophers. In *Mind, matter, and method: essays in philosophy and science in honor of Herberg Feigl,* ed. P. K. Feyerbend and G. Maxwell. Minneapolis: University of Minnesota Press.

KOESTENBAUM, P. 1973. Phenomenological foundations for the behavioral sciences. In *Discovering man in psychology: a humanistic approach,* ed. F. Severin. New York: McGraw-Hill Book Company.

KOFFKA, K. 1935. *Principles of Gestalt psychology.* New York: Harcourt, Brace, and Company.

KOHLBERG, L. 1969. Stage and sequence: the cognitive-developmental approach to socialization. In *Handbook of socialization theory and research,* ed. D. A. Goslin. Chicago: Rand-McNally and Company.

KOZOL, J. 1967. *Death at an early age: the destruction of the hearts and minds of Negro children in the Boston public schools.* Boston: Houghton Mifflin Company.

KRAEPELIN, E. 1905. *Lectures on clinical psychiatry.* 2d ed. London: Balliere, Tindall, & Cox.

KUSHNER, M. 1965. The reduction of a long-standing fetish by means of aversive conditioning. In *Case studies in behavior modification,* L. P. Ullmann and L. Krasner, eds. New York: Holt, Rinehart and Winston.

LAING, R. D. 1961. *The self and others: further studies in sanity and madness.* London: Tavistock Publications.

————. 1965. *The divided self: an existential study in sanity and madness.* Baltimore: Penguin Books.

————. 1968. *The politics of experience.* New York: Ballantine Books.

LOWRY, R. J. 1973. *A. H. Maslow: an intellectual portrait.* Monterey, Calif.: Brooks/Cole.

MANNHEIM, K. 1952. *Essays on the sociology of knowledge.* London: Routledge and Kegan Paul.

MASLOW, A. 1954. *Motivation and personality.* New York: Harper & Brothers.

————. 1968. *Toward a psychology of being.* 2d ed. New York: Van Nostrand Reinhold.

————. 1970. *Motivation and personality.* 2d ed. New York: Harper & Row.

MAY, R. 1958. *Existence: a new dimension in psychiatry and psychology.* New York: Basic Books.

————. 1969. *Love and will.* New York: W. W. Norton and Company.

MCLUHAN, H. M. 1964. *Understanding media: the extension of man.* New York: McGraw-Hill Book Company.

MILGRAM, S. 1974. *Obedience to authority: an experimental view.* New York: Harper & Row.

MISIAK, H. and SEXTON, V. S. 1973. *Phenomenological, existential, and humanistic psychologies: a historical survey.* New York: Grune & Stratton.

NEILL, A. S. 1960. *Summerhill: a radical approach to child-rearing.* New York: Hart Publishing Company.

ORNE, M. T. 1962. On the social psychology of the psychological experiment: with particular reference to demand characteristics and their implications. *American Psychologist* 17: 776–83.

ORNSTEIN, R. E., ed. 1974. *The nature of human consciousness: a book of readings.* New York: The Viking Press.

————. 1976. *The mind field: a personal essay.* New York: The Viking Press.

————. 1977. *The psychology of consciousness.* New York: Harcourt Brace Jovanovich.

PAGE, J. D. 1975. *Psychopathology: the science of understanding deviance.* 2d ed. Chicago: Aldine Publishing Company.

PETERSON, S. 1971. *A catalog of the ways people grow.* New York: Ballantine Books.

PLOWDEN REPORT, THE. 1973. In *The open classroom reader,* ed. Charles E. Silberman. New York: Vintage Books/Random House.

POLANYI, M. 1958. *Personal knowledge: towards a post critical philosophy.* Chicago: University of Chicago Press.

POLSTER, M. 1975. Gestalt approach: the case of Allen. In *Three psychotherapies: a clinical comparison,* ed. C. A. Loew, H. Grayson, and G. H. Loew, New York: Brunner/Mazel.

POSTMAN, N. and WEINGARTNER, C. W. 1969. *Teaching as a subversive activity.* New York: Delacorte Press.

REICH, C. A. 1970. *The Greening of America.* New York: Random House.

REICH, W. 1976. *Character analysis.* New York: Pocket Books/Simon and Schuster.

RIMM, D. C. and MASTERS, J. C. 1974. *Behavior therapy: techniques and empirical findings.* New York: Academic Press.

ROGERS, C. R. 1969. *Freedom to learn: a view of what education might become.* Columbus, Ohio: C. E. Merrill Publishing Company.

————. 1970. *Carl Rogers on encounter groups.* New York: Harper & Row.

ROGERS, C. and STEVENS, B. 1967. *Person to person: the problem of being human.* Lafayette, Calif.: Real People Press.

ROSENTHAL, R. 1966. *Experimenter effects in behavioral research.* New York: Appleton-Century-Crofts.

ROSENTHAL, R. and FODE, K. L. 1961. The problem of experimenter outcome-bias. In *Series research in social psychology,* ed. D. P. Ray. Symposia Studies series, No. 8. Washington, D.C.: National Institute of Social and Behavioral Science.

————. 1963. Three experiments in experimenter bias. *Psychological reports* 12: 491–511.

ROSZAK, T. 1969. *The making of a counterculture: reflections on the technocratic society and its youthful opposition.* Garden City, N.Y.: Doubleday and Company.

————. 1975. *Unfinished animal: the acquarian frontier and the evolution of consciousness.* New York: Harper & Row.

RUITENBEEK, H. M., ed. 1972. *Going crazy: the radical therapy of R. D. Laing and others.* New York: Bantam Books.

SARTRE, J. P. 1948. *The psychology of imagination.* New York: Philosophical Library.

————. 1956. *Being and nothingness.* London: Methuen.

————. 1965. *Essays in existentialism.* New York: Citadel Press.

SCALLETT, L. 1976. What the Supreme Court said . . . and what it didn't. In *Paper victories and hard realities: The implementation of the legal and Constitutional rights of the mentally disabled,* eds. V. Bradley and G. Clarke. Washington, D.C.: The Health Policy Center, Georgetown University.

SCHAFER, R. 1976. *A new language for psychoanalysis.* New Haven: Yale University Press.

SCHUTZ, W. 1967. *Joy: expanding human awareness.* New York: Grove Press.

————. 1971. *Here comes everybody: bodymind and encounter culture.* New York: Harrow Books/Harper & Row.

SCOTT, E. P. 1976. Civil commitment statutes in the courts today. In *Paper victories and hard realities: The implementation of the legal and constitutional rights of the mentally disabled,* eds. V. Bradley and G. Clarke. Washington, D.C.: The Health Policy Center, Georgetown University.

SEEMAN, J. 1969. Deception in psychological research. *American psychologist* 24: 1025–28.

SEMMES, J. 1968. Hemispheric specialization: a possible clue to mechanism. *Neuropsychologia* 6: 11–16.

SEVERIN, F. T., ed. 1965. *Humanistic viewpoints in psychology: a book of readings.* New York: McGraw-Hill Book Company.

SHAFFER, J. B. P. and GALINSKY, M. D. 1974. *Models of group therapy and sensitivity training.* Englewood Cliffs, N.J.: Prentice-Hall, Inc.

SHAH, I. 1974. The teaching story: observations on the folklore of our "modern" thought. In *The nature of human consciousness: a book of readings,* ed. R. E. Ornstein. New York: The Viking Press.

SHEEHY, G. 1974. *Passages: predictable crises of adult life.* New York: E. P. Dutton.

SINGER, E. 1970. *Key concepts in psychotherapy.* 2d ed. New York: Basic Books.

SKINNER, B. F. 1971. *Beyond freedom and dignity.* New York: Alfred A. Knopf.

SULLIVAN, H. S. 1953. *The interpersonal theory of psychiatry.* New York: W. W. Norton and Company.

———. 1954. *The psychiatric interview.* New York: W. W. Norton and Company.

———. 1962. *Schizophrenia as a human process.* New York: W. W. Norton and Company.

SZASZ, T. 1961. *The myth of mental illness.* New York: Hoeber-Harper.

———. 1963. *Law, liberty, and psychiatry.* New York: The Macmillan Company.

———. 1965. *The ethics of psychoanalysis: the theory and method of autonomous psychotherapy.* New York: Dell Publishing Company.

———. 1977. *Psychiatric Slavery.* New York: The Macmillan Company.

TOMKINS, C. 1976. Profiles: new paradigms. *The New Yorker* (Jan. 5, 1976), 30–51.

WALLACE, R. K. and BENSON, H. 1972. The physiology of meditation. *Scientific American* 226: 85–90.

WATTS, A. 1951. *The wisdom of insecurity.* New York: Vintage Books/ Random House.

WEBER, L. 1971. *The English infant school and informal education.* Englewood Cliffs, N.J.: Prentice-Hall, Inc.

WHEELIS, A. 1974. *How people change.* New York: Harper Torchbooks/ Harper & Row.

WHITAKER, C. A. and MALONE, T. P. 1953. *The roots of psychotherapy.* New York: Blakiston.

WHORF, B. J. 1956. *Language, thought, and reality: selected writings.* Cambridge: Technology Press of Massachusetts Institute of Technology.

WOODWARD, K. 1976. Ideas: getting your head together. *Newsweek* (Sept. 6, 1976), 56–62.

Index